The Wonder of Worship

Why We Worship the Way We Do

The Wonder of Worship

Why We Worship the Way We Do

Keith Drury

Wesleyan Publishing House, Indianapolis, Indiana
Triangle Publishing, Marion, Indiana

The Wonder of Worship: Why We Worship the Way We Do
Keith Drury

Direct correspondence and permission requests to one of the following:

Wesleyan Publishing House
7990 Castleway Drive
PO Box 50434
Indianapolis, IN 46250

> Website: www.wesleyan.org/wph
> E-mail: wph@wesleyan.org

Triangle Publishing
Indiana Wesleyan University
4301 South Washington Street
Marion, Indiana 46953

> Website: www.trianglepublishing.com
> E-mail: info@trianglepublishing.com

Scripture quotations are from the *Holy Bible: New International Version* (NIV)®
(North American Edition), copyright © 1973, 1978, 1984 by the International Bible
Society. Used by permission of Zondervan Publishing House. All rights reserved.

Drury, Keith
The Wonder of Worship: Why We Worship the Way We Do

ISBN 0-89827-243-2

*Editor's note: The dates given in this book are all in the Christian era (A.D.)
unless otherwise noted. (A.D. is the abbreviation for the Latin phrase, anno
domini—"in the year of our Lord".)*

Graphic Design: Gary Phillips
                     Susan Spiegel

Printed in the United States of America
Evangel Press, Nappanee, Indiana

To
My students who reach for the future
without discarding the past.
And to their parents
who preserve the past
without rejecting the future.

Contents

Acknowledgments

Each of us is the product of interaction with God and others. No book can be written alone. This book could not have been completed without the aid and support of so many friends and associates. My associates in the religion department at Indiana Wesleyan University were a constant encouragement. Dr. Steve Lennox urged me to write this book. Dr. Ken Schenck often stood in my doorway, coffee cup in hand, honing and improving my rough ideas. Dr. Jim Lo was a reliable and regular source of inspiration, as were Dr. Bud Bence, Dr. David Smith, and my other colleagues.

Karen Eilers gave a long summer to reading and critiquing the manuscript from a lay perspective. The extent to which a chapter is clear is largely due to her work on the manuscript.

Bobbie Sease has contributed so much to my past book projects, and once again, her work editing this manuscript has considerably improved the end product.

Vanetta Bratcher, Juli Knutson, and Aimee Williams assisted with proofreading. Robert W. McIntyre reviewed the entire manuscript.

Nathan Birky and Don Cady have supported this and my other writing projects with such steady (sometimes nagging) prodding that I have continued to write for others—even after my primary focus in life has shifted to teaching and mentoring my own students.

And to those who read the manuscript from a scholarly perspective, correcting errors and important things I overlooked, I am most grateful: Dr. James F. White, Dr. Robert E. Webber, Dr. Clarence (Bud) Bence, Dr. Kenneth Schenck, Dr. Stephen Lennox, Dr. David Riggs, Dr. Todd Guy, and Dr. Robert Black. Thank you for your improvements to this book.

Keith Drury
Epiphany 2002

Preface

Teaching university students the subject of worship for a half-dozen years has brought me several realizations. First, I've learned how little the average person knows about our worship history—the roots of our current worship practices. Worship to many of my students (almost all of whom come from conservative evangelical churches) is a contemporary experience largely cut off from its roots. Many assume that the church has always worshiped in about the same way up to the 1980s and that recent innovations were the first time worship has ever shifted styles. To my delight, these same students light up when they discover the rich history of worship streams feeding into the present. Following a reading in class, one girl burst out in astonishment, "Why, they've *always* changed worship!" Knowing our roots of worship brings perspective and maturity to planning and leading worship.

Second, my students are not alone in knowing little about our past worship practices. This is also true of their parents. While the parents may have more historical knowledge, that knowledge is often limited to the last fifty years. Many of these parents (and others of their generation in the church) have succeeded in changing the worship styles practiced by *their* parents. Having finished their "revolutionary work," they have set about the business of defending their innovations (now considered to be traditions by their children). But their view of history is a short one—just fifty years or so. When adults become aware of the overall flow of worship history, they often gain a deeper maturity and perspective in assessing the effectiveness of their own innovations—and in dealing with the *next* generation's suggested changes.

So, this book is for both my students and their parents (and, of course, other church leaders). It is designed to be both a "reader" for students in college worship classes and a study book for parents in Sunday school classes or small groups.

I have tried to write for the average reader, keeping this book easy-to-read, so that any person—college student or adult— can grasp its contents. I have also tried to remain unbiased, allowing the reader to make up his or her mind about the issues. However, no writer is totally without an opinion or a leaning toward one or another view. Each of us writes from personal experience. Even as I attempt to remain impartial, I should outline my background and the personal assumptions that have influenced the making of this book.

1. I have a Revivalist-Holiness-evangelical background. I was reared and continue to serve in a church with strong roots in the Methodist Revivalist-Holiness Camp Meeting tradition. My denomination considers itself "evangelical" and a member of the "Holiness Movement." I suspect that this background has nudged me to inflate the importance of the Revivalist and Camp Meeting streams in worship. On the other hand, as an insider I doubtless feel more free to criticize this aspect of worship history, as well. But you should know that I am not Anglican or Catholic—I am a Wesleyan rooted in the worship of Camp Meeting Revivalism.

2. I am present-biased. While I love worship history, I am more concerned with the present and the future than the past. This is precisely why it is important to study the history of worship—to know how to build today's church on a good foundation as it enters the future. I don't believe that everything we now do in worship is wrong, or that the solution is to turn back the clock to the way we worshiped three hundred years ago. I don't even believe that getting back to "early church worship" is our best course. True, our present worship could use considerable upgrading. However, I believe that has been true in every age— even during the first century.

So, this book does not give equal treatment to subjects based on their role in all of history. If I had done that, I would certainly have given more space to baptism and the Eucharist (and little to the altar call or the testimony meeting). My intention is not to cover worship history in some mathematically precise treatment. Rather, I start with our current worship practices—the things we do in worship today—and trace them back to their roots. Thus, I include a whole chapter tracing the "greeting handshake." My hope is that the reader will see that almost all of our present practices have some historical roots. And a familiarity with these roots increases our chances of intelligently designing and redesigning future worship.

3. I am Protestant. Many Protestants tend to inflate the importance of the early church and post-Reformation periods of history, treating the in-between time as the "Dark Ages." For them, the "Dark Ages" began in 313 when Constantine converted and continued until the 1500s when Martin Luther "restored the church again." I don't believe this is true. However, like most other Protestants, I am probably guilty of depreciating the thousand years between 500 and 1500.

On the other hand, having been raised in a somewhat anti-Catholic environment, I may veer off on the other side of the road at times, as I try to correct some of the myths we Protestants have about the Middle Ages and Catholicism.

4. I am an American. This book is especially written for people in the Americas. Many European histories of worship inflate their own role in history (of course, they *did* have a corner on just about everything for 1,500 years). European worship histories easily overlook the wild and crazy happenings in North America's short worship history. I probably do the reverse by upgrading the importance of worship happenings here in America.

5. I am Charis-friendly. I am friendly to the recent Charismatic world-wide movement. A book on worship cannot ignore a movement that represents as much as one third of the world's Christians. I am not a Charismatic, but I value this stream as part of the current worship milieu of Christianity.

6. I don't want to answer all your questions. If I have done my job right, you will finish every chapter with more questions than when you began. This book is not an exhaustive, conclusive history of worship. It is just a "reader"—something to introduce you to deeper thinking and study. My hope is that you will come to the "Books to Read Next" chapter, near the end of this book, hungry to know more—callously tossing aside this introductory book and devouring deeper works by the likes of James F. White, Robert Webber, Bernhard Lang, and others reviewed in that chapter.

7. *I am an educator.* My craft involves more teaching than writing. I get up each day, prepare for my courses, go to class, and coach students into learning. I do not approach this book as a church historian—there are plenty of excellent worship history books out there—but I write as an educator. This book's primary intent is to get you to *learn* and to *think*. It is an educational tool—for classroom or church. Each chapter begins with a contemporary story to engage your interest and get your mind in gear for the subject. The story is followed by a series of questions designed to arouse your curiosity—to generate your interest in attempting to find answers. (The chapter does not try to answer all the questions as if it were a legal brief. Instead, it attempts to open doors for the reader, encouraging him or her to begin thinking about the answers.)

Each chapter then moves through the history of the particular worship practice (baptism, preaching, etc.). While this necessarily involves some repetition, as an educator I see such repetition as a good thing. Usually, I begin with the biblical practices, then trace them down to the present. After this sweep of history, each chapter closes with a series of discussion or learning questions. These questions will help the reader (or a class) think deeper and clarify personal positions on a variety of issues in worship. Many chapters also include actual historical quotations—enabling the reader to decide on an individual basis what an early church writer meant.

8. *I am indebted to many other writers.* As I mentioned above, this book includes a separate chapter reviewing quite a few superb worship histories—books you will want to read next. The three writers who have influenced me most are James F. White, Robert Webber, and Bernhard Lang. To these three scholars I am deeply indebted for molding and influencing my thinking. They have written excellent texts for study and I hope you'll buy their books next. What I have written here is a "reader" to get you started—to get you moving on your journey toward a deeper study of the rich roots of Christian worship.

Part I
The Primary Elements of Worship

What are the primary elements of worship? That is, what are the elements we consider indispensable, the things we'd do no matter what—even if we dropped other parts of our worship service?

This section focuses on five primary elements. You might argue for other elements to be added, but for the purpose of this reader as outlined in the Preface, we have settled on these five:

- **Music/Praise**
- **Public and Private Prayer**
- **Scripture and Preaching**
- **Baptism**
- **Lord's Supper**

1

1
Music/Praise

*Karen had graduated from college in 1979 with a music degree. She was having a hard time adjusting to singing the simple melodies that were projected on a large screen at her church. She pleaded with Shawn, her worship leader: "Can't we sing at least **some** hymns? These simple praise choruses have no depth. Isn't God a God of variety and four-part harmony too?" Shawn smiled and replied, "Someday . . . someday your style of music might come back." Feeling strangely old all at once, Karen shrugged hopelessly and walked slowly to her car. "But God expects our best—and these simple melodies are not the best we can offer Him."*

How did music come to be such a dominant part of worship? Was it always that way? Have musical styles changed in the past as often as they've changed recently? When did we start using music in worship? Is it "biblical"?

Music is a central part of today's worship. However, that was not always so. This chapter could have been titled "Praise," since that is probably the "primary element" of worship. But, we are looking at the elements of worship from today's perspective. And since music is the primary form of praise today, we have titled this chapter "Music/Praise."

Old Testament Music

Music and worship are intertwined inextricably. Music is such a powerful medium of expression that it was bound to be used in worship, and it has been—in almost all religions of the world. The Jews of the Old Testament are no exception.

As soon as the Hebrew people became Israelites—immediately after they crossed the Red Sea —they held a worship celebration. Miriam led the singing, complete with tambourines and a trail of dancing, singing women accompanists. Before the Tabernacle or Temple or even the Ten Commandments were reality, there was praise through music.

Martin Luther (1500s)

"...next to the Word of God, the noble art of music is the greatest treasure in the world. It controls our thoughts, minds, hearts, and spirits...Our dear fathers and prophets did not desire without reason that music be always used in the churches. Hence, we have so many songs and psalms. This precious gift has been given to man alone that he might thereby remind himself that God has created man for the express purpose of praising and extolling God...A person who gives this some thought and yet does not regard music as a marvelous creation of God, must be a clodhopper indeed and does not deserve to be called a human being; he should be permitted to hear nothing but the braying of asses and the grunting of hogs."

From Luther's *Forward* to Georg Rhau's *Symphoniae*, a collection of chorale motets published in 1538. Retrieved 7/21/01 from www.classicalmus.hispeed.com/articles/luther.html

When Samuel met a collection of prophets descending from a holy site, musicians were leading them with lyres, tambourines, flutes, and harps—an ancient orchestral procession. When King Saul lost control of his emotions, David played his harp to soothe him.

In the tabernacle–tent and in Solomon's Temple, music became formal and extravagant, including full-time professional musicians (1 Chronicles 15:22). The complexity and splendid performances lifted the hearts of the people. The Levites appointed singers and choirs who were accompanied by instruments, including lyres, harps, rams' horns, metal trumpets, flutes and reeds, tambourines/hand drums, and cymbals (1 Chronicles 15:16). The Temple musicians used strings, wind and percussion instruments. The Temple choirs were splendid, and the Jewish hymnbook, the Psalms, provided the text for the performances. These were probably sung in a chant-like form or with a simple melody.

Music in the many local synagogues was less extravagant and professional than in Jerusalem's impressive Temple. Local synagogue worship leaned toward Scripture and prayer more than celebration and praise, but there was always some singing. At the very least, the worshipers chanted the Scriptures without accompaniment. One or two cantors probably led recitations in a rhythmic chant-like tone, and the people responded with easy-to-remember responses—antiphonal singing of sorts. The notion of "parts" or varied complex harmonies was still centuries away. If you had asked a first-century Jew if he sang, he would surely say he did, but that singing would probably sound to us more like a chant than melody or harmony.

New Testament Music

The New Testament, of course, begins with an angelic host saying: "Glory to God in the highest, and on earth, peace, good will . . ." (Luke 2:14 KJV). The disciples sang a hymn with Jesus—presumably a Psalm—as they left the Last Supper and headed out to the garden (Matthew 26:30). The most famous song-singing service was that of Paul and Silas in the jail at Philippi (Acts 16:25-26).

When the Apostle Paul wrote the Ephesian Christians, he assumed the Spirit-filled Ephesians would "be speaking to yourselves in psalms and hymns and spiritual songs, singing and making melody in your heart to the Lord" (Ephesians 5:19 KJV). When he corrected other excesses in Corinth, he mentioned, "When you come together, everyone has a hymn," while others would offer a variety of other contributions to the informal stew of early church worship (1 Corinthians 14:26).

5

Of course, the New Testament was not written down until decades after Christ rose from the dead. Until it was available in written form, the gospel was handed down orally. It is likely the first-century church—before it had a written New Testament—preserved and passed on some of these stories through hymns and songs. What that means is the earliest portions of the New Testament may have been sung for years before it was even read. It makes sense—it is much easier to remember Scripture by singing it than by reciting it. Luke records several hymns that are likely candidates for such sung Scripture, but perhaps the best example is from chapter two of Philippians (the "Kenosis Hymn"), which Paul recorded.

Many other possible Scripture hymns had circulated as sung pieces before being written down.

The Early Church

The early church was a singing church. These believers sang hymns that told stories and affirmed what they believed. The "Kenosis Hymn" previously mentioned is an excellent example of a creedal song. The first "Apostles' Creed" may have been sung before being written, since chanting/singing was the preferred method of memorizing things. Certainly the early Christians continued the synagogue practice of singing/chanting the Psalms of the Old Testament. Participation was a governing principle of early church worship, so it seems likely that the worshipers may have sung "Amens" or "Alleluias" as part of their worship.

However, don't get the idea that their singing was always a thunderously joyful celebration. The Christian church was not an authorized religion for several centuries, so worship music was perhaps subdued. But they did celebrate, as we can gather from the reports on the Corinthian church.

By the 300s Christian worship was legalized, freeing the church's worship considerably. The Christians no longer were forced to meet quietly, dispersed throughout the city in quiet cells or at various homes across the city. They could now unite, gather in large groups, and construct magnificent church buildings.

6

Physical settings affect the kind of music we use in worship. Groups of thirty to forty (or at the most 100 in some North Africa locations) Christians quietly assembling in a private home use a different kind of music than 1,000 Christians gathering for multiple services in a massive, metropolitan basilica. The simple songs quietly sung in private homes became increasingly more complex and professional. By the late 300s, Ambrose introduced antiphonal singing—with one part of the congregation "answering" the other. Antiphonal singing is probably not something a small group in a home setting would think of doing. (Ambrose, a Western bishop, may have been "beaten to the punch" by Ignatius of Antioch before him in the East.) It had been a part of the "super-church"

Old Testament Temple, of course, but now was reintroduced. However, don't get the idea that their music was anything like the complex choir piece you may have heard last Sunday. The tunes were simple folk tunes and only the melody was sung. If we actually heard them today, we might not consider them "real music." Most early church leaders rejected instruments in worship, perhaps due to then pagan association.

John Calvin (1500s)

"To sing the praises of God upon the harp and psaltery, unquestionably formed a part of the training of the law and of the service of God under that dispensation of shadows and figures, but they are not now to be used in public thanksgiving."

On Psalms LXXI (1500s). Retrieved 7/21/01 from http://www.swrb.com/newslett/actualnls/InstCalv.htm

The Middle Ages

In the thousand years from approximately 500-1500, the role of music continually grew both in importance and excellence. Performance replaced participation as the goal. While the Eastern church dragged its feet in adopting the aesthetic value of music (i.e., beauty itself inherently being important to worship), the Western church considered the beauty of music important enough to provide it a principal role in worship.

In the late 600s, Pope Gregory II gathered the many melodies of his day into what are now known as "Gregorian Chants." These simple melodies were sung unaccompanied. The text was dominant and affected the rhythm of the vocal line. While variations existed, the "Gregorian Chant" was the dominant musical style for almost a thousand years.

7

When the organ appeared in the 500s, it was at first opposed by the Christians as pagan and inappropriate for churches. The organ came to be used to signal praise in the emperor's court (in a sense filling the role of the traditional trumpet flourish). However, it soon appeared at the Pope's court, used for a similar purpose—to signal the entrance of the Pope. By the 700s and 800s, it had emerged in the church but did not yet rule, and by the 900s it was used in the Benedictine monasteries.

Martin Luther (1500s)

"I always loved music; whoso has skill in this art, is of a good temperament, fitted for all things. We must teach music in schools; a schoolmaster ought to have skill in music, or I would not regard him; neither should we ordain young men as preachers, unless they have been well exercised in music."

Table Talk, of Universities, Arts, etc. DCCXCIV.
Retrieved 7/17/01 from Christian Classics Ethereal Library,
Calvin College, Grand Rapids. http://www.ccel.org/l/luther/table_talk/ table_talk42.htm

The organ eventually found solid footing in the church. The Christians were at first suspicious and thus limited its use to sounding out the note to kick off the chant—a sort of elaborate pitch pipe. However, it gradually came to accompany the singing itself, eventually using its full range of pitches to increase the complexity of the relatively simple musical format of the chants. By the 1100s, the organ was widely accepted. By 1300, every significant church possessed an organ.

For a thousand years the church had survived without singing "harmony." Instead, worshipers sang their songs in a single tone or "melody." From 1000-1100, polyphonic music emerged. By the end of the 1200s, the polyphonic music revolution had swept the Christian church. Complex musical pieces were produced by talented professional composers and were sung by gifted professional musicians. Five centuries later, the leading composers of the day, including Haydn, Mozart, and Beethoven, wrote religious masses along with their secular work. Musical masses were performed as entire services, with music instead of the spoken word becoming the medium of the mass.

Monks could read and write, so monasteries became a focus of musical development and promotion. In the early 1100s, Bernard of Clairvaux wrote the text for "Jesus the Very Thought of Thee" and "O Sacred Head Now

Wounded." St. Francis wrote "All Creatures of our God and King" in early 1225.

In one sense, this period was the height of complexity and quality in church music. The composition was professional and the music was performed with a penchant for excellence. Composers were paid for their work, and their professional compositions were performed by paid singers. Kettledrums, violins, and full orchestration became a common part of worship. Aristocrats could attend these services and "go home proud" of the quality of their church's worship.

The church often oscillates between the two ends of the performance-participation axis. During the Middle Ages, performance and professionalism tended to displace participation and involvement, especially in the music. The congregation increasingly became an "audience" whose only task was to listen, then come forward at the end of service to receive the Eucharist.

John Calvin (1537)

"There are psalms which we desire to be sung in the Church, as we have it exemplified in the ancient Church and in the evidence of Paul himself, who says it is good to sing in the congregation with mouth and heart. We are unable to compute the profit and edification which will arise from this, except after having experimented. Certainly as things are, the prayers of the faithful are so cold, that we ought to be ashamed and dismayed. The psalms can incite us to lift up our hearts to God and to move us to an ardor in invoking and exalting with praises the glory of his Name."

John Calvin, Articles Concerning the Organization of the Church and of Worship at Geneva, Proposed by the Ministers and the Council January 16, 1537. Trans. J. K. S. Reid, Library of Christian Classics, XXII, 53-54.

Reformation

The Reformers changed doctrine more than worship—at least, that was their initial intent. Invariably, Protestant worship gravitated away from Roman Catholic traditional worship even in musical forms. The Reformation was a great movement, and great movements almost always develop great music.

Martin Luther, who began penning hymns in 1523, was probably the first great evangelical hymn writer. Many churches still sing his "A Mighty Fortress is Our God." The first "hymnals" as we know them emerged in Luther's time and included his hymns along with those written by others.

Reformation choirs still sang complicated polyphonic compositions, but simple congregational singing again came to the forefront. By the late 1600s, the Pietistic movement in Germany had influenced a shift in musical lyrics. Songs of that time emphasized objective truths about God—they were musical creeds of sorts. The Pietistic movement nudged songs more toward subjective personal experience. This was a minor blip on the historical screen at the time, but it was the first foretaste of what would become a massive trend two or three centuries later.

Charles Finney (1835)

"Choirs. Afterwards, another innovation was brought in. It was thought best to have a select choir of singers sit by themselves, so as to give an opportunity to improve the music. But this was bitterly opposed. How many congregations were torn and rent in sunder by the desire of ministers and some leading individuals, to bring about an improvement in the cultivation of music, by forming choirs! People talked about 'innovations,' and 'new measures,' and thought great evils were coming to the Churches, because the singers were seated by themselves, and cultivated music, and learned new tunes that the old people could not sing."

Lectures on Revival XIII: "How Churches can help Ministers." Retrieved 7/17/01 from CCEL, Calvin College, http://www.ccel.org/ f/finney/ revival/

Zwingli was probably the most accomplished musician of the Reformation period. But when he discovered that the wonderful organ in Zurich's cathedral was being used for classy, non-gospel entertainment, he destroyed it. Radical Reformers and the "Free Church movement" attempted to strip all the "extras" from the Catholic mass. John Calvin even eliminated all music from worship. However, the resulting service was so cold and sterile that Calvin relented and restored singing, but required that it be simple, modest, and without showiness. For groups like the Puritans, singing was accepted, but musical instruments were considered excessive.

1700s

At the turn of the eighteenth century, most hymn lyrics were largely limited to Bible texts, especially to the Psalms. The notion of singing words written by a modern person (instead of the inspired Word of God) was yet to be accepted. Two "outsiders" (or really people on the fringes of the church) changed all that: Isaac Watts and John Wesley (along with his brother Charles).

Isaac Watts, considered the "Father of English Hymnody," moved beyond Scripture to paraphrasing and rearranging Scripture into modern hymns. He told the Bible in his own words. Many churches still sing his "When I Survey the Wondrous Cross" and "O God Our Help in Ages Past."

John and Charles Wesley were more radical and more subjective than Watts. The Wesleys wrote and promoted hymns based on scriptural

11

Charles Finney (1835)

"And there are many churches now who would not tolerate an organ. They would not be half so much excited to be told that sinners are going to hell, as to be told that there is going to be an organ in the meeting house..."

"Measures to Promote Revivals" (1835). *Lectures on Revivals of Religion*, ed. William G. McLoughlin (Cambridge, Mass.: Harvard University Press, 1960).

ideas, but not necessarily Scripture itself. They promoted catchy melodies (sometimes popular barroom tunes) and lusty congregational singing. Many congregations still sing Charles Wesley's "O For a Thousand
Tongues to Sing."

1800s

As the nineteenth century saw revivalism emerge, music came to be
used in even more powerful though controversial ways. Charles Finney,
lawyer-turned-preacher, taught the use of "right means" to bring about
a revival. Finney used the first part of the service—where music was
emphasized—to warm up the audience for the sermon. Music as testimony and witness increased, along with a generous dose of sentimental-
ism and subjectivism. William Bradbury launched what was then called
"Sunday School hymns" (now called gospel songs) and included the tune
along with the words of a song, an innovation at that time. Gospel songs
swept the church, though not without great resistance to forcing all songs
into one mold by actually specifying the tune for each.

The Camp Meeting movement and Revivalism, along with Holiness and
Pentecostal worship, kept energetic gospel singing alive. The "song service" (the first part of the service) became an exciting and animated part
of revivalist meetings.

Modern Times

Fanny Crosby, the premier gospel songwriter, took gospel songs even
further into subjective testimony style. To this day, many churches still
sing her "Blessed Assurance" and "I Am Thine, O Lord." D. L. Moody
recruited Ira Sankey to travel with him as his singer on campaigns; thus
Sankey became the first modern "song evangelist" to kick off the trend
of matching preachers and singers in meetings. (Actually one could
argue that Thomas Hastings, Charles Finney's music leader, may have
been the first.) The Jesus People in the 1960s and 1970s led a return to
simple Scripture choruses (accompanied by guitar), reversing the trend
away from Scripture to experience. A temporary trend, it was not widely
adopted, though it may have become the forerunner of the later "praise
chorus movement" that also returned to the practice of singing Scripture.

The Charismatic movement most directly spawned the late twentieth century "praise and worship" movement with "praise choruses," moving the focus from personal experience back to God again. Somewhat ironically, the "praise and worship" movement is itself highly subjective and experiential, yet the songs of this movement have returned to the simple melodies and objective truths of an earlier era. One might argue that this movement uses repetitive music to create a kind of subjective altered state of feelings, even though the words themselves are objective.

The piano had eventually joined the organ as one of two primary instruments, especially in evangelical and revivalist churches. In some camp meeting churches, the piano and organ were joined by a brass band. Later the organ began to lose ground to the piano, but then both lost ground to what was dubbed "the worship team": a collection of attractive singers with microphones, accompanied by guitars, an electronic "keyboard" and a drum set.

Where will worship music go in the future? The answer is partly found in another question: Where will the culture go? Worship music often reflects the culture's music, though admittedly there is a delay in the church's adaptation of cultural patterns. Music is a cultural expression, as is most of worship. The musical forms and instruments of worship in West Africa will differ from that of Nebraska simply because the cultures are different. Each will use different rhythms, styles, instruments, and traditions. And the musical forms of a downtown church full of middle-aged folks will differ from that of a brand-new church full of singles and younger couples, because their cultures are also different. As musical forms change and old musical instruments fade away, worship music will also shift. Just as the organ, kettledrums, accordion, and xylophone found places in various cultural expressions of worship, so will the electronic keyboard, guitar, and other instruments find a place as musical culture shifts. Ultimately, worship is an expression of the people—and that articulation is almost always expressed in a way that is culturally comfortable.

13

To think about . . .

1. What new discovery did you make from reading this chapter about music in worship?

2. Since the early church apparently sang quietly and in a subdued manner for fear of attracting attention to their secret gathering, should we try to "get back to doing things the way the early church did them"? Was this house-church setting *ideal* or a mere necessity of the day?

3. What do you think about the notion that the early church first preserved Scripture in song, before it was later incorporated into the writings of the apostles? If this is true, would it be "cheating" on the apostles' part to include in the Bible texts that were already sung, or would it be OK?

4. Think about the transition from small house-church music to large basilica "super-church" singing, which took place between 300 and 500. What are the comparative advantages and disadvantages of both small house-churches and large super-churches when it comes to music?

5. What about singing only the melody in unison versus singing "parts" in polyphonic style? Make a chart of the advantages and disadvantages of both styles.

6. Reflect on the resistance, then reluctance, then grudging acceptance, and finally approval of the organ in the Middle Ages. What insights and generalizations would you make from this account that might relate to other "innovations"?

7. So many songs mentioned in this chapter have lasted hundreds of years, while others have disappeared. Which modern songs do you think might last several hundred years into the future? Why? What gives a song endurance through time?

8. Discuss these shifts: (1) from objective hymns, (2) to gospel-tes-

timony songs, (3) to God-directed praise choruses. What are the advantages of each? Disadvantages? Relating to these three shifts, how would you draw a pie diagram of your own church? What would you shift if you could?

9. Some think the preferable worship musical style for adults is "frozen in" during their 20s and early 30s. That is, whatever worship style adults preferred in their 20s and 30s will become their lifetime preference or their "tradition." Test this notion on yourself and friends. Where it is true, ask what contributes to this phenomenon.

10. What compromises and halfway points have you seen that exist between styles of worship? How should a church handle the diverse worship "needs" or "preferences" of a congregation?

11. This chapter was titled "Music/Praise" but the author believes the real primary element should be "praise." Music is presently the primary means of praise. So, to learn more about the real primary element, make a list of all the ways we can accomplish praise *without* music.

15

2

Public and Private Prayer

Kathy was a highly disciplined, stay-at-home mother of four chil-
dren, including two preschool kids. She had made a commitment
to Christ in high school, met her future husband Justin while in
college, and had gotten married the evening of her graduation.
Kathy always had her "time alone with God" every morning before
breakfast; that is, until her second child was born. From then on,
she struggled to stay awake in the evenings and couldn't drag
herself out of bed in the mornings before her children.

Deciding she would have her devotions while the children took a
nap worked fine for her first two children, but even that went out the
window when her brood increased to four. There just was no time
for herself . . . or for devotions anymore. Her children and family
demanded all her available time. Kathy felt guilty about her slipped
devotional habits, but saw no light at the end of the tunnel—at least
until the kids went off to school. She did notice one thing. She was
voraciously hungry for church and all that went with it. She couldn't
wait for Sunday school class because the first half of the class was
devoted to prayer. Her Mothers of Preschoolers group on Tuesday
mornings was also a lifesaver. But she felt her prayer life was a
total failure.

How much prayer is enough? Is private prayer at home better than public
prayer at church? Can we worship without praying very much or without
praying at all? If we pray, are we in fact worshiping when we do? What
role does prayer play in worship? How have individuals and the church
at large viewed prayer down through the centuries? Is more prayer
always better? Can there ever be too much prayer?

Roots of Christian Prayer

In all religions, people speak to their god and ask him or her to do something. These are prayers of petition. In ancient times, it was assumed that the god had power to change things in the life of human beings, and thus prayer was a common activity. Indeed, prayer may be the most elemental of all means of worship. All people in all religions pray. In fact, many people with no religion at all still pray. Surveys repeatedly show the vast majority of people—even those who never attend church—pray regularly, many on a daily basis. Prayer is a universal means of worship. While Christians may claim a unique rite in the Lord's Supper or in baptism, when we pray, we join all of humanity past and present in this act of worship.

While prayer most commonly consists of asking God to do things, it does include other elements: praise, thanksgiving, listening, and honest confession.

If Christians were forced by some despot to strip away the elements of worship one by one—singing, preaching, Communion, and so forth— prayer would likely be the last to go. For prayer may be the most elemental form of worship—of pledging allegiance to God and asking Him to act in our world.

Prayer in the Jewish Community

Like all religious people, the early Jews were a praying people. They practiced *personal prayer*, or what we today might call "devotions" or "time alone with God." The Jews also had a series of *worship ritual prayers* mostly related to the sacrifices in the Temple—these were corporate prayers. Finally, when the Jews faced a serious threatening national crisis, they would come together to offer *prayer for national deliverance*.

The synagogue ritual was focused on the Torah but was begun with a series of eighteen or nineteen prayers, including praise, petition, and a closing set of prayers of thanksgiving. The eighteen prayers that were standardized by the year 80 probably existed earlier. Thus, the first apostles were familiar with praying as a *corporate worship activity*—public prayer. They were also familiar with habits of private prayer. The Jews practiced a *daily ritual schedule of personal prayer*. The Jews did not practice "morning devotions" as we know them, but set aside time for prayer at different times during the day (usually three). The Psalms mention prayer at three appointed hours: *"evening, morning, and noon"* (Psalm 55:17). Daniel was, of course, most famous for his insistence on maintaining this thrice-daily habit—even in a foreign land and at the risk of death (Daniel 6:10). While the writer of Psalm 119 "ups the ante" from three to seven with *"Seven times a day I praise you"* (Psalm 119: 164), praying three times daily was apparently the most common practice in Jesus' day.

The Christians saw no need to depart from this pattern of three-times-a-day prayer, though Paul urged the Thessalonians to "pray continually" (1 Thessalonians 5:17). Thus, the Christians practiced prayer, both public and private. In their house-to-house worship services, they primarily prayed prayers of praise and petition. In their private lives, they continued the Jewish habit of three-times-a-day prayer.

The two-pronged emphasis we have today developed from these roots: public and private prayer. We use corporate prayer as an element of our collective worship. We use private prayer as an element of our private devotions.

Public Prayer in the Early Church

The simple services of the early church included a variety of corporate prayers plus the set ritual prayer—the "Our Father" or "Lord's Prayer." In early Christian worship, prayer was peppered throughout the worship plan. These prayers included prayers of praise and petition, along with thanksgiving and some confession. Prayer was so frequent in their worship it seemed to act like the lubricating oil between the various working parts of the worship engine. There was not just one item on the worship agenda titled "Pastoral Prayer." Instead, prayer was offered frequently throughout the worship service. The "Our Father" took its place as a weekly common ritual prayer, in a sense summarizing the whole New Testament just as the Ten Commandments had summarized the Old.

Private Prayer in the Early Church

Prayer was not limited to church services for the early Christians. These Christians believed in prayer, and they continued the Jewish practice of praying three times a day too. This thrice-daily prayer ritual became

19

the "daily office" or "people's office" of the Christian church. It would develop into private and family devotions later on. The "daily office" did not have to take the form of private devotions. It could have been an assembly meeting from the start, and we know for certain that it developed into several public daily services. However, gathering three times a day for joint prayers may have been difficult in some settings. After all, when the Jews prayed three times daily, the whole nation offered cultural support for it—much like the Muslim nations that maintain the practice of collective prayers throughout the day. If everyone else is closing up shops to go to pray, you can afford to close up too. However, for the Gentile Christians in a pagan world, these joint prayers—or some of them—may have rapidly changed into thrice-daily personal prayers. That is, rather than gathering three times every day with other Christians for prayers, these Gentile Christians may have practiced their thrice-daily prayers personally, more like personal devotions than public prayers.

The Didache (about 100)

"Neither pray ye as the hypocrites, but as the Lord commanded in His Gospel, thus pray ye: Our Father, which art in heaven, hallowed be Thy name; Thy kingdom come; Thy will be done, as in heaven, so also on earth; give us this day our daily bread; and forgive us our debt, as we forgive our debtors; and lead us not into temptation, but deliver us from the evil one; for Thine is the power and the glory for ever and ever. Three times in the day pray ye so."

The Didache 8:2-3. Retrieved 7/17/01 from Indiana Wesleyan University server, Marion, Indiana. http://www.indwes.edu/courses/rel435/didache.htm

The early Christian believers were urged to pray the Lord's Prayer—the "Our Father"—three times each day. *The Didache*, an early church worship and membership training manual of sorts, includes the prayer and instructs Christians to pray it three times daily, though no hours were specified. In the third century, Tertullian instructed Christians to pray at sunrise, sunset and the third, sixth, and ninth hours. Cyprian joined in with his own instructions for prayers three times daily. *The Apostolic Tradition*, dated at 217, "raised the ante" back to Psalm 119's seven

times a day by establishing set times and a "memory agenda" for some
of these prayers:

1. When rising for the day
2. Nine a.m. — when Christ was nailed to a tree
3. Noon — when it became dark
4. Three p.m. — when Christ died
5. Bedtime
6. Midnight
7. At the cock's crow — when Peter denied Christ

Origen (early 200s)

"Each person should organize his prayers according to these top-
ics. Praise; thanksgivings; forgiveness; request; concluded with a
doxology."

On Prayer 33:1.

These prayer times may have been personal prayers or gatherings of
Christians; we don't know for sure. Perhaps it depended on the local situation. One thing we can surmise: as the Christians won entire cities to
Christ, it became easier to gather for these prayers. Perhaps they discovered what most Christians in every age since have discovered — prayer
with others is of greater power than solitary prayer. For when it comes to
corporate prayer, "the sum is greater than the parts."

We do know that by the 300s, Eusebius of Caesarea reported what
appeared to be a joint service at dawn and in the evening, at two of
the traditional three appointed times of prayer. And by the late 300s, the
"Apostolic Constitutions" directed a daily assembly every morning and
evening for "singing psalms and praying in the Lord's house." At about
this time (the late 300s), Egeria, a Spanish nun who toured the Holy
Land, reported that the Christians there sang "morning hymns" at daybreak, plus held regular services every day at the "apostolic hours" (at
nine, noon, and three o'clock).

So, what do we know about prayer in the early church? We know that

21

the early Christians made prayer a significant part of their public worship services—not just a single agenda item, but distributed throughout the service. Among other prayers, they prayed the Lord's Prayer together in worship. Even more impressive was their practice of daily prayers— the "daily office." These early Christians had "devotions" three times a day, comprised of the Lord's Prayer each time and presumably their own petitions. As time passed (or maybe even from the start), these daily prayers became daily assemblies of the Christians, and a daily morning and evening service emerged, including hymns along with the prayers.

Eusebius (late 200s)

"Throughout the whole world in the churches of God hymns, praises, and true divine delights are arranged for God at morning sunrise and in the evening…"

Eusebius of Caesarea

The Middle Ages

Prayer as an element of public worship continued throughout the Middle Ages into today's mass. Protestants who attend a Roman Catholic or Orthodox mass often feel convicted by how much prayer is offered compared to the average evangelical church. The mass placed prayers throughout the service. Through frequent prayer, worshipers were reminded that the worship service was oriented toward God, not just a horizontal transaction between the priest and people.

The daily "people's office" continued in the Eastern part of the church as a gathering for the ordinary people to have "devotions at church" each day. In the Western (later, Roman Catholic) part of the Christian church, daily prayers morphed from being an activity for ordinary people to something monks and nuns would take up.

If more prayer is always better, then the nuns, monks, and friars of the Middle Ages earned the prize. They took prayer and worship seriously. They really believed that prayer was a central duty of a man or woman, so much so that they gave themselves over to a life of prayer. That is not to say monks and nuns did nothing but pray—for medieval monasteries

Apostolic Constitutions (late 300s)

"Assemble yourselves together every day, morning and evening, singing psalms and praying in the Lord's house,"

Apostolic Constitutions, Book II, Section VII, pp. 422-423.

were wonderful places of learning, medicine, agricultural research and training. However, monasteries were primarily places of prayer. Ordinary people who cared about spiritual things and wanted to take prayer and worship seriously knew what to do: they joined an order. The rest of the ordinary folk left it to the monks and nuns to do the heavy praying.

In some ways, this division of labor was similar to our current understanding of "spiritual gifts" or "many parts/one body" theology. Everybody could not take prayer so seriously, but *some* could. Modern churches often follow the same pattern by setting apart the "old saints"

John Calvin (1500s)

"… we ought always to raise our minds upwards towards God, and pray without ceasing, yet such is our weakness, which requires to be supported, such our torpor, which requires to be stimulated, that it is requisite for us to appoint special hours for this exercise, hours which are not to pass away without prayer, and during which the whole affections of our minds are to be completely occupied; namely, when we rise in the morning, before we commence our daily work, when we sit down to food, when by the blessing of God we have taken it, and when we retire to rest. This, however, must not be a superstitious observance of hours, by which, as it were, performing a task to God, we think we are discharged as to other hours; it should rather be considered as a discipline by which our weakness is exercised, and ever and anon stimulated."

Institutes of Religion. Retrieved 7/18/01 from *Christian Classics Ethereal Library*; Calvin College, Grand Rapids.
http://www.ccel.org/pager.cgi?file=c/calvin/prayer/
prayer1.0.html&from=RTFToC59&up=c/calvin/prayer/prayer.html

23

for a prayer ministry, privately recognizing that most ordinary people can't or won't give so much time to prayer. However, the monks and nuns weren't older folk. Young men and women oriented to spiritual things went off and joined a monastic order to give their lives to something lasting and worthy: prayer and worship. These nuns and monks (mostly lay people, not priests, mind you) gathered at set times through the day to pray, sing psalms, and hear Scripture read.

In the 300s, St. Basil's "long rules" called for eight hours of prayer daily. In fact, until recent Roman Catholic reforms in the twentieth century, many monks and nuns still spent up to six hours every single day in prayer. St. Benedict developed the dominant plan for monastic devotions in the early 500s. His plan was to last for fourteen hundred years—into the 1960s. James White[1] outlines St. Benedict's plan for eight services as follows:

1. End of workday – *(Vespers)*
2. Before bedtime – *(Compline)*
3. Middle of night – *(Nocturns, Vigils, Matins)*
4. Daybreak – *(Lauds)*
5. Soon after daybreak – *(Prime)*
6. Mid-morning – *(Terce)*
7. Noon – *(Sext)*
8. Mid-afternoon – *(None)*

Benedict's plan prevailed in the monasteries and was copied by many local priests, though few ordinary folk attended these services. The "people's office" had become the "monastic office." Regular people increasingly left the praying to the "prayer ministry"—the prayer professionals, the monks and nuns. Common folk might drop off some food or other gifts at a monastery, hoping that the professional *pray-ers* would lift their requests to God. Increasingly, prayer became something done by those called to full-time prayer.

Local priests copied the eight services in their own parishes, but few ordinary people showed up for these daily services. This resulted in the

[1] James White, *Introduction to Christian Worship* (Nashville: Abingdon Press, 1980), 128.

priest holding his devotions alone in the church building.

By the 1100s, St. Benedict's plan was shortened by some orders as the pace of life started to speed up. By the 1200s, the Franciscans truncated the plan to an even briefer edition, which was recited in a "choral" way. In the 1500s, the Jesuits loosed their members altogether from the choral recitation, providing the model of what would become once-a-day "personal devotions" in our modern, fast-paced world.

The Reformation

While prayer was a concern of the Reformers, Scripture was more central. In prayer, men and women speak to God; in Scripture, God speaks to us. Which is more important? During the Reformation, daily prayers were reinstated for the ordinary people, but Scripture took a more important place in those daily services.

Church of Scotland (1647)

"Besides the publick worship in congregations, mercifully established in this land in great purity, it is expedient and necessary that secret worship of each person alone, and private worship of families, be pressed and set up; that with national reformation, the profession and power of godliness, both personal and domestick, be advanced."

Church of Scotland, *The Directory for Family-Worship*, I, II, IV (1647). The Confession of Faith; Directories for Public and Family Worship (Philadelphia, 1829), 595-596.

25

Zwingli restored daily services, but not primarily for prayers so much as for daily exegesis of Scripture. His twice-daily services provided fourteen different sermons a week, plenty of Scripture for the laity to chew on! Luther offered two daily services: one at the end of the workday and the other in the evening, before bedtime.

The Church of England offered morning prayers and evening prayers to its members. These services included prayer along with hymns and

Scripture readings. The attendees read through the Psalms once a month and the entire Bible in a year by offering three readings: each time starting at Genesis, Matthew, and Romans.

In general, the Reformation attempted to reverse the medieval trend of moving daily prayers and services away from the ordinary folk to the monasteries. Regular working people were now expected to attend church in the morning and evening to pray, to hear Scriptures read, and to sing.

The Modern Era

Luther had reminded us of the priesthood of all believers. That is, nothing is needed to provide a path between humans and God—we can "go direct." While this concept was not intended to make the church less important, it invariably did exactly that. An increasing number of Protestants saw no reason to go to church for their daily prayers—why not have them right here at home as a family matter with myself as priest? Thus was birthed what would later come to be called "family devotions." In this setup, the father served as the priest and the family as parishioners. This practice was especially popular with Puritans, the Scottish Presbyterians, and some English folk during Queen Victoria's rule. Daily public prayer had moved from the church to the home, and the father was now the presiding priest at the family altar.

Protestant principles can seldom be stopped partway on the journey to their logical ends. If Luther taught the priesthood of all believers, why would there need to be a father to preside between God and us—couldn't we as individuals go directly? The Enlightenment brought the notion of individualism to an even greater peak and made this transition easier. With this enhancing of the individual came the evangelical movement. In this movement, *individuals* make *personal* decisions to receive Christ as their *personal* Savior, thus popularizing the notion that religion is primarily a personal thing and not a church or family matter. It is no wonder that "personal devotions" would come to replace church or family devotions, although on a smaller scale both church devotions and family devotions continue today.

This move from daily prayers at church, to family prayers at home, to individual private devotions has been especially popular in America, where individualism is a central doctrine of life. "Daily devotions" for many evangelical Americans is the central sacrament of their religion. They believe it is the *chief* way to receive God's changing grace and the *primary* route to spiritual growth. When asked how to grow closer to God, the average evangelical will seldom answer, "Receive the Lord's Supper more." Even "Attend church more often" is an infrequent response by evangelicals. By far the most common response to this question is something like, "Read my Bible and pray more often." American evangelicals especially value private devotions, sitting all alone in prayer far away from a church or small group. This privacy penchant puts us out of step with history, our theology of the church, and the New Testament, but leaves us exceedingly in tune with the values of our culture.

Private Prayer Today

Devotions reign supreme in American evangelicalism, or at least the notion rules. Although far more Christians believe in personal devotions than actually have them, daily prayers are a feature of evangelical Christianity. While study of Scripture, reading devotional literature, or doing "homework" for a discipleship class often competes with prayer in daily devotions, prayer is still an important element. Some Christians, especially younger ones, are experimenting with pure-prayer devotions several days a week, which upgrades the importance of prayer in devotions. Having prayer corporately has surfaced again, though usually not at church. Instead, small groups meet throughout the day or even interdenominational groups gather at the workplace. After all, a Christian should be able to pray with someone from just about any other Christian denomination. Private prayer is doing pretty well among today's evangelicals.

27

Public Prayer Today

What about public prayer in evangelical worship? It's not faring so well. Minimalist evangelicals have reduced the role of prayer in their services and placed most all of the prayers on the platform rather than in the pew. Though a service might be opened in prayer and the offering might be blessed, usually one prayer is given significance—the "pastoral prayer." In the pastoral prayer, the minister (or designee) serves as priest representing the people's collective needs to God. Some evangelical churches feature pastoral prayers several minutes in length—almost rivaling a special song. If prayers are going to last more than a few minutes, soft musical accompaniment is often played in the background.

However, most evangelicals have streamlined the prayer part of the worship service in line with one pastor's remark: "You can't keep people interested when their eyes are closed." The final prayer might be a benedictory prayer at the close of the service, but that is sometimes a review of the sermon's points more than actual serious God-directed praying. An attendee at such an evangelical church would assume prayer is a minor part of worship and participatory prayer even less important. Face it, many evangelical ministers, like the monks and nuns of old, do all the praying on the platform for the people. While private prayer may be thriving among evangelicals, public prayer as an act of worship is not doing quite so well. Worship scholar James White once observed, "It is frustrating to visit a church that has introduced puppets but has overlooked corporate prayer."[2] Amen.

However, all of the signs are not bad for prayer. An increasing number of evangelical and Charismatic churches are reintroducing the Lord's Prayer as a regular feature of worship. More Christians are coming to believe that Jesus might have actually meant it when He instructed us to pray that prayer. Other churches now make their "pastoral prayer" an extended time of prayer, inviting the congregation to come to the altar to pray and seek personal help from God. For many Revivalist churches, this "open altar" time is replacing their traditional "altar call" at the end of the service. Still other churches divide their people into small prayer groups during worship so the people can pray for each other's needs. "Quaker silence" for personal prayer is starting to make a comeback— even in some Quaker churches. While the midweek "prayer meeting" has fallen away in most Revivalist churches (or morphed into a weekday teaching time), modern Sunday school classes now make heroic efforts at reintroducing prayer as the first part of their class time (though most of the time is spent in discussing requests, not in actual prayer). Some

---

[2] James White, *Christian Worship in North America* (Collegeville, MN: The Liturgical Press, 1955-1995), 41.

evangelical churches are introducing prayer litanies, projected on the screen and sandwiched between choruses. Many of the more recent "praise choruses" are not really praise songs at all but sung prayers. Could it be that prayer will make a comeback as a significant part of evangelical worship?

To think about . . .

1. What new discovery did you make after reading this chapter on the development of prayer through history?

2. We should be involved in both public and private prayer, of course. But if you had to "tilt" toward one of the two, which would you pick? Why?

3. If one of the two kinds of prayer needs to be upgraded more than the other in your own local church (corporate or private prayer), which one needs more work? In your own life?

4. The bad *pray-er* in the New Testament is the Pharisee who prays a self-glorifying prayer of thanksgiving, not the sinner who prays a humble prayer of confession/supplication. Think about this, then give several examples of how thanksgiving prayers can be used wrongly for self-glorification or other purposes out of line with God's values.

5. Is *more* prayer better than less? That is, were the monks and friars right? Would we all be better off if we could give our lives to full-time prayer?

29

6. List some possible reasons why many evangelical churches do not make prayer a greater part of their worship experience. Which of these is the primary reason in your opinion?

7. Medieval folk often "delegated" their praying to the monks and nuns. Is it OK for busy people to get others to do their praying for them? Is it all right for young people going on a mission trip to expect others—especially older people—to give greater time

praying for their trip than they do themselves? Is this a fair "division of labor" or not?

8. Think back over the past week, then list every time you prayed or were present during public prayer during the last seven days. Discuss your results with someone else. Is it more than you thought? Less? When were the best times to pray?

9. Discuss how prayers moved from church to family altar to private devotions. For each of the three forms of prayer list several advantages.

10. If you were going to practice saying the Lord's Prayer like the early Christians did, three times a day, when would you pray it in your daily routine?

11. What one thing might you do to improve prayer in your personal life?

12. What one thing might your local church do to improve the prayer in its public services?

3
Scripture and Preaching

Pastor Karin had trained for the ministry at a solid seminary in the Reformed tradition. There they taught her to spend at least fifteen hours a week preparing an "expositional sermon" for Sunday morning. In her first church she found how difficult this was going to be. She had to attend committee meetings, make hospital calls, catch up on office work, and be present at district meetings. Her people even expected her to attend birthday parties for their children. Worse, when she tried to be "expositional," her people tended to doze off. Yet anytime she told stories or funny illustrations, they perked up and complimented her preaching. Over the course of her first two years as pastor, Karin gradually abandoned what she had been taught in seminary, moving instead toward "Help-for-Monday" sermons with lots of humor and contemporary stories. She felt badly about doing this, but figured it was a matter of survival.

Last summer Karin attended a seminar at a large successful church on the West Coast. The graying pastor said, "Forget trying to preach Scripture—people won't listen today to strange words that take ten minutes to explain—you've got to 'exegete life,' not Scripture." She felt better for a while, but confessed to her school chum Jessica, "The people love my messages now, but I still feel like I've abandoned something important."

Had Karin abandoned a vital element of worship? Do we have to have Scripture in worship? Or, can we speak the truth separate from Scripture? Who says Scripture is a required element for worshiping God? Can't we "go direct" to God without the mediation of a book? How did Scripture become a part of worship?

Scripture for the Patriarchs

Adam, Noah, Abraham, Isaac, Jacob, and Joseph had no Scripture, yet they worshiped God. At least, they had no *written* Scripture. Essentially Scripture performs the role of a "word from God" in worship. The Patriarchs got their word directly from God. God spoke, the Patriarchs listened and responded in worship, sacrifice, and obedience to God's Word. God said to make an ark, and Noah made one. God told Abraham to move, so he did. The Patriarchs heard God's Word directly and responded. Their Bible was the direct voice of God. During the time of the Patriarchs, the Ten Commandments had not yet been given. All the Patriarchs had was God's direct voice.

The Israelites' Scripture

The written Scriptures appeared in connection with Moses and the emerging of the "Israelites." One might argue the first written Scriptures were not on paper at all but on stone—the Ten Commandments. Moses brought these written laws from God down from Sinai and commanded the people to follow them. However, there wound up being more than just the Ten Commandments. The Torah—the first five books of the Old Testament—presented elaborate details for daily living, including one's relationships with others and God. "The Law" became the written basis of God's covenant with Israel. At times the Law was valued and central to Israel's life. At other times it was completely overlooked and "lost" for all practical purposes.

The first five books of the Old Testament are not the only sacred writings for the Jews. A sacred songbook, the Psalms, joined the Torah, though the Torah continued to be the most sacred of the writings. Prudent words of wisdom were collected in the Proverbs and books like Job, and these too are part of Scripture. (Job may even be one of the oldest books of the Old Testament.) Once Israel entered the Promised Land and established a kingdom, prophets emerged with words of chastisement, correction, and prediction. Their words came to join the Torah in constituting the sacred literature of the Jews. But Scripture did not take center stage until the synagogue emerged.

The Synagogue and Scripture

In synagogue worship Scripture became the central focus. For several

The Apostles' Creed

I believe in God, the Father almighty,
> creator of heaven and earth.

I believe in Jesus Christ, his only Son, our Lord.

He was conceived by the power of the Holy Spirit
> and born of the Virgin Mary.

He suffered under Pontius Pilate,
> was crucified, died, and was buried.

He descended to the dead.
> On the third day he rose again.

He ascended into heaven,
> and is seated at the right hand of the Father.

He will come again to judge the living and the dead.

I believe in the Holy Spirit,
> the holy catholic Church,
> the communion of saints,
> the forgiveness of sins,
> the resurrection of the body,
> and the life everlasting. Amen.

Retrieved 7/21/01 from: http://www.mit.edu/~tb/anglican/intro/lr-apostles-creed.html

thousand years, the Old Testament people didn't have a synagogue. At first they worshiped as a family or clan. Then they worshiped corporately in the Tabernacle and Temple, along with family worship. When the Jews were carried away into Babylonian captivity, they probably invented the local synagogue to preserve their religious heritage in a religiously hostile environment. Apparently, they brought this idea with them as they returned from exile, for every town had a synagogue or place of prayer (the idea is more related to an "assembly" than a building) in Jesus' day. At the single national Temple, the worship focused on elaborate rituals and animal sacrifice. In the many local synagogues, worship focused on Scripture—the reading and study of the Torah. The synagogue's "tone" was that of looking back and remembering what God had done, primarily through reading the Torah and through prayer. This practice was designed to pass on the "corporate memories" of a people.

Knowing what God had done in the past was assumed to help the people know who they were, resulting in faith for the present and hope for the future.

The Christian's first-century "service of the Word" was based largely on the Jewish synagogue pattern—after all, the first Christians were Jews and continued to worship for the most part in the way to which they were accustomed.

The typical synagogue service after the year 80 (and especially after 200) opened with a creed (the Shema) as recorded in Deuteronomy 6: 4-9. Next, the congregation was led in a series of nineteen prayers—the tefilah—including three of praise, thirteen of petition, and a closing set of three prayers of thanksgiving. Next, the service turned its full attention to the Scriptures. This section of the service began with the singing of hymns and psalms from Scripture; then the Torah (and sometimes the writing of the prophets) was read aloud. The readings were explained by the darshan or "searcher," whose job it was to search for the real meaning of a passage and explain it to the congregation. This synagogue focus on Scripture strongly influenced early Christian worship if this later format reflected the style at the time of Jesus.

The Early Church and Scripture

In addition to the synagogue pattern, the early Christians had a second model of worship. "Upper room worship" included an intimate meal, fellowship, perhaps a hymn or two, and the breaking of bread. This bread breaking was a spiritual ritual that developed into the agape meal and included the Lord's Supper. This second model—the upper room model—was less focused on Scripture and more on sacred actions and fellowship.

The very first Jerusalem Christians met in the (Jewish) Temple and from house to house. However, as the gospel spread throughout the world, believers often met in the Jewish synagogues as "completed Jews" until they were eventually expelled.

Once the Jewish Christians were on their own, house churches sprang up. These featured a two-part service: first, a "Service of the Word" based on the synagogue pattern and focused on Scripture and prayer; and second, a "Service of the Table," which followed the first service and was based on the upper room pattern—the blessing and receiving of the Lord's Supper.

The typical early Christian service probably began with corporate prayers, then the singing of hymns and psalms. These hymns and psalms may have been Scriptures delivered in a song-like chant, so Scripture in worship probably emerged in the music before it was ever read aloud. Somewhere in the service, perhaps next, the Christians recited a creed or oath. The creed most likely was some early edition of the Apostles' Creed—a statement of belief. However, from one piece of early evidence—a letter by the Roman governor Pliny—it appears that the Christians may also have recited some sort of oath binding themselves to a particular lifestyle. This oath was not so much about what they believed as how they would live—including binding themselves not to "commit fraud, theft, or adultery," among other things.

After the prayers, hymns, and creeds/oaths, a "reader" came forward to present the Scriptures. At first, Scripture was for them the Old Testament in a Greek translation. However, soon the "memoirs of the apostles" (probably the gospels) and other writings, especially those of Paul, joined the Old Testament for reading in worship.

The "reader" was not an unprepared volunteer who ran over the verses on the way to church that day, but someone who held a sacred position in the early church. In fact, it is likely that the readers actually kept "their assigned books" (e.g., Galatians, Ephesians, Mark) at their homes and brought these books with them to the assembly. These readers were supposed to master the books—learn them thoroughly—so that when they read, the message came through dramatically. It is likely they changed their voices, took parts, and were so well prepared that their reading was more like a modern dramatic presentation than a droning litany of boring words.

In the Eastern Church, the position of "reader" was an ordained position—the reading of Scripture was not taken lightly. *Hearing* Scriptures read was more important than studying them. After all, much recent

35

research suggests the Scriptures were not originally intended to be studied bit by bit at all, but rather to be *heard* in community. Contemporary Christians are used to reading and studying ten verses in depth. The early church knew nothing of this method. The readers delivered large sections—maybe even an entire book—at one sitting in a riveting, dramatic style. Some Scriptures may even have had prompting notes in the text for the reader to use in presenting the text out loud to the assembly of Christians (e.g., "let the reader understand," Matthew 24:15). Paul's message in Galatians or John's in Revelation has a significantly different impact when read aloud in a communal setting than if read in solitude.

The role of Scripture for the early Christians did not stop with the *hearing* of Scripture. Following the reading of Scripture, the congregation's "president" or presiding leader then explained and applied the Scripture to the lives of the congregation. Here we have the birth of Christian preaching. However, don't look for examples in the New Testament. Most of the record we have of New Testament preaching is evangelistic in nature and targeted to the Jews or Gentiles. We have little record of Paul's messages to Christians—even though he once preached all night. We presume the content of his preaching was similar to the content of his epistles. Thus, we surmise the content of the president's message to the congregation would be an explanation of the Scriptures and their application to the lives of the attendees.

Following this sermon came the offering. Then the *catechumens* (candidates for baptism) were dismissed. Only baptized Christians stayed for the second part of worship—the "Service of the Table" or Lord's Supper.

By 300, the "order of worship" had settled in, and the notion had emerged that every service should have three readings: one from the Old Testament, another from the Epistles, and a third from the Gospels—a practice followed by most Christians ever since. Even before the Emperor Constantine converted to Christianity, the Christian "Service of the Word" included at least three readings: one from the Old Testament (followed by singing of one or more psalms), one from the Epistles (also followed by the singing of one or more songs or responses), and finally the reading from a gospel (followed by a sermon). After the sermon, the catechumens were dismissed and the "Service of the Table" began.

The Middle Ages

Many Protestants believe that medieval worship was a service of magical, superstitious hocus-pocus without Scripture. They also think the Reformation is what brought Scripture back into worship. Not true. The mass of the Middle Ages was packed with Scripture. The typical medieval mass followed the opening greeting with Psalm 43, which set the tone for the penitential atmosphere in medieval worship: "Why are you downcast, O my soul?" After an antiphon, psalm, and the *Gloria Patri* (Glory be to the Father), the congregation recited the *Kyrie eleison* (Lord, have mercy) and then the collect, a prayer offered before the reading of Scriptures (though in Latin). Next came the Old Testament readings, the reading of the Epistles, and then the gospel readings, followed by a sermon. After the sermon, the congregation recited the Nicene Creed and continued into the second part of the service, the Eucharist.

Martin Luther (1523)

"The reading of the Epistles and Gospels is necessary, too. Only it is wrong to read them in a language the common people do not understand."

Formula Missae (1523). Trans. Paul Zeller Strodach and Ulrich S. Leupold, *Luther's Works* LIII.

However, the reading of Scripture was not the only way the medieval churchgoer got a dose of Scripture. They literally went to church inside the Bible! Medieval churches featured fabulous frescoes and stained glass windows portraying scenes from the Bible. Today's multimedia worship experiences can't yet touch what these churchgoers experienced. The worshipers stood inside a virtual Bible—with the entire story from creation to the final judgment wrapped around them in full color. Remember this was long before TV, rear-screen projectors, or laser light shows. Nothing competed with this gorgeous display of the entire story of the Bible. It is true that worship was not in the common language of the people, and thus seemed (cognitively) irrelevant. However, what do you suspect they did when the priest droned on in a language they didn't understand? You bet! Their eyes and minds wandered to their surround-

37

ings. In medieval times wherever you looked—at the walls, the windows, even at the ceiling—you got Scripture. Thus, even if you could not read, as was the common condition, you got plenty of the Scripture story from your surroundings. One might even argue that there was more Scripture in a medieval church than is found in the average "Bible-believing evangelical church" today.

Reformation

The Reformation was more about doctrine than worship, but the Scriptures were central as a doctrinal matter. It is generally accepted that every group must have an authority. For instance, a nation may have a "constitution" it holds sacred and to which it submits. So, what is the authority for the Christian? Christians for some 1,500 years had lodged that authority with the church—meaning gathered councils and established structures, including the prime bishop, the pope. That brought abuses, of course. The Reformers, however, lodged authority in Scripture. *"Sola scriptura"* was their cry: "Only Scripture."

The Reformers refused to allow the church to rule on matters not specifically mentioned in the Scripture. That is, the rules of faith and living were to be taken directly from Scripture where the Bible was explicit in that regard, and not from the church's interpretation or application of that Scripture in some implicit way.

So, what happened to Scripture in the Reformation? Several things. First, about 1450, Johannes Gutenberg invented movable type, making mass production of books possible and replacing the expensive, handmade copies used for the previous several thousand years. It is important to remember that up to this time ordinary medieval Christians never "read the Bible." Even if they could read (and most couldn't), they couldn't get one—for an ordinary farmer to get a copy of the entire Bible would be like an ordinary worker today trying to save up to buy a jumbo jet. It was out of the question. The Scriptures came to you at church unless you were a rich person, a scholar, or a monk. The printing press changed this. Within a hundred years of this invention, the Reformation was under way. It was no accident. (It was not the first time—or the last time—that technology would influence doctrine and practice in worship.)

Second, the Reformers insisted that worship be in the common language of the people, including all Scripture reading. Thus, the reading of the Scripture began to "leap off the page" and directly enter the lives of the worshipers. Some of Luther's followers even thought that to preach anything but Scripture was to invite too much human thought—and thus their entire sermon was simply the reading of Scripture. During the Reformation, Scripture moved closer to the people. The Reformers promoted every Christian to the rank of "priest"—the "priesthood of all believers." All believers now had the right and responsibility to understand and apply the Bible to their own lives. No longer was a person simply to accept what the church declared to be the meaning of the Bible. (Of course, each of the Protestant denominations soon made individual lists in their *disciplines* or *manuals* of what the Bible really meant. As the Catholics like to point out to us, this relocated the authority from the Pope to a democratic group in many cases.) Nevertheless, in the Reformation, Scripture moved closer to the individual, and its reality became clearer.

John Calvin's worship service started with a prayer of confession, after which the pastor pronounced an absolution. The congregation then sang the Ten Commandments and followed this with extemporaneous prayer. Psalms were chanted, after which came the collect—a prayer for illumination as the congregation approached the Scriptures. After the Scripture lesson, the pastor presented the sermon, followed by a long pastoral prayer of intercession and a congregational recitation of the Lord's Prayer. The Service of the Word closed with a blessing by the pastor, which Calvin prescribed was to be followed every week by the Lord's Supper. Calvin's followers, however, were not so keen as he was on this aspect and mostly ignored his plan for weekly Communion.

Modern Era

One would think that the Reformation would have launched a movement for more Scripture in Protestant worship. It did for some (at least more preaching, though that does not always mean more Scripture). But for many modern evangelicals there is far less Scripture in their worship services than ever before.

Many mainline churches like the Episcopal Church have retained the

39

three-fold pattern of reading Scripture—reading each week from the Old Testament, the Epistles, and the Gospels. These churches usually follow a *lectionary*, an organized coordinated plan of Bible readings for worship. Other churches, notably Presbyterian churches, have held fast to a *pedagogical* style of worship, making the teaching of Scriptures central to worship as they offer a three-part service: preparation for the Word, preaching of the Word, and response to the Word. As for Roman Catholic use of Scripture, Vatican II in the 1960s had a massive impact on Catholic worship by returning the mass to the common language. Many Protestants are shocked to discover on visiting a Catholic mass that there is more Scripture there than in their own evangelical churches.

The Puritans (1644)

"All the Canonicall Books of the Old and New Testament, (but none of those which are commonly called Apocrypha) shall be publiquely read in the vulgar Tongue, out of the best allowed Translation, distinctly, that all may heare and understand...is requisite that all the Canonical books bee read over in order, that the people may be better acquainted with the whole Body of the Scriptures: And ordinarily, where the Reading in either Testament endeth on one Lords day, it is to begin the next...Beside Publique Reading of the Holy Scriptures, every person that can reade, is to be exhorted to reade the Scriptures privately (and all others that cannot reade, if not disabled by age or otherwise, are likewise to bee exhorted to learne to reade; and to have a Bible."

A Directory For the Publique Worship of God, *Of Publique Reading of the Holy Scriptures* http://www.athens.net/~wells/dpwg/reading.htm

Quakers had introduced direct revelation to individuals in worship, which took its place along with Scripture. Camp Meeting Revivalism *used* Scripture—especially Scripture stories—to persuade people evangelistically, but many revivalist preachers did not consider expositing Scripture and its meaning as their primary task. Camp Meeting

Revivalism worship produced a three-part service: preparing the soil in music, an evangelistic sowing of the seed, and the "altar service" where the harvest was reaped. (This was sometimes termed three services: the "song service," the "preaching service," and the "altar service.")

Help-for-Monday practical sermons in some evangelical churches make minor use of Scripture, basing their development more on pop psychology or how-to-succeed writings than the Bible, though they might find *illustrations* of their points in Scripture. Many evangelical churches have discarded the millennia-old, three-part reading from the Old Testament, the Epistles, and the Gospels. Some Protestant preachers even say, "Because of limited time I'll not read this lengthy section of Scripture," and then go on to give their own sermon for the next twenty minutes. "Expositional preaching" from time to time makes a temporary comeback, then fades until another generation reinvents it and tries it again.

There is, however, some restoration of Scripture in Protestant churches. In the late twentieth century, the "Praise and Worship" movement introduced the "Praise Chorus" and extended periods of pure singing. Writers of these praise choruses increasingly gravitated toward direct use of Scripture, as the "Jesus People" had once done in the 1960s. As we have seen, Scripture as song is an ancient practice of worship and this new, updated version has upgraded Scripture's use in worship for many churches. Other churches use live drama to communicate Scripture stories in a pageant style, and many others are projecting Scripture on a screen while it is being read, sometimes even projecting it throughout the message. In a few (admittedly, very few) Protestant churches, biblical art or sculpture is returning to worship, though more commonly in a modern form of image projection or by video. Especially popular among these churches is the use of the "Jesus Film" or other "Video Bible" efforts to portray the Bible story of the day.

41

A recent form of worship is "entertainment worship," requiring the "audience" to be constantly captivated and interested by what is happening on the "stage." In this form of worship, the reading of Scripture is often eliminated. As one well-known, super-church pastor likes to say, "Reading to modern men and women is what you do to put them to sleep."

In Scripture we hear God speak and see what He has done in history. Hearing God speak is somewhat different than hearing a pastor talk. Church history professor Bud Bence calls worship "a conversation with God." That is, worship is both speaking to God and hearing from God. Worship is not a one-way human monologue or performance with God as the audience. It is God and His church communicating. While God communicates in other ways (through creation, through an inner voice, through the words of others), most Protestants believe God communicates most clearly and reliably through Scripture. Believing that is easy. Practicing it in worship is harder, isn't it?

To think about . . .

1. What new discovery did you make after reading this chapter on Scripture and preaching in worship?

2. Since the Patriarchs "heard directly from God" and had no written Bible, are we just as free today to "hear directly from God" the "Word of the Lord"? Or does having a written Bible now restrict direct revelation? If God speaks just as clearly today as then, why use a Bible at all in worship when we can simply hear His up-to-date prophets speak for Him?

3. Scripture was not the centerpiece of Temple worship as it was in synagogue worship. Is there a place for "Temple worship" today—where pageantry, sacred acts, and song play a greater role than Scripture? If so, where? How?

42

4. It seems that some early Christians recited an "oath" weekly about how they'd live—not just what they believed. If you were to write such an oath for your own church today, one the congregation would recite every week as a promise before God, what would you include? Write a short lifestyle oath you think would be good.

5. The early church had a designated, prepared "reader" to ensure the prominence of Scripture in worship. What are some things we might do today to increase the effectiveness of Scripture reading in worship? The popular preacher who said, "You can't read to modern

people" is right in a way. So, how do we communicate what God has said in the Scriptures to modern TV-video-Internet-visual-action kinds of people?

6. In what way would "the message" of Scripture be heard differently if a well-trained and practiced reader read *the entire book* of Mark in a worship service? What would we "get out of it" compared to short readings and expositions of a few verses? What might be lost?

7. The Christian church has read from three sections of the Bible through most of history. What is good about this practice? What is bad about it? Should we adopt this practice?

8. In what ways could a modern church reintroduce the sort of visual communication of the Bible that the medieval church had "built in"?

9. How would you explain the curious observation that many "Bible-believing churches" use less actual Scripture in their worship than "liberal" and mainline churches do?

10. If "entertainment worship" were to become our destiny and we *had to* adapt to this style of worship, how could Scripture be used so that it would not be lost or eliminated from worship?

11. This chapter treats "preaching" as a subset of "Scripture." That is, rather than having two chapters—one on preaching and another on Scripture—the author treats preaching as falling under the heading of "Scripture." Why do you think he did this? Do you agree or disagree?

43

4
Baptism

Grace was a single mother of two, someone who "just didn't have time" to attend church. However, her friend Freda, who lived in a nearby apartment, kept inviting her to go along, promising, "We've got a great program for your girls." One Sunday she finally joined Freda. At church she met several delightful people who made her feel welcome—they were not at all the sort of folk she expected to meet. Almost every week after that (except when one of the girls was sick), she rode with Freda. She eventually joined the "Look-Us-Over" class for newcomers taught by Pastor Fred, a snowy-haired pastor in his 60s. In the fourth class she attended, Pastor Fred outlined "What It Means to Be Converted." Grace still wasn't completely sure, but at the end of the session she checked a box saying she'd like to talk further about "being saved." Later that week, she told Freda in her kitchen over a cup of coffee that she'd checked the box. Freda talked simply and fluently about her own experience with Christ, and there, in Freda's kitchen, Grace "became a follower of Christ in a new way," as she put it. When Pastor Fred visited her house on Thursday to "talk more about conversion," she reported, "I've already done that." He replied, "GREAT! So now you're ready for baptism." Grace was taken aback. "I've already done that, too. When I was a little baby at church in Wisconsin, my parents had me baptized. Do I have to do it again?"

45

Where did this strange practice of putting water on people (or putting people under water) come from as a rite of acceptance into the Christian community? Is infant baptism just as good as adult baptism? When one is baptized as an infant and then later becomes a follower of Christ, does he or she have to be re-baptized, or can the infant baptism "count"? Does anything spiritual actually "happen" when one is baptized, or is it

Didascalia Apostolorum (about 250)

[Woman deacons are to] "anoint the women...for the ministry of a woman deacon is especially needful and important."

R. Hugh Connolly, ed., *Didascalia Apostolorum* (Oxford: Clarendon Press, 1969), 147.

only a symbol of something that has already happened? Why do modern Christians still cling to this strange and ancient initiation ritual?

Nobody is a Christian by birth; a person *becomes* a Christian. How did the first-century person become a Christian? "By faith" is the easy answer, of course. What was the process? Did they "go to the altar" or "come forward"? What sign or symbol was accepted as the dividing line between the old life and the new life—that designated the new believer as a full Christian and part of the church? The sign was baptism.

THE EARLY CHURCH

The Jews and Baptism

Consider initiation among the Jews. How does one become a Jew? Most present-day Christians would say, "Be born to a Jewish family." This is a racial answer—"Jews are born Jews like the Chinese are born Chinese." Being born Jewish was only one way to become a Jew. There was another way. In the times of the early church, a pagan could convert to Judaism by becoming a Jewish "proselyte." The Ethiopian eunuch (Acts 8) was probably such a proselyte to Judaism.

How did one become a Jewish proselyte? There was a specified process. Conversion first required extensive study and preparation, which was then completed by a symbolic act—an "induction sign." That sign for the Jews was circumcision. As adhered to since the time of Abraham, all Jewish males were to be circumcised. In ancient times, the Egyptians had practiced circumcision (not at infancy) but by the time of Christ it appears to have been uniquely Jewish. Circumcision was considered so particular to the Jews that it became the symbol of their separation from the rest of the world. The Jews referred to their Philistine neighbors as "the uncircumcised." To the Jewish male, circumcision symbolized Jewish identity—whether he had been born Jewish or had converted to Judaism. To become a Jew—for a man—was to become circumcised. The Jewish male was thus "marked for life," making it both the sign and the act of initiation. (Women had a separate ritual of initiation, but we will deal with that later.)

Didache (about 100)

"Now about baptism: this is how to baptize. Give public instruction on all these points, and then 'baptize' in running water, 'in the name of the Father and of the Son and of the Holy Spirit.' If you do not have running water, baptize in some other. If you cannot in cold, then in warm. If you have neither, then pour water on the head three times 'in the name of the Father, Son, and Holy Spirit.' Before the baptism, moreover, the one who baptizes and the one being baptized must fast, and any others who can. And you must tell the one being baptized to fast for one or two days beforehand."

The Didache, VII. Retrieved 7/17/01 from Indiana Wesleyan University server, Marion, Indiana. http://www.indwes.edu/courses/rel435/didache.htm

The Christians adopted or adapted many practices of the Jews. The question came up: Should the new church adopt circumcision as its initiation rite? It did not. Christian *baptism* eventually replaced Jewish circumcision as the rite of initiation and incorporation.

47

Baptism was not new to the Jewish people. Indeed, there is some evidence that male proselytes to Judaism might have been baptized along with being circumcised probably as an act of ceremonial cleansing rather than specifically a rite of initiation. For female proselytes to Judaism,[3]

---

[3] Obviously, women proselytes could not be circumcised. Thus, baptism would have been their *only* sign of conversion to Judaism. For Christians, the sign of baptism has no sexual preference—being identically performed on men or women. This gender-neutral initiation act is a hint of the greater access and equality for women that is embedded in Christianity—albeit delayed even to this day.

Justin Martyr (about 155)

"Then they are brought by us where there is water, and are regenerated in the same manner in which we were ourselves regenerated. For, in the name of God, the Father and Lord of the universe, and of our Saviour Jesus Christ, and of the Holy Spirit, they then receive the washing with water."

First Apology. LXI Ante-Nicene Fathers, CCEL CD-ROM produced by Wheaton College.

however, baptism was even more likely used as the symbolic rite of conversion. The notion of baptism was around even before John the Baptist baptized the Jews, for baptism was used as a rite related to induction for Jews. John baptized Jesus in the Jordan River (Matthew 3:15). Jesus' disciples also baptized the Jews (John 4:2), though apparently Jesus himself abstained from performing the rite for some reason. The book of Acts is packed with baptisms, starting with the mass baptism of 3,000 Jewish converts in a single day, the day of Pentecost (Acts 2).

Thus, the rite of baptism was not new to the Jews. However, it was a significant shift to drop circumcision and replace it with baptism as the sign of belonging to the community. Although many of the Jewish converts to Christianity probably continued to circumcise their sons, baptism became the new sign of initiation. The practice of circumcision as a Christian rite eventually died out, and baptism reigned supreme as the initiation ritual for new Christians.

The Baptismal Blueprint

So, what did they say when baptizing new believers? At first, the phrase used was invariably "in the name of Jesus."[4] However, before long, this simple formula apparently gave way to a more Trinitarian one: "in the name of the Father and of the Son and of the Holy Spirit." By the time the Gospel of Matthew was written (after at least several and maybe all of Paul's journeys were already completed), Matthew records the Great Commission in Trinitarian terms. Perhaps the Trinity was assumed in

[4] See Acts 2:38; Acts 8:12; Acts 8:16; Acts 10:48; Acts 19:5; Romans 6:3.

the earlier pattern, but ever since that time, Christians have followed the Trinitarian formula with only a few exceptions.[5]

Baptism was not the only sign or sacred act related to initiation. Usually the "laying on of hands" also accompanied baptism. Laying on of hands was already established as an Old Testament practice, signifying a blessing or transfer of power. It was common among the apostles in the New Testament and was often related to receiving the Holy Spirit. Other acts soon joined the baptism rite, such as having the person drink a mixture of milk and honey, and anointing the person with oil.

Hippolytus (about 217)

"For whether it be a newborn infant or a decrepit old man—since no one should be barred from baptism—just so, there is no one who does not die to sin in baptism. Infants die to original sin only; adults, to all those sins which they have added, through their evil living, to the burden they brought with them at birth..."

The Apostolic Tradition, XV-XXI. Trans. Geoffrey J. Cuming, *Hippolytus: A Text for Students* (Bramcote, Notts.: Grove Books, 1976), 15-21.

The Didache provides us with a glimpse into the actual baptism practices of the early church less than one hundred years after Christ. It shows that baptism itself was prescribed with specificity, yet not so narrowly that options weren't offered. For instance, the "rules" preferred *running water* to a still pool; *cold water* was preferable to warm water and *immersion* preferable to pouring. However, while baptisms were to be in cold running water and by immersion, if circumstances did not provide for one or another of these preferred means, one might use still or warm water and baptize by pouring the water on the head three times.

49

---

[5] Luke's recording of the baptism formula "in the name of Jesus" (or *into* the name of Jesus) was recovered by groups such as the United Pentecostal Church (sometimes referred to as "Jesus-only people"), some of whom insist that the "name-of-Jesus" formula is the only authorized way to be baptized, and other formulas for baptisms "don't count."

Apostolic Constitutions (about 375)

"Now concerning baptism...thou shalt beforehand anoint the person with the holy oil, and afterward baptize him with the water, and in the conclusion shall seal him with the ointment; that the anointing with oil may be the participation of the Holy Spirit, and the water the symbol of the death of Christ, and the ointment the seal of the covenants. But before baptism, let him that is to be baptized fast; for even the Lord, when He was first baptized by John, and abode in the wilderness, did afterward fast forty days and forty nights."

Apostolic Constitutions, XXII. Retrieved 7/17/01 from New Advent server http://www.newadvent.org/fathers/07157.htm

Infant Baptism

As for baptizing infants, sources from the early period of the church are sketchy. Advocates of infant baptism argue that the "whole household" baptism of the Philippian jailer certainly included his children, but we can't say for sure. The Jews had taken their sons to be circumcised on the eighth day, so perhaps some Christians wanted a similar rite for their Christian children, and thus had them baptized on the eighth day as would become the practice hundreds of years later. But we have no evidence of that in the first century. We do know that some Christians practiced infant baptism by the early 200s, because Tertullian and others wrote at that time arguing against the practice.

Preparation Period

As we have seen, the early church offered a two-part church service. The first part was the "Service of the Word" and was open to everyone. At the end of this first service, all those not yet baptized were dismissed, because Holy Communion was reserved only for baptized Christians. The candidates for baptism, called *catechumens*, went through elaborate study and preparation for baptism. *The Didache* illustrates the extensive training they must have received in the "two ways."[6] This study and preparation for

---

[6] The "two ways" seems to be a collection of "membership commitments" on the proper lifestyle and attitude of a Christian juxtaposed with the other way—the way of darkness, the old life and attitudes.

Egeria (about 384)

"I feel I should add something about the way they instruct those who are to be baptized at Easter. Names must be given in before the first day of Lent, which means that a presbyter takes down all the names before the start of the eight weeks for which Lent lasts here, as I have told you. Once the priest has all the names, on the second day of Lent at the start of the eight weeks, the bishop's chair is placed in the middle of the Great Church, the Martyrium, the presbyters sit in chairs on either side of him, and all the clergy stand. Then one by one those seeking baptism are brought up, men coming with their fathers and women with their mothers. As they come in one by one, the bishop asks their neighbours questions about them: 'Is this person leading a good life?'...And if his inquiries show him that someone has not committed any of these misdeeds, he himself puts down his name...but if someone is guilty he is told to go away, and the bishop tells him that he is to amend his ways before he may come to the font. They have here the custom that those who are preparing for baptism during the season of Lenten fast go to be exorcized by the clergy first thing in the morning..."

Trans. John Wilkinson, *Egeria's Travels* (London: SPCK, 1999), 161-162. Also posted in an earlier edition by M. L. McClure and C. L. Feltoe under the title "The Pilgrimage of Etheria" at CCEL http://www.ccel.org/m/mcclure/etheria/etheria.htm

baptism could last as long as three years. During the entire training period, the catechumen could attend only the first part of worship (the service of the Word), then would be required to leave before the Lord's Supper portion of the service. The catechumen did not get a chance even to observe the closed Communion during the second half of the service.

The Baptismal Service

Easter Sunday was the primary day for baptisms, though they could occur at other times (most notably also on Pentecost Sunday). The baptism started when the candidate and others began fasting one or more days before they were to be baptized. On the Saturday night before

Easter, the candidate began an all-night vigil, watching and waiting for his or her day of baptism. Scripture was read just before dawn, then the bishop prepared the holy oil for anointing. The candidate was sometimes given a mixture of milk and honey to drink. The candidate completely undressed, renounced the Devil, and was thoroughly rubbed down with the oil of exorcism. (Early instructions have emerged that directed deaconesses to do the exorcism rubdown for women.) This exorcism was a significant event and not a mere "attending ritual" to the whole process. The candidate then was taken into the water and asked a few questions that paralleled what we know today as the "Apostles' Creed" in question format.

Coming out of the water, the candidate dressed in a fresh white robe and met the rest of the congregation. The Bishop anointed the head of the newly baptized person with oil, made the sign of the cross on his or her forehead, and gave the kiss of peace to each one before the new Christians took their "First Communion" with the congregation.

THE MIDDLE AGES

By the end of the 400s, Christianity had triumphed in the Roman Empire and had stomped out most of its competition. The empire became a "Christian nation" with one unifying religion—Christianity. As the Philippian jailer had decided the matter of faith for his "whole household" 400 years before, now the Roman emperors decided the matter of faith for a whole empire. When "everyone" is a Christian, whom do you baptize? Occasionally a foreigner or Jew converted, and one might witness an adult baptism, but for the most part the only new people were the infants being born into a community. So adult baptism gradually disappeared and the common practice remaining was infant baptism. Infant baptism was not hard to accept, partly due to the common understanding of Augustine's theology as consigning unbaptized babies to hell. What loving parents would delay their child's baptism if it meant that the unbaptized child would suffer eternally in hell upon death? However, pagan worship survived although in an "underground" format. Adults were still baptized partly due to the notion of delaying baptism until greater need in adulthood to wash away sins. In the 500s the emperor Justinian made infant baptism compulsory and adult baptisms "dried up" in the church by and large.

In the eastern part of the church (later to become the Eastern Orthodox Church), the local priest performed the baptism and confirmation as a single act. However, in the Western (Roman) church, the baptism service was split into two segments. The actual baptism, performed by the local priest soon after birth, was occasionally postponed until Easter. *Confirmation* only occurred when the bishop finally showed up—as a sort of finishing act. Outside Italy there weren't enough bishops to go around, so this second part of the ceremony was increasingly delayed. In the early Middle Ages, infants received their first Communion immediately after baptism. The priest would dip his little finger into the wine and place it into the infant's mouth. However, this practice was later abandoned.

By the late Middle Ages, infant baptism had become a private family matter instead of a public ceremony. Most infants were baptized on the eighth day, following the pattern of Jesus' circumcision. The bishop normally confirmed the baptized child by age seven, also in a private family ceremony. If the bishop had not shown up by age seven, most priests permitted children to start taking Communion before confirmation, pending the later ceremony.

Menno Simons (1539)

"Young children are without understanding and unteachable; therefore baptism cannot be administered to them without perverting the ordinance of the Lord, misusing His exalted name, and doing violence to His holy Word."

Foundation of Christian Doctrine. Trans. Leonard Verduin, *The Complete Writings of Menno Simons* (Scottdale, Pa.: Herald Press, 1956), 120, 126-127.

By the end of the Middle Ages, Christian culture predominated. Almost all "new converts" were babies who were baptized in private ceremonies soon after birth. Confirmed by bishops at about seven years of age, they became full participants as adults in Communion. Occasionally, an infidel converting to Christianity would require an adult baptism, but this was so rare that few Christians ever got to witness one.

THE REFORMATION

Luther and the initial Reformation brought two significant changes to baptism. First, baptisms were no longer to be private family affairs. Instead, they were conducted in a public service where the entire congregation could participate. Second, as in other liturgies, baptism was to be performed using the common language of the people. Beyond these two major changes, the Reformers tended to trim off any other excessive symbolism in the ceremony, simplifying it and making it less mysterious.

The Church of England (Anglican) kept most of the Catholic baptism ceremony with a few changes. They did insist that the child be dipped fully beneath the water three times. John Wesley started out with this Anglican practice but later accepted the practice of sprinkling children with water.

Reformer John Calvin followed Luther's pattern of continuing to baptize infants, but went a bit further than Luther in stifling any attending rituals that seemed too Catholic or mysterious.

Most modern Christians must be reminded that the Reformation was not about ending infant baptism and introducing personal conversion along with adult baptism. The Baptist movements and the evangelical revival

John Wesley (1784)

"Baptism is not only a sign of profession, and mark of difference, whereby Christians are distinguished from others that are not baptized; but it is also a sign of regeneration, or the new birth. The baptism of young children is to be retained in the church."

Articles of Religion (1784). Article XXVII revised in John Wesley's Sunday Service (United Methodist Publishing House, 1984), 312.

brought these ideas to the forefront. Reformers, captivated by "Covenant Theology," continued to baptize their babies along with any adult converts. Still, the forces set in motion by the Protestant Reformation would lead to other changes in baptism—changes more radical than Luther and the first Reformers might have imagined.

The Anabaptists introduced the radical new idea of adult baptism. These groups insisted that child baptism was invalid, for it did not signify personal and individual faith. Thus, for them, the only valid baptism was that of a cognizant adult coming to personal faith in Christ. However, the Anabaptists did not insist on immersion. Baptism by pouring was their preferred method. The English Baptists (following the Anglican insistence on infant immersion?) were the ones who went a step further, insisting that adults be fully immersed in the water.

The Quakers, always willing to take Protestant principles to their logical or illogical extremes, simply eliminated baptism altogether, preferring instead the "baptism of the Spirit."

Perhaps the greatest change ushered in by the Reformation was not related to baptism so much as to confirmation. The Reformers, mesmerized by systematic belief systems, delighted in sound catechism for their young. Catechism became the inculcation of true beliefs into the participants. Right belief became paramount. Thus, confirmation became the public acceptance of that belief system. Baptism and confirmation had always reflected two ends of one continuum: grace (reflecting what God had done) and knowledge (reflecting personal beliefs). Some Reformers' emphasis on right belief systems may have actually tilted the baptism-confirmation continuum toward the knowledge end of the grace-knowledge axis. Where this happened it was out of character with the basic systems of most Reformers, who emphasized "God's part" more than "the human part" in salvation and sanctification.

MODERN ERA

Wesley's evangelical movement, American Camp Meeting Revivalism, the modern evangelical movement, and generic pluralistic crusades and conferences have brought increasing acceptance of variety in matters of baptism. While the Salvation Army and Quakers still do not practice the rite, others seem willing to allow for variety in forms and means of baptism. Both infant baptism and adult baptism are being practiced, with some from both traditions adopting the rites of the other side.

Though early camp meeting schedules invariably included an opportunity for baptism, Camp Meeting Revivalism may have actually been a culprit in bringing about a decline in the importance of baptism to the average Christian.

Camp meetings and Finney's Revivalism introduced to the modern church a new and seemingly more powerful rite—the "altar call." An altar call seemed even better than baptism as an initiation rite. In powerful, emotional "altar services," unbelievers were invited forward to kneel at the altar and become "seekers." They would "go down" (not in the water, but "down to the altar") by bending their knees. These seekers would be submerged in a sea of altar workers who helped them "pray through." After a period of being submerged under this sea of saints, they would rise up, standing on their feet to testify about their newfound peace and relationship with God. The symbolism of the altar call was powerfully akin to baptism and far simpler: it required no tank of water, no heaters to be turned on the day before, no wet clothing, no preparation—just a simple mourner's bench at which to pray.

Thus, in many revivalist evangelical churches the altar call came to replace baptism as the symbolic initiation rite. It is at the altar where converts make their public commitments. It is at the altar where they are "born again." It is at the altar where they are extended the right hand of fellowship. All this was accompanied by powerful ritual symbols and emotionally memorable songs. For individuals "saved" in this ritual setting, their baptism became merely a formal reminder of the real experience they'd already had—the altar call conversion experience.

To think about . . .

1. What new discovery did you make after reading this chapter on the development of baptism?

2. We know pretty clearly how the early church performed baptisms. Is this method some sort of ideal we should seek to emulate, or are we free to adapt baptism to our own culture and preferences?

3. What do you think about the practice of infant baptism? Why?

4. If a person becomes a believer as an adult after having been baptized as an infant, is it OK for him or her to embrace this earlier baptism, or does that person have to be baptized again?

5. What are the advantages today of practicing immediate "celebration baptism" instead of a delayed "confirmation baptism"? Dangers?

6. Does anything spiritual actually happen at baptism, or is it merely a symbolic gesture of something that has already happened?

7. Most all churches consider baptism a "sacrament." What is a sacrament and what does this mean for baptism?

8. If you've been baptized, what did you "get" from it? Would you recommend it for all believers? Why or why not?

9. In some churches the altar call came to fulfill many of the ritual meanings of baptism. Is this a good thing or bad? As the altar call and public conversion gradually diminish in these churches, will this have a corresponding influence on baptism? How?

5
Lord's Supper

Larry arrived just in the nick of time for the service this morning. As he slipped into the pew during the first song, an older lady beside him pointed out the hymn number. He thumbed the pages and joined the congregation in singing. Lifting his eyes for the first time since coming in, he spied the Communion table in the front of the church. It was covered with a white linen tablecloth and the Communion set on top was also covered with a white cloth. "Shoot!" he thought to himself. "It's Communion Sunday—the pastor won't have studied much this week and this'll be a mostly wasted service."

Why is it some Christians—especially evangelicals—are disappointed on Communion Sunday? Why does this rite seem like an "imposition" on the regular plan of services? When did Communion start and how has it developed through the years? Is it time to drop this ancient symbolic act as totally irrelevant to the modern world? Or should it be renewed and restored as a weekly practice like it was in the early church?

Sign-Acts

Human beings are symbolic creatures. We see significance in symbols and signs. Many of us have mementos of past events tucked away somewhere in our dressers or attics—coins from a trip abroad, a stone from the top of a mountain, or a napkin from our first date. These mementos represent an important memory or event. Putting on a wedding ring is a fine example of such a human sign-act and the ring itself becomes a symbol. Such tangible objects possess a far deeper meaning than is apparent in either the action or the objects.

The Jews and Sign-Acts

We are indebted to the Jews for the notion that God and humans can communicate through certain physical objects, though these objects must never be confused with God himself. *Sign-acts* are tangible symbolic actions representing deeper intangibles. They blend the spiritual and physical in a profound way. The pillar of fire, the cloud, and the Ark of the Covenant were tangible expressions of communication between God and humans. For the Jews, imagine the overpowering sign-act of slaughtering hundreds of live animals, then burning them as a sacrifice to God. When Jeremiah put on a yoke and smashed the hardened pot, he was performing sign-acts. The Jewish Passover meal, a sign-act recalling their rescue from Egypt, was packed with smaller sign-acts. The Jews ate unleavened bread, which reminded them of the hurried exodus from Egypt. The bitter herbs recalled their bitter life under the taskmasters in Egypt. Circumcision, of course, was the sign-act of initiation for the Jews—the meaning went far beyond the action itself. For the Christians, the chief sign-acts were baptism and the Lord's Supper.

The Lord's Supper and Passover

Was the Lord's Supper an adapted "Passover-become-weekly" rite—a reinvented Passover sign-act? We do not know for sure. The institution of the Lord's Supper indeed began on the Jewish Passover (or the day before). The two rites were somewhat similar—both included a meal, a hymn, bread, and wine while the participants reclined at a table. The Passover recalled God's mighty act of delivering the Children of Israel out of Egyptian bondage. The Lord's Supper focused on God as the deliverer and Jesus Christ as the once-for-all sacrificial Lamb. But we don't know if one is based on the other. If the Jewish converts saw the Lord's Supper as a redesigned Passover, it would have been a significant change for them to move from celebrating this supper once a year to cel-

ebrating it weekly. There is no mention of the Passover's "bitter herbs" in either the New Testament accounts or in early church sources. So, if the Lord's Supper derived from the Passover, it did so with innovative adaptations. It is more likely that the Lord's Supper was adapted from the Jews' traditional weekly meal in preparation for the Sabbath.

The Lord's Supper in the New Testament

Matthew, Mark, and Luke tell of the institution of the Lord's Supper, but John's gospel is totally silent on this subject. Why? This is curious— wouldn't you think that such an important rite would be included in all four Gospels?

There are several explanations for John's silence on the Lord's Supper. Perhaps it was due to the secrecy surrounding Communion. As discussed earlier, in the early church Communion was closed to everybody except baptized Christians. Candidates for membership were required to fulfill their preparation first, and "seekers" were dismissed before the Communion portion of the service. Interestingly, this two-part service, with only baptized Christians being able to attend the second part of worship, resulted in a sort of first-century "reverse altar call." All the unbaptized had to leave the meeting at the halfway point. We do not know for sure why John omitted the story of the institution of Communion. For whatever reason, the other gospel writers were specific in telling the story.

The Christian Lord's Supper

Christians discarded circumcision as the mandatory initiation rite and replaced it with the sign-act of baptism, signifying one's cleansing from sin, burial with Christ, and resurrection to new life. The second sign-act with profound meaning for these Christians was the Lord's Supper or "Communion." The term "Lord's Supper" is recorded by Paul in 1 Corinthians 11:20, though Luke uses "breaking of bread" in Acts (2:46; 20:7).

The Jews had a weekly common meal in preparation for the Sabbath. Groups of friends often met together on Friday afternoons to eat, fellowship, and get ready for the Sabbath, which began at dusk. As the Sabbath was about to begin, the leader of these Jewish groups would preside over a ceremony called *the sanctification*, the blessing of the wine, before they drank it. The custom of the day among both Jews and Romans was to end their common meal with wine, a "toast" of sorts. Many Romans had a similar ceremony after a meal, pouring out a cup of wine as an offering to the family gods.

61

The Christians used bread and wine for their Communion service. It all started with a common meal, the *"agape meal"* or love feast. At the end of the meal, the person presiding—the president—would lead the gathered group in the Eucharist or Lord's Supper. The bread and wine would be blessed, and then all would partake of the elements, remembering the body and blood of Christ.

It is quite possible that the earliest Christians in Jerusalem celebrated the Eucharist daily, not just weekly. However, by the end of the first century, the Christians were taking the Lord's Supper weekly on the Lord's Day, Sunday. The entire Lord's Supper remembered the atoning death of Jesus and His resurrection. Communion was not something they heard about, talked about, or recited, but something they *did*—a sign-act. Since the Reformation, Protestants have tended to fill up the sign-act service with words, thus tilting worship from the experiential more toward the rational. In the early church, the act itself communicated the meaning.

A Secret Service—"Word and Table"

Our earliest pictures of the first Christians have them meeting from house to house, breaking bread together, with an apparently open invitation to anyone who would believe and join them. Baptism was performed immediately, and new Christians were incorporated into the gathering-fellowship of the church, including their regular "breaking of bread" and/or Lord's Supper.

The relationship between the bread breaking—the Lord's Supper—and the agape meal is not completely clear. The best guess seems to be that the Christians met for a common meal that included the wine and bread as a special rite. That is, "after supper [they] took the cup" and prayed (1 Corinthians 11:25 NIV).

Justin Martyr (about 155)

"This food we call Eucharist, of which no one is allowed to partake except one who believes that the things we teach are true, and has received the washing for forgiveness of sins and for rebirth, and who lives as Christ handed down to us. For we do not receive these things as common bread or common drink; but as Jesus Christ our Saviour being incarnate by God's word took flesh and blood for our salvation, so also we have been taught that the food consecrated by the word of prayer which comes from him, from which our flesh and blood are nourished by transformation..."

First Apology. Ante-Nicene Fathers CD-ROM produced by CCEL, Wheaton College.

This soon changed. All of the very first Christians were Jews. The Jews took only a small step of faith to become Christians. Jews simply *repented* of their sins (something they already understood from John the Baptist's preaching); *believed* Jesus was indeed the Messiah (messianic thinking was already strong in the minds of first-century Jews); and were *baptized* (with which they were already familiar through John's practice and their own proselyte conversion practices). A Jewish convert did not need a lot of "cleaning up" or preparation for full participation in the church

However, as Christianity spread throughout the first century, a new category of converts became integral to the church—the pagan Gentiles. At first they represented a small portion of the church, but eventually they made up the majority of the church population. Before the Christians (perhaps especially the Jewish core groups in many churches?) were able to accept them into the day's equivalent of "full membership," these new Gentile converts needed additional discipleship in the rudiments of Judeo-Christian religion. The result was delayed baptism and a two-part communion service: "Word and Table." As we discussed earlier, the first part of this service—the "Service of the Word"—included prayers, Scriptures, and a sermon to prepare participants for the second part of the service: the Lord's Supper. The first part of the service was public and open to everyone, both baptized Christians and "seekers" who wanted to become Christians.

However, before the Lord's Supper was served, every person not yet baptized was dismissed. The second part of the service, the "Service of the Table," was exclusively for baptized Christians—a "secret service" of sorts. This two-part service, "Word and Table," prevailed until there were no longer any unbaptized Christians. Once Christianity became the compulsory religion of the empire and everyone was baptized, there was no longer anyone to dismiss. In the early church, the first time a person witnessed the Lord's Supper was when he or she partook of Communion—at that person's "First Communion" immediately following baptism.

63

The Agape Meal Is Dropped

As mentioned above, the first Christians took the Lord's Supper in the context of a common meal, a sort of first-century, carry-in dinner. The early Christians eventually exchanged the daily common meal of the Jerusalem Christians for a weekly common meal. You might argue that meeting from house to house to "break bread together" refers primarily to the common meal more than the "Lord's Supper," which was probably a part of that meal. There is little talk elsewhere in Acts of this common meal.

Ignatius of Antioch (about 115)

"To the Smyrneans,

Let that be deemed a proper Eucharist, which is [administered] either by the bishop, or by one to whom he has entrusted it...It is not lawful without the bishop either to baptize or to celebrate a love-feast; but whatsoever he shall approve of, that is also pleasing to God, so that everything that is done may be secure and valid."

Letters. Ante-Nicene Fathers CD-ROM produced by CCEL, Wheaton College.

However, Jude 12 alludes to such "love feasts," so they must have continued in some places. The church in Corinth also must have had such a regular meal, for Paul addressed problems in their practice of the agape meal or love feast in his first letter to them. Apparently, the rich members of the church were partying and eating sumptuously, while the poor in the church hungrily watched. This selfish practice made a mockery of the unity the Lord's Supper was supposed to reflect. Paul scolds these affluent members, asking, "Don't you have homes to eat and drink in?"—a rhetorical question that seems to restrict the common meal practice. Perhaps the eventual disappearance of the agape meal as the context for the Lord's Supper and worship may have been due to these abuses. Or perhaps the agape meal was dropped for pragmatic reasons.

We do know that in some locations the agape meal was split from the Lord's Supper and moved to another time slot before eventually disappearing altogether. The Lord's Supper survived, of course, without the attending common meal. However, the potential for cliques and class warfare alluded to in 1 Corinthians may have been only one cause. The Roman government may have been another.

Pliny (about 112)

"...they were accustomed to meet on a fixed day before dawn and sing responsively a hymn to Christ as to a god, and to bind themselves by oath, not to some crime, but not to commit fraud, theft, or adultery, not falsify their trust, nor to refuse to return a trust when called upon to do so. When this was over, it was their custom to depart and to assemble again to partake of food—but ordinary and innocent food. Even this, they affirmed, they had ceased to do after my edict by which, in accordance with your instructions, I had forbidden political associations."

Letters 10.96-97 in a letter to Emperor Trajan. Retrieved 7/16/01. Posted on University of Pennsylvania server by James J. O'Donnell, Professor of Classical Studies, University of Pennsylvania. http://ccat.sas.upenn.edu/jod/texts/pliny.html (Read the full text of the Pliny letter in chapter 22 of this book.)

In Roman culture, a regular common meal indicated that the group was an established, approved organization or trade union—an "official gathering of an organization." The Christian church was not an approved religion or society. While the Romans often looked the other way at the unauthorized Christian gatherings, it is possible that when the church thrived and grew strong, the gathering attracted enough attention to cause unease among Roman officials. That is, the Romans may have wondered, "What is this new group up to in their secret meetings?" A successful, growing group could be a threat to Roman power, so they would have been tempted to intervene and shut down the unauthorized gathering.

65

This was true just after the turn of the first century in Bithynia. We have a surviving letter from Pliny the Younger, the Roman governor of Pontus-Bithynia from 111-113. Pliny exchanged letters with the Roman Emperor Trajan on a variety of administrative matters, and two of these letters refer to Christianity. The Pliny-Trajan correspondence gives us an independent Roman view of Christian worship just after the turn of the century and not too long after the final books of the New Testament had been written. The letter reveals a political reason for dropping the agape meal in the context of reporting to his Emperor how Pliny was attempting to stamp out this spurious group (the Christians) and to lead a revival of the old pagan religions (which had been losing ground to the Christians). Pliny explains it was the Christians' custom to (after an early morning worship) "assemble again to partake of food—but ordinary and innocent food." That is, these Christians apparently met early in the morning for worship, went home, and then came back together again for an agape meal. They had removed the love feast from their morning worship by this time, and they soon abandoned even the evening meal, at least in Bithynia.

Ignatius of Antioch (about 155)

"To the Ephesians,
At these meetings you should heed the bishop and presbytery attentively, and break one loaf, which is the medicine of immortality and the antidote which wards off death but yields continuous life in union with Jesus Christ."

Letters. Ante-Nicene Fathers CD-ROM produced by CCEL, Wheaton College.

Pliny assured the Emperor that following his edict forbidding "political associations," the church had given up its evening meal. Evidently, the Romans saw the growing clan of Christians as a potential political threat and their common meal as signifying their organized (political) strength. Thus, the Christians (at least in Bithynia) abandoned the agape meal.

At other locations, the agape meal may have been held on Saturday night as preparation for Sunday, reminiscent of the Jewish preparation for the Sabbath. While the tradition may have lasted several hundred years in a few places, it did not last as a significant and permanent part of the weekly celebration for the Christians.

For whatever reasons—abuse, politics, pragmatism, or something else—soon after the close of the New Testament era, the agape meal faded. By the first Church councils (300s), it had totally disappeared. (However, the agape meal became an "innovation-by reintroduction" in the 1700s for the Brethren, Mennonites, Moravians, and John Wesley, who reintroduced the feast as a means of worship and fellowship.)

Two things happened during the 300s-400s that changed the Lord's Supper significantly and would cement a new style throughout the Middle Ages. First, Christianity was legalized, then required; and eventually "everyone became Christian." The Christians had succeeded in evangelizing an empire. They no longer were forced to meet in homes, limiting their numbers to no more than forty or fifty people in a group. They now had large buildings, some as huge as those in the Roman Empire itself. They had enormous congregations, too—they were "super-churches." Serving Communion in a gigantic, cathedral-like structure to a thousand people is quite different from taking Communion with thirty of your best friends in the warm atmosphere of a friend's home.

Second and quite simply, the church eventually ran out of converts. Once whole nations became Christian, who was left to evangelize? Besides doing missionary work (which they did), the only "new prospects" were the children being born. So, while the two-part service continued, there was nobody to dismiss—everyone but "Jews and infidels" had already been baptized and were free to partake of Communion. The intimate, secret service of the early church with its few participants had now become a far-reaching, more public service with gigantic crowds participating.

67

Middle Ages

In the Middle Ages, the Eucharist became the centerpiece of worship. The Communion table increasingly functioned as an "altar," and the elements were more and more seen as a literal reenacted "sacrifice" of the Lord. By the 800s, the idea had spread that the bread and wine were actually changed into the physical body and blood of Christ. By 1215, the Church found the right term for this change: "transubstantiation," a doctrine that was defended by Thomas Aquinas and others.

Thomas Aquinas (1200s)

"I answer that, the presence of Christ's true body and blood in this sacrament cannot be detected by sense, nor understanding, but by faith alone, which rests upon Divine authority. Hence, on Lk. 22:19: 'This is My body which shall be delivered up for you,' Cyril says: 'Doubt not whether this be true; but take rather the Saviour's words with faith; for since He is the Truth, He lieth not.'"

From: *The Summa Theologica of St. Thomas Aquinas*,
Second and Revised Edition, 1920. Trans. Fathers of the English Dominican Province.
Online Edition © 2000 by Kevin Knight.
Retrieved 7/22/01 from http://www.newadvent.org/summa/407501.htm

Communion had long lost its roots as the conclusion to a common meal among friends in an intimate setting. It now was something set apart from the people, up in the chancel of an awesome cathedral—sometimes even set apart by a rood screen (a fence or screen that separated the chancel from the nave) so the people could barely see what was going on. The Eucharist became a mysterious and magical "sacrifice," and the laity's job was simply to wait until invited to line up at the end of the mass to receive the elements. Even then, the wine was often withheld from the laity, who took the bread alone as their Communion. However, don't get the idea that these Christians had Communion every week. Many medieval priests were lax at serving Communion, even during the mass. It would take the Reformation and later worship movements to try to restore weekly Communion to the people.

The Reformation

Martin Luther condemned Catholic abuses of the Lord's Supper, including the notion that the elements actually transformed into the body and blood of Christ. However, he did stress the "Real Presence" of Jesus in the Communion service. To Luther, the presence of Jesus was not a result of some magical transformation of the bread and wine, but he believed that Christ really was present just the same. Luther saw the primary effect of the Lord's Supper as being forgiveness of sins, as the Puritans also did later on. That is, when taken properly, the Lord's Supper functioned much as "confession." Communion was an opportunity to confess sins and receive forgiveness while participating in the symbolic act that reminded us of the means of our forgiveness, "the body and blood of our Lord."

Ulrich Zwingli (1526)

"And this he signified by the words: 'This is (that is, represents) my body,' just as a wife may say: 'This is my late husband,' when she shows her husband's ring."

On the Lord's Supper. Trans. G. W. Bromiley, LCC, XXIV, 195, 213, 234-235.

Zwingli (always ready to go further than Luther) did so here, discarding Luther's notion of "Presence" and even accusing Luther of "superstition." Others would go even further than Zwingli—the Quakers, for instance. Quakers so vehemently rejected sacramental practices that they stripped away all outward sign-acts, including baptism and the Lord's Supper. They practiced a "spiritual Communion," where no physical elements were used, and baptism by the Holy Ghost, not water. (Many modern evangelical churches have for all practical purposes adopted this Quaker view of Communion, though they might grudgingly offer Communion a few times a year, and then only in an "off service.") Every time Quakers gathered, they believed they were "communing" with the Lord and each other.

69

Calvin tried to find balance between the extremes. He called his followers to "guard against two faults . . . too little regard for the signs . . . [or] extolling them immoderately"; that is, avoiding both the Catholic magical view and the radical spiritualizing view. To Calvin, Christ was spiritually but not physically present. Calvin tried to restore weekly Communion, but his followers didn't follow him in this.

Along with attempting to restore the agape meal, John Wesley was an advocate of "frequent Communion" and tried to restore its weekly

Church of England (1563)

"The Supper of the Lord is not only a sign of love that Christians ought to have among themselves one to another; but rather it is a Sacrament of our Redemption by Christ's death: insomuch that to such as rightly, worthily, and with faith, receive the same, the Bread which we break is a partaking of the Body of Christ; and likewise the Cup of Blessing is a partaking of the Blood of Christ."

Church of England, *Articles of Religion* (1563); *Book of Common Prayer* (London, 1784). From *John Wesley's Sunday Service* (1784). (Nashville: United Methodist Publishing House, 1984), 312-313.

celebration. However, like the other Reformers, his success was mixed. The people had taken Communion infrequently for so long that the Lord's Supper actually seemed out of place (!) in a Christian service.

Others argued that the more frequently one took Communion, the less meaning it would have. Wesley argued that this was not true of prayer or other "means of grace," and it was not true of Communion either. To the question, "How often should I take Communion?" he answered simply, "As often as you can." For Wesley, Communion was more than Luther's purification from sin. To him, it was a "means of grace"—an ordinary channel by which God enables and changes people. Thus, to Wesley, Communion was a sanctifying work, not just about forgiveness of sins.

Some in the frontier churches and the Churches of Christ succeeded in recovering a weekly Communion using a common loaf. Alexander Campbell insisted that "all Christians" as "a holy and royal priesthood . . . may bless the Lord's Table, its loaf and cup," freeing up the rite in a democratic way for anyone to officiate.

The Lord's Supper Today

Many evangelicals consider Communion to be a memorial or remembrance of Christ's death and nothing more. Few expect any work of grace or purification from sin in this rite. For most, Communion is a mere token stripped of all mystery. This kind of thinking is more a product of the Enlightenment than the Reformation. In attempting to escape the mysterious and magical elements of Communion, modern evangelicals have sometimes stripped the rite of so much of its meaning that it seems strangely out of place in a service—something we now do that used to mean something but no longer does. Thus, it is relegated to off nights or Christmas Eve family services, or occasionally added to a wedding ceremony to borrow from its mystery and beef up the ceremony's sense of the sacred.

John Wesley (1784)

"I also advise the elders to administer the supper of the Lord on every Lord's day."

Letter of September 10, 1784, bound with *Sunday Service* (1784). *John Wesley's Sunday Service* (Nashville: United Methodist Publishing House, 1984).

On the other hand, a fresh "Word and Table" movement among evangelicals, featuring a weekly Lord's Supper, is returning to the two-part service of the early church. The current younger generation is especially keen on mysterious and ancient sign-act experiences. Their contemporary Eucharist services include elongated praise songs, candles, medieval ambiance, and the "Stations of the Cross" as an attempt to include sign-acts in worship. Worship is indeed becoming a verb for this generation.

Considering all of history, we'd have to say the weekly Lord's Supper is making a significant comeback. There is a greater hunger for this rite among the laity, as well as an increased awareness among all of how sacred acts signify deep mysterious truths. In a culture that can explain everything and has removed just about all mystery from life, the unexplained change that happens in people when taking a bit of bread and wine in a special way returns an element of mystery to an otherwise explainable religion.

To think about . . .

1. What new discovery did you make from reading this chapter about the Lord's Supper?

2. Why might the writer of the Gospel of John have omitted the story of the Lord's Supper from his Gospel? What is your theory?

3. How did Communion change when the early church moved from cell meetings in homes to large gatherings in basilicas? Compare or contrast this historical shift to your own experiences in taking Communion through the years—in large and small groups. Is one better than the other?

4. If a first-century Christian were transported to our modern Communion service, what do you think would most surprise this visitor?

5. What do you think of the early church's "secret service," excluding all but baptized Christians from the second part of the service? What would happen if a church tried this today? Have you ever been to a church that practiced "closed Communion"? If so, describe it.

6. How would Communion change if we practiced it at the end of a carry-in dinner, as the first Christians did? Would this be better or worse?

7. During the Middle Ages, Communion was removed and distanced from ordinary people. In what ways can churches do this even today?

8. Concerning the presence of Christ, what do you think actually happens during Communion?

9. Does Communion do any good for the person taking it? That is, can anything actually change as a result of the Lord's Supper? Or is it totally a token of a past event and not a changing agent to the person individually?

10. What are the nuances of the three common terms for this sign-act: Communion, Lord's Supper, and Eucharist? What does each term say to you?

11. In your opinion, how often should a church serve the Lord's Supper? Why? How should it be served?

Additional Sources on the Lord's Supper

The Didache (about 100)

"Now, about the Eucharist: This is how to give thanks: First in connection with the cup: 'We thank you, our Father, for the holy vine of David, your child, which you have revealed through Jesus, your child. To you be glory forever.'

"Then in connection with the piece [broken off the loaf]: 'We thank you, our Father, for the life and knowledge which you have revealed through Jesus, your child. To you be glory forever...'

"You must not let anyone eat or drink of your Eucharist except those baptized in the Lord's name. For in reference to this the Lord said, 'Do not give what is sacred to dogs.'"

The Didache, IX-X, XIV. Retrieved 7/17/01 from Indiana Wesleyan University server, Marion, Indiana. http://www.indwes.edu/courses/rel435/didache.htm

73

Martin Luther (1529)

"Now, what is the Sacrament of the Altar? Answer: It is the true body and blood of the Lord Jesus Christ in and under the bread and wine which we Christians are commanded by Christ's Word to eat and drink. As we said of Baptism that it is not mere water, so we say here that the sacrament is bread and wine, but not mere bread or wine such as is served at the table. It is bread and wine comprehended in God's Word and connected with it."

The Large Catechism. Trans. Theodore G. Tappert, *The Book of Concord* (Philadelphia: Fortress Press, 1959), 447.

John Calvin (1559)

"Now here we ought to guard against two faults. First, we should not, by too little regard for the signs, divorce them from their mysteries, to which they are so to speak attached. Secondly, we should not, by extolling them immoderately, seem to obscure somewhat the mysteries themselves..."

Institutes of the Christian Religion, IV, 17. Trans. Ford Lewis Battles, Library of Christian Classics, XXI, 1364-1404.

Part II
Other Elements of Worship

Worship has seldom been limited to what we have selected as the five "primary elements." Depending on the culture, the needs of the people, and a host of other factors, worship often reaches out and uses other elements. They are not really secondary—for at times these elements of worship dominate while even the primary elements recede. This section selects four of these additional elements for our study. Why these and not others? Because they are common elements in present-day worship, or have even dominated American worship in the last one hundred years or so. Learning about them will help us better understand our worship, ourselves, and our predecessors. These four elements are:

- **The Altar Call**
- **The Greeting Handshake**
- **Personal Testimony**
- **Ecstatic Expression**

6

The Altar Call

*Marty was reared in a totally secular family. He had attended
church only twice before college: once for his cousin's wedding, and
the other time for a bluegrass concert. Marty's college roommate
was his total opposite. He got up every single Sunday and went to
church, never bugging Marty to join him. Finally, after an entire
semester, Marty offered, "I just might go to church with you someday . . ." And the following Sunday he did.*

*"This isn't that bad," Marty thought to himself halfway through the
service. Sure, it was a waste of good sleep-in time, but the preacher
was interesting—actually more so than most of his profs. However,
Marty wasn't ready for the way the service ended. Everything was
carefully orchestrated; the pastor instructed the people to stand and
close their eyes. The praise band slipped back to their instruments
and started playing quietly, increasing the emotional effect of the
pastor's hushed voice. As the lights dimmed, the pastor actually
asked Marty to walk out right in front of everyone and kneel at the
altar. Well, he didn't exactly mention Marty's name, but it seemed the
pastor was talking right to Marty.*

*Marty wanted to disappear into the floor. He felt his ears turn red,
and he sensed everyone was looking right at the back of his head to
see if he'd go up front like the preacher was asking him to do. He
felt increasingly uncomfortable and on the spot. "If I get out of here,
I'll never come back, for sure," he thought to himself. Marty didn't
know what was happening—he just wanted it to end.*

Marty had experienced his first "invitation" or "altar call." When did
this practice of inviting people forward to pray actually begin? Has the
church always used it, or is it a recent innovation? If Jesus were here
today, how would He give an invitation? When is it improper manipula-

tion, and when is it a useful device to help people receive Christ?

The Gospel clearly demands a decision. It is the ultimate either/or proposition. It demands you choose Christ or reject Him. Christians—especially evangelists—are to present these claims to others and call for a response. Thus, it is natural that there would emerge some *means* of showing that response—some rite or device to show the prospect had indeed accepted the Gospel and repented. The public altar call became that rite in 1800. Until then, there were other response-rites.

Early Church

Jesus is often considered as having given the first invitation when He approached Peter and Andrew on the shores of Galilee and commanded them to come and follow Him (Matthew 4:18-19). They left their nets and followed Christ. However, this invitation is more an invitation to deeper discipleship than an initial invitation to be saved. Jesus was calling them to join Him in itinerant preaching and teaching, to become fishers of men.

Probably a better altar call story occurred on the day of Pentecost. Peter preached a sermon that produced 3,000 new believers. However, he did not invite the Jews to come forward to pray at a mourner's bench, but commanded that they *repent and be baptized*. Thus, the first invitation in the Christian church—the rite of response—was baptism.

In fact, baptism has been the primary response ritual for much of church history. "Do you believe? Then respond by repentance and baptism."
As Christianity grew, the rite of baptism developed. New converts were given instruction, and when they were proven worthy, they were baptized and received into full communion. "Want to become a Christian in 250? Repent of your sins and join our group of catechumens who are in study and preparation to be baptized." This was the invitation of the day.

Middle Ages

Once Christianity grew and dominated the Roman Empire, few adult converts were to be made; infants were baptized into the church not long after birth. Baptism moved from an adult rite to an infant rite. Sure, there was an occasional convert from another religion or a foreign land, but by and large there was no act of conversion beyond embracing one's infant baptism and going to church to demonstrate it. "Confirmation" of that infant baptism became the closest thing to a response-rite. There are many individual accounts of conversion, but there was no public rite associated with these decisions.

However, Catholic missionary work saw adult converts step forward to be baptized. In some cases, whole tribes were lined up and commanded to convert or be killed. In such cases, the chief (if he was still alive) converted, and his people followed dutifully, thousands receiving baptism at one time. "Want to become a Christian in 1200? Prepare for baptism—convert into the Roman Catholic Church." Thus, baptism was still the sign of conversion, the "response device" to the Gospel, the only altar call they had.

That is not to say other ways to respond were unavailable. In a sense, every Christian was invited to "come forward" and "go to the altar" every week to receive the Eucharist. It was a weekly response device. However, this response was not for initial conversion so much as a rite of continual consecration. In the Middle Ages, salvation was found in the church alone, and most entered the church first through baptism as an infant and later through confirmation.

Yet, there was a call to deeper discipleship in the Middle Ages, an altar call of sorts. If you were serious about spiritual things, you joined a monastic order. These were the spiritually committed people who "went deeper" in the matters of God. However, this going forward to a monastery was not a call to conversion (though that term was indeed used to denote the total conversion of lifestyle the monk or nun was to expect), but a call for deeper commitment.

79

For well over a thousand years, if you heard the Gospel and wanted to respond, the way to do that was to move toward baptism. Baptism was the "altar call."

Reformation

Many modern Christians are disappointed when they discover that the Reformers were less like their own church than they thought. Most modern evangelical worship patterns stem from Camp Meeting revivalists, not from Reformation forefathers. The Reformers did not invent the public altar call and did not use one.

Even great evangelists like John Wesley and George Whitefield did not use an altar call. Wesley and Whitefield preached personal conversion, but they did not invite people to respond publicly. They called for a personal and private response, not a public trip to the altar. In all of his preaching, Wesley never once gave an invitation for people to publicly receive Christ. Like Wesley, English Methodist preachers called for a decision, but they did not call people to come forward. A hundred years later, opponents of the altar call would enjoy pointing out that the Wesley-Whitefield revivals did quite well reviving nations without an altar call, thus concluding that the "new methods" of inviting people forward in front of everybody else were quite unnecessary.

The New England "awakening" under Jonathan Edwards reached Northampton, Massachusetts, in 1734. However, this "Great Awakening" occurred without an altar call or invitation to publicly receive Christ ever being given. It would take the 1800s and American Camp Meeting Revivalism to introduce what we now know as the "altar call."

However, there were some earlier rites or "precursors" of the altar call. The pre-Reformation Anabaptists insisted on *adult* baptism as a sign of personal conversion. Infant baptism was not good enough—a person needed to express *personal* faith in Christ and be baptized as a cognizant adult. They believed that this practice was a return to the biblical means of response to the Gospel—baptism. Such an adult baptism rite was a public affair and thus was a kind of proto-altar call of sorts. Still, before the 1800s the altar call/invitation did not exist in any form that we would recognize. Three ideas would have to take hold before the modern altar call could emerge.

Three Ideas Enabling the Altar Call

Idea #1: The Individual as Paramount
For much of history, people saw themselves chiefly as members of a group, not primarily as individuals. So long as people considered themselves primarily part of a group—my family, tribe, nation, or

social class—the chances of responding *personally* to the Gospel were limited, though entire groups might respond at once. Humans have always held both ideas in tension—individuality and group identity. The Enlightenment enabled the emergence of the individual to such an extent that it "trumped" one's group identity, enabling a move toward more *personal* conversion of the *individual*.

At times in history, a father simply decided the faith of the entire family (as perhaps the Philippian jailer did). Entire clans—even nations—would "become Christian" when their clan leader or king converted. Today, we can't imagine such a thing. Indeed, most Christians today wouldn't even "count" such conversions as real without involving each individual's personal will. Yet, through much of human history, individuals have left many of their decisions to others—the king, clan leader, or father. The Enlightenment way of thinking changed this; people began seeing themselves increasingly as individuals, not merely as part of a group. The ideas of human choice, free will, and making decisions to master one's own destiny prevailed. In this atmosphere of thought, inviting an individual to receive Christ—even if the rest of your family, tribe, or friends did not—became more plausible.

Idea #2: Immediate Salvation
The Puritan heritage of most early Americans required a personal confession of faith for membership. However, to the Puritans—and many others at the time—conversion was not an immediate experience but something that happened gradually, over years of attending church and sitting under the influence of Scripture. Revivalism would change this notion. By the end of Revivalism's sweep across the country, most Americans would come to believe a person could hear the Gospel, repent, and be converted, all in the space of an hour or less. Most people came to accept instantaneous conversion, something that would later fall under the familiar "Four Spiritual Laws" approach. The notion of an "Hour of Decision" emerged. Where belief in instantaneous conversion prevailed, an altar call to "receive Christ tonight" became a logical means of closing an evangelistic appeal.

Idea #3: Assurance
The final idea essential to the emergence of the altar call can be espe-

cially credited to John Wesley's teaching: the notion that you can *know for sure* that you are saved. The popular view of Wesley's day was that God alone knew who was saved or lost, and that humans could never know for sure these matters of eternal destiny. Wesley argued that a person could know for sure whether he or she was saved; the Holy Spirit would witness to a believer's heart this assurance. This idea is so common today that to state the earlier view would sound incredulous, but personal assurance of salvation was a minority view until Wesley came on the scene.

When these three ideas combine, you get the following: Each person is responsible for a *personal decision* to receive Christ; a person can be *saved instantaneously*; and a person can *know for sure* that he or she is saved. This combined system prevailed in the minds of the American people. In this milieu of thought, the modern altar call became reality.

James McGready (1800)

"The floor was covered with the slain; their screams for mercy pierced the heavens."

From a personal letter by James McGready, describing the effect of his preaching on the Red River worshipers, June 1800. Bernard A. Weisberger, *They Gathered by the River* (New York: Quadrangle, The New York Times Book Co., 1958), 25.

Western Camp Meeting Roots

82

Preaching has always attempted to persuade listeners to repent. However, that repentance usually occurred after a long period of mourning or "conviction" and not as a public spectacle. People were saved as a result of preaching, but the actual event occurred in the woods, in their barns, at their bedsides, or someplace else—not in front of everyone else at church. (Some American Presbyterians argued that the moment a pastor observed the rise of emotional conviction, he should dismiss the person from the service and ask him to seek the Lord privately.) Thus, people "prayed through" on their own, though prompted by the preaching. Camp Meeting Revivalism kept this "praying through" in the public service. It started in what was the Wild West of the time—Kentucky. In June 1800 at Red River, Kentucky, Methodist James McGready preached so powerfully that his listeners were overcome with conviction. But the listeners did not leave to go pray in the woods or at home—they stayed in church. Sinners did not "go to the altar" but fell to the floor crying out to God for mercy. People wailed and cried to God. Their repentance was a public affair at the end of the message, not a private affair after the service. While this sort of crying out had happened before in history, what happened in the next few years enables one to see the connection between the Red River meeting and the altar call.

While McGready had not given attendees an "invitation" to fall on the floor in response to their guilt, the stage was set for Gasper River and Cane Ridge, Kentucky, where the Camp Meeting would be born—and the "altar call."

In Gasper River and Cane Ridge, Kentucky, great camp meetings emerged almost spontaneously the following year. Many claim that the Cane Ridge Camp Meeting of August 1801 had 20,000 attendees! Though Revivalists tend to pad attendance figures, this figure could be accurate. If there were 20,000 attendees, it is impressive—remembering the whole state of Kentucky had only 250,000 people at the time!

The Kentucky camp meetings approached emotional pandemonium. People shouted, shook, ran, and barked up trees, "treeing the devil." A single preacher could not reach all 20,000 listeners, so preachers spread out around the grounds, and their audiences wandered about from service to service to add to the confusion (and excitement).

83

Peter Cartwright (1801)

"To this meeting I repaired, a guilty, wretched sinner. On the Saturday evening of said meeting, I went, with weeping multitudes, and bowed before the stand, and earnestly prayed for mercy."

Peter Cartwright, *Autobiography* (New York: Abingdon Press, 1956), writing of his conversion at a camp meeting in Kentucky in May 1801.

The frontier people shared a common understanding of the process by which one was saved: intense, convicting preaching, deep personal feelings of guilt or "conviction," a sense of "lostness" and despair, crying out for mercy from God, then experiencing a transforming conversion that produced a changed person who lived a better life.

All across the camp meeting grounds in four to seven locations, preachers railed simultaneously. At each location, sinners might fall under conviction and begin to cry out to God for mercy. So, where would they pray? The traditional response-rite had been to "go out," not to "come down." "Mourners" of both sexes left camp and entered the woods to pray alone with God. This left the camp meetings open to charges of immorality (perhaps not totally without cause).

So, who thought first of the practical idea to gather all the "mourners" together in one place and aid them in their repentance and prayers? Whoever it was, it apparently happened in 1801 for the first time in these Kentucky camp meetings, as far as we now know. The "altar call" as we know it may have been invented to bring order to the chaos of solo-seekers in multiple-preaching locations at these meetings.

For whatever reason, the altar call was born as a means especially suitable to camp meeting evangelism. Peter Cartwright, who told of his own conversion in Kentucky at the time, describes going with "weeping multitudes" to pray before the stand.

Frances Trollope (1829)

"Again a hymn was sung, and while it continued, one of the three was employed in clearing one or two long benches that went across the rail, sending the people back to the lower part of the church. The singing ceased, and again the people were invited, and exhorted not to be ashamed of Jesus, but to put themselves upon the 'anxious benches' and lay their heads on their bosom. 'Once more we will sing,' he concluded, 'that we may give you time.'"

An English woman's observations on a Kentucky service in 1829. Frances Trollope, *Domestic Manners of the Americans* (New York: Alfred A. Knopf, 1949).

Frontier religion was a rough-and-tumble emotional affair. Gathering together with other "mourners" to seek God's mercy and forgiveness fit with the experiential culture of frontier folk. But it was in Kentucky that this response device got its modern launch.

Adaptations and additions to the altar call soon arrived. After all, this rite was not a thousand years old but a recent innovation developed for practical reasons. At first, the altar call involved simply going up near the pulpit to pray. Soon several benches were included near the front where mourners could sit as they pondered their eternal fate—the "mourner's bench." Sometimes, these benches were set apart from other benches with a railing—scoffers called the end result "the hog pen." The "mourner's tent" also made its eventual debut. This would later become the "inquiry room," to be used by Billy Graham and others more than one hundred years later.

Thus, the modern altar call was most likely born in 1801 in Kentucky—in a western camp meeting setting. However, it would be picked up and popularized in the East by handsome, six-foot-tall Charles Finney. This lawyer-turned-preacher usually gets most of the credit for inventing the altar call.

Roots in Eastern Revivalism

Charles Finney (1792-1875) was converted on his twenty-ninth birthday. He had bought a Bible in order to study the Mosaic roots of the law. After reading it, he was convicted and became anxious about the state of his soul. While pondering the Gospel, he was struck with an idea that would change his life (and the evangelistic methods of America's churches) ever after. It dawned on Finney that all that was keeping him from being saved was *his own* consent. That is, God had done His part on the cross long ago, and God had extended the invitation to whosoever will—all that remained was Finney's own *personal decision.*

Later that evening in a dark room, Finney "met Christ face to face," and in a moment was converted. Soon after, he hit the road with his evangelistic crusades designed to get people saved. Since people could be saved in a moment and could know it for sure, and since the only thing holding them back was *their own* consent, he would use his skills as a lawyer to persuade them to accept Christ immediately. If a good lawyer could persuade a jury to give a verdict in an hour, why couldn't a good preacher persuade his audience to render a far more important verdict—their decision on their own eternal destiny—in the same amount of time?

Finney was ordained by the Presbyterians (though grudgingly on their part) and started his evangelistic work. He introduced a variety of "new measures" to facilitate evangelism. These included such innovations as protracted meetings and the naming of sinners in public prayer. He also introduced in "Yankee" New York the western camp meeting's "anxious bench," though he was attacked for its use. His first use of the anxious bench was probably at Evans Mills, New York, in 1825, just three years after his own conversion, and twenty-four years after the Kentucky Cane Ridge camp meeting.

Finney's Presbyterian colleagues roundly criticized him for his Revivalist methods (recognizing that they were largely incompatible with traditional Calvinist theology). Ignoring his detractors or condemning them, he simply went on converting New York and America. Presbyterian preacher Finney took America's gradual slide away from traditional Calvinism and turned it into an outright flight. Much of America—including many Presbyterians—became "practicing Arminians."[7] When the fires of Revivalism died down, most of America—no matter what they claimed as their doctrine—would wind up somewhere in the middle of the continuum between radical Calvinism and radical Arminianism.

However, Finney did not limit his invitation methods to the anxious bench alone. He experimented with a variety of public response methods. These included an inquiry meeting following the main service and an invitation to those who were repenting to come and stand before the

---

[7] Arminianism is a slightly revised Calvinism that puts greater emphasis on the "free will" of humans to "choose Christ" and be saved, rather than being saved by God's action and selection alone. Arminians also propose that it is conceivable that a person could later choose against Christ and eventually even be lost. In a more general way, Calvinists place greater emphasis on "God's part" in matters while Arminians tend to also emphasize the "human's part." Finney's approach to revival placed great emphasis on human measures, so much so that he proposed a list of these measures guaranteed to bring revival, almost like a recipe. This approach made Finney a Calvinist in theology and an Arminian in practice; thus, the term "practicing Arminian."

pulpit. However, there was always an opportunity to "close the deal."

Gradually, the altar call became a popular response rite to the Gospel. "Want to get saved in 1850? Go to the altar and repent." Many of Finney's fellow ministers (including Baptists) resisted the altar call, but the tradition swept over the land nonetheless, and the resisters were left to grumble quietly to their ever-shrinking congregations. The leading edge of American Christianity had adopted this new rite of conversion.

Charles Finney (1835)

"It is exceedingly important that he who leads the meeting should press sinners who may be present to immediate repentance. He should crowd this hard, and urge the Christians present to pray in such a way as to make sinners feel that they are expected to repent immediately. This tends to inspire Christians with compassion and love for souls. The remarks made to sinners are often like pouring fire upon the hearts of Christians, to awaken them to prayer and effort for their conversion. Let them see and feel the guilt and danger of sinners right among them, and then they will pray."

Lecture VIII, "Meetings for Prayer." Delivered by Charles Finney to the congregation of the Chatham Chapel, New York City, 1835; reported in the *New York Evangelist*, J. Leavitt. Retrieved 7/22/01 from http://www.gospeltruth.net/1835Lect_on_Rev_of_Rel/35revlec08.htm

By 1860 when D. L. Moody began his revival work in Chicago, the altar call was well established as the popular method of "reaping the harvest." Dwight L. Moody was probably the most influential "preacher" in the closing years of the 1800s, though he was never actually ordained. America had hundreds of other professional evangelists who organized local campaigns in villages, small towns, medium-size cities, and gigantic metropolises like New York. At this time an aspiring evangelist, Moody started his tour with village campaigns and worked his way up to larger cities as his fame and effectiveness grew. Moody was the king of them all, preaching campaigns in large cities by demand. While Finney had earlier held his campaigns in churches, Moody now held his gigantic, urban, citywide campaigns in public arenas.

Moody's altar call invited people to come forward publicly, then go to an "inquiry room." In the inquiry room, the seekers prayed with counselors who helped them repent and receive Christ.

In 1875 Thomas Harrison, a contemporary of Moody, offered an even simpler invitation—those with a desire to be saved were simply invited to stand up. That was all. They did not have to come forward. Their friends did not have to wait. They did not have to hear a litany of memorized verses from an over-prepared counselor. They just had to stand up to indicate they were repenting and receiving Christ as their Savior at that moment.

To make standing up easier, other evangelists had the entire audience stand, bow their heads, and close their eyes. Then penitents were asked to "slip up their hands" quietly, enabling an even more private response to the call. In 1906 in Boston, evangelist Gypsy Smith called for raising a hand with the much-copied phrase, "Put your hand up for Jesus—He put two up for you."

In 1895 Billy Sunday took up the mantle of J. Wilbur Chapman, who had returned to local church ministry following his own campaign ministry. Sunday had been a hard-drinking, rough-living baseball player before he was converted. Conversion radically changed his life. He landed a job helping J. Wilbur Chapman with citywide campaigns just two years before Chapman's retirement from itinerant work. Billy Sunday took over the work (and the contacts) and hit the road as an evangelist himself. Starting at smaller towns and cities, he worked his way up to giant metropolitan cities like New York.

Billy Sunday was the premier entertainer-evangelist of his day. Few have rivaled him before or since. Sunday knew how to communicate to the common person. He could captivate, entertain, energize, and persuade a crowd. For this evangelist, the whole sermon was the altar call—the entire event was designed to persuade the sinner to come forward at the end of the service. Sunday swept the nation and was the must-see attraction of his day. At his peak in 1917-1920, he "knocked 'em dead" in major American cities, including an extended campaign in New York City.

Sunday made sure the entire service was a crescendo to the climax of the altar call. He was especially good at appealing to specific groups—to veterans, students, trade union members, or even Scotchmen—in his series of pleas between the verses of altar call songs led by his musical sidekick, Homer Rodeheaver.

But the crowd is fickle. After 1920, the country tired of Billy Sunday. He kept up the same show but found himself getting invitations to smaller towns and villages. The country had moved on to other entertainment. However, even his detractors had to admit that he effectively persuaded thousands of people to respond to his invitations. Copycat preachers and professional "evangelists" imitated his style for decades.

So, how would these citywide crusades preserve the fruits of their labor? Most evangelists were not in the church planting business. New Christians who did not get into a church might easily have fallen away, like seeds on shallow soil. To preserve the harvest and provide a means of local follow-up, evangelists like J. Wilbur Chapman and Benjamin Fay Mills introduced the "decision card." The cards could be given to local pastors for follow-up, and the converts could be accurately counted. Such counting in some cases led to the preposterous development of cost-per-convert calculations, with various evangelists vying to present the lowest cost per convert.

However, the "decision card" itself provided a new means for an invitation. Attendees could sign an attendance card with the invitation for sinners to "check the box for 'I have accepted Christ as my Savior today.'" Conversion could now be as simple as checking a box. Others made it easier still—"with every head bowed and all eyes closed—take that card you all completed when you came in. Now if you want to accept Christ tonight just quietly tear a little piece off at one corner . . ." What started out in Kentucky as public wailing on the floor for personal sin had morphed back into a private affair—simply and quietly tearing off a small corner of an attendance card.

Modern Use of the Altar Call

Some churches and movements have specialized in the altar call. Indeed, there are some revivalist evangelicals who would sooner sacrifice the

Lord's Supper than the altar call. The Camp Meeting movement continued to use the altar call for evangelism and to call "backsliders" back into the kingdom. Even when local churches abandoned the device, their people could attend a camp meeting and experience time travel—observing a "real altar call" like it used to be done.

The Holiness Camp Meeting movement also used the altar call to invite Christians to seek a second work of grace—entire sanctification, or being cleansed and filled by the Holy Spirit. Phoebe Palmer, the mother of the American Holiness Movement, had proposed an "altar theology." The notion was that "the altar sanctifies the gift." That is, believers who put their "all on the altar" would receive cleansing and empowerment from God. The believers' only job was to consecrate their all, and God would do the rest.

While the "altar" to which Palmer was referring was a theoretical altar, many of her followers did their total consecration at the mourner's bench in the front of the tabernacle—an actual altar. The altar at camp became the functional place where Christians said, "I surrender all." People were filled with the Spirit at the same sort of altar where they had been saved—receiving both by faith in a similar experience. In the Holiness camp meetings, the "altar service" was the final service of a three-fold camp meeting liturgy: the "song service," "preaching service," and "altar service." Thus, the altar was used primarily for three purposes: (1) to "get saved" at conversion, (2) to "be reclaimed" if one had backslidden and abandoned his or her faith, and (3) to "be sanctified."

However, not all churches kept the altar call. The Restoration churches (Campbell, Stone, the "Church of Christ" movement) used the altar call at first but then dropped it as unbiblical, restoring what they considered to be the early church practice—inviting people to come forward to be baptized. Some Baptist churches have a similar altar call today—inviting sinners to come forward to commit to baptism and church membership.

Pentecostal churches, with deep roots in the Camp Meeting, Holiness, and Afro-American worship styles, kept the altar for evangelism and "baptism in the Holy Spirit." However, Pentecostals (and the later Charismatics) made the entire altar area sacred space. The *area* around the altar (and sometimes the aisles) became a holy place where worshipers could expect to encounter God, get healed, speak in tongues, and receive His blessings and gifts.

As evangelical churches reach more professional people and others from the upper strata of the socio-economic ladder, they tend to downplay the altar call, opting for more private rites of conversion. (However, most of these churches insist that the altar call continue to be used as a device for their youth.) The personal evangelism movement tried to get people saved in their homes, not at church. These churches adapted the altar call by inviting people "who have made a decision for Christ this week" to come forward as a public testimony to that already-made decision.

More recently some churches have introduced an on-stage "new converts' interview" as their public rite of conversion, with the pastor or emcee interviewing new converts. Still other churches have merged this public testimony into the baptism event, having the new converts testify to their faith before they are baptized . . . which returns the church full circle to the practice of the first Christians—using baptism as the public rite of witness and conversion.

So, where to from here? Will the altar call survive? Should it? The Gospel does indeed call all men and women everywhere to repent. "What will you do with Christ?" is the question. There is a decision to make. There will probably always be some sort of rite for making that decision. At certain periods and places in history, the response has been public, immediate, and dramatic. At other times, it has been private, gradual, and subdued. But there will always be some means of responding—for the Gospel demands it.

91

To think about . . .

1. What new discovery did you make from reading this chapter on the development of the altar invitation?

2. Most movements and denominations that specialize in using a dramatic-response altar call seem later to exchange it for a more subdued method. Why do you think this happens?

3. Of the three issues of thinking that facilitated the introduction of the modern altar call—the individual, immediate salvation, assurance—which is strongest in today's belief system? Which is weakening? How might this affect the altar call?

4. List all of the "response rituals" you have ever observed. Which do you prefer? Which are better for which kind of audience?

5. This chapter illustrates how theology and methodology are intertwined. List several theological positions and how each relates to evangelism and the altar call.

6. What do you think of the relationship between the two public rites: baptism and the altar call?

7. What do you think about the idea of preserving a public altar call for youth and children, while adults downplay it for their own age group?

8. This chapter describes much about the Camp Meeting movement and Revivalism. What new insights did you gain on these two movements and their roles in American religious practice?

9. It seems that socio-economic level and various response devices are related. Have you seen this tendency? How? Why?

10. How has the more recent "open altar" prayer time during the pastoral prayer affected the traditional end-of-service altar call?

11. Many modern people do not believe in instantaneous change but accept only slow improvement, long-term therapy, twelve-step process groups, and "recovering" gradually. How does this affect their thinking during an altar call?

12. What was really happening to Marty in the opening story? Was this church mistaken in its approach, or was it OK? If you were Marty's roommate, what would you say after church?

7
The Greeting Handshake

*Kenneth, a middle-aged man, had been persuaded by his wife Nancy
to attend church. Over time he made church attendance a regular
habit and came to like it, though his faith was still underdeveloped.
After the opening set of choruses each week came the part of the
service Kenneth hated. As the keyboard played "I'm So Glad I'm
a Part of the Family of God," Pastor Shawn exuded, "Now, turn
to someone, shake their hand, or give them a hug and say 'You
look great today!'" Kenneth stood woodenly, fixing his eyes straight
ahead and hoping nobody would offer to shake his hand. But someone always did and occasionally he'd even get hugged, though his
imposing form and perennial scowl during this part of the service
usually signaled most of the huggers to pass by.*

How did this greeting handshake (or hug) become a part of Christian
worship? Is it an old custom or a recent innovation?

The modern greeting handshake started out as a kiss between Christians
accompanied by a verbal greeting. It then morphed into kissing a common object. Later when the kiss was dropped, an exchanged verbal
greeting took its place. This part of the service finally wound up as a
handshake, a hug, or "passing the peace."

The "Holy Kiss" in the New Testament

Ancient Middle Eastern people were accustomed to greeting each other
with a kiss. In some Mediterranean cultures, the kiss was reserved for
family, but in the Middle East it was given to any dear friend or associate. The kiss in New Testament times was a greeting something like
our modern handshake. It was often given mouth to mouth, a sign of
intimate greeting between two people that had no more sexual overtones
than today's handshake. Today, when your friends arrive at your home
for dinner, you offer to take their coats and extend your hand as a greet-

ing. You do this without thinking—it is our custom. The kiss was just such a common custom in the ancient Mediterranean world, though the kiss meant a bit more than our handshake. It was perhaps similar to a quick hug we might give a brother we have not seen for several years. A kiss was the first-century Middle Eastern way of showing friendship with another person.

Justin Martyr (100s)

"Having ended the prayers, we salute one another with a kiss. There is then brought to the president of the brethren bread and a cup of wine mixed with water."

First Apology, chapter 65, "Administration of the Sacraments," ANF, vol. 1, page 340.

Jesus was kissed. At least we assume He was. In fact, one time He complained when He wasn't kissed upon entering the Pharisee's house (Luke 7:45). Of course, the most infamous kiss He received was from Judas in the garden—a kiss of betrayal.

Early Christians and the Kiss of Peace

When the early Christians incorporated this greeting into their worship service, it was a natural cultural greeting, not some new notion. The early church was a fellowship of intimacy. They considered themselves brothers and sisters—all part of one family, one body. To greet your brother or sister with a kiss publicly and symbolically illustrated how you felt related in the body of Christ.

The Christians, however, did not introduce the liturgical kiss directly from the culture without apostolic support. The Apostle Paul commanded the Christians in Rome, Corinth, and Thessalonica to greet each other with a "holy kiss" (Romans 16:16; 1 Corinthians 16:20; 2 Corinthians 13:12; 1 Thessalonians 5:26). The Apostle Peter commanded it also, calling it the "kiss of love" (1 Peter 5:14). Whatever we call it, the early Christians had plenty of scriptural support for the worship kiss. However, it was not an ordinary kiss, but a "holy" kiss, or a "kiss of love"—a liturgical greeting with more meaning than an ordinary greeting. This was especially true outside the Middle East in other Mediterranean cultures, where the kiss was reserved only for family. Thus, the early Christians began to regard the kiss as a part of the worship service. To them, it signified the importance of their intimate relationship with each other as part of the body of Christ.

Athenagoras (100s)

"The apostle calls the kiss holy. When the kingdom is worthily tested, we dispense the affection of the soul by a chaste and closed mouth, by which chiefly gentle manners are expressed. But there is another unholy kiss, full of poison, counterfeiting sanctity...And often kisses inject the poison of licentiousness."

Paedagogus. Trans. B. P. Pratten. Book 3, Chapter 11, ANF, 567.

In the early church, the greeting kiss was apparently shared with both sexes—between all men and women, all brothers and sisters. Perhaps this practice led to some abuses; we don't know for sure. We do know that during the second and third centuries, boundaries and restrictions were established on the practice. The kiss was to be given with a "chaste and closed mouth" and anyone wanting to kiss a second time was forbidden to do so. The kiss was further limited to a same-sex greeting with men giving a kiss only to other men and women to women. Were some members wandering off into some sort of hanky-panky during the liturgical kiss? Who knows? Even if there weren't abuses, such a kiss might have led to charges of impropriety from those outside the church, thus bringing about these restrictions.

97

In any event, and in spite of any abuses (and perhaps because of the restrictions), the kiss was able to remain a part of the Christian liturgy for a long time. As we have seen, the early church had a two-part service. The first part was open to all, including candidates for baptism. The second part, called the "Service of the Faithful," was reserved only for baptized Christians who would take the Lord's Supper together. It was in this second closed service that the "holy kiss" or "kiss of peace" was practiced. It was placed in the liturgy, usually just before or after the offering (which was not a collection of money at first, but the offering of the elements of Communion by bringing them forward).

Athenagoras

"On behalf of those, then, to whom we apply the names of brothers and sisters, and other designations of relationship, we exercise the greatest care that their bodies should remain undefiled and uncorrupted; for the Logos again says to us, 'If any one kiss a second time because it has given him pleasure, [he sins]'; adding, 'Therefore the kiss, or rather the salutation, should be given with the greatest care, since, if there be mixed with it the least defilement of thought, it excludes us from eternal life.'"

A Plea for the Christians, Chapter XXXII. Retrieved 7/22/01 from http://www.newadvent.org/fathers/0205.htm

The Greeting Kiss through the Middle Ages

In the 300s, Christianity was first legalized, then favored, and finally established as the exclusive state church. This ushered in a great era of church growth. For the next five hundred years, the kiss was retained in the service. In the Roman rite, it followed the "fraction" or breaking of the bread during the Lord's Supper. Most other rites kept the kiss before or after the offering of Communion elements. In the Eastern Church (later *Orthodox* Church), the offering was an impressive procession transporting the Communion elements forward in "The Great Entrance." The kiss followed this procession just before the Nicene Creed was recited.

The 1100s brought a unique innovation to the liturgical kiss. Instead of kissing one another, everybody kissed a *paten* or sacred tablet made of precious metal or ivory on wood. The bishop or presiding priest kissed the paten, then passed it on to the next highest-ranking cleric who added his kiss. It was then passed on down the line by rank until all the people had greeted each other by a holy kiss via the paten. In other places the "holy kiss" passed away completely as the mass took on a mysterious or magical character. Progressively, the mass became focused on something mystifying (performed by the priest) happening up front. The congregation's job was to attend, be quiet, watch, and listen.

Apostolic Constitutions (300s)

"Then let the men give the men, and the women give the women, the Lord's kiss."

Book II, LVII. Retrieved 7/19/01 Christian Classics Ethereal Library; Calvin College Ante-Nicene Fathers http://www.ccel.org/fathers2/ANF-07/anf07-41.htm#P5323_1937285

Modern Use of a Greeting Sign

Most probably a verbal greeting accompanied the kiss of peace from its earliest days, just as today's handshake invariably accompanies a "How are you?" or similar greeting. We know that when "passing the peace" emerged again in modern times, the greeting became, "Peace be with you," to which the response was, "And also with you." Or, some use the greeting, "The Lord be with you," to which the response is, "And also with you." "Passing the peace" eventually returned to the church while the kiss itself largely disappeared as a liturgical act.

Justin Martyr (about 155)

"We, however, after thus washing the one who has been convinced and signified his ascent, lead him to those who are called brethren, where they are assembled. They then earnestly offer common prayers for themselves and the one who has been illuminated and all others everywhere, that we may be made worthy, having learned the truth, to be found in deed good citizens and keepers of what is commanded, so that we may be saved with eternal salvation. On finishing the prayers we greet each other with a kiss. Then bread and a cup of water and mixed wine are brought to the president of the brethren..."

First Apology. Trans. Edward Rochie Hardy, LCC, I, 285-287.

Congregations in the Free Church, Revivalist, and Camp Meeting traditions tend to drop the formalized greeting, yet retain the handshake in one form or another. Congregations with Charismatic leanings often move beyond the handshake to offer a hug during the greeting time. Sometimes, Charismatic leaders urge their folk to line up across the aisles and join hands to signify a similar unity and connection with each other. Many congregations now designate a few people to offer a handshake to all—what they call "greeters."

There are, of course, congregations that resist any sort of interpersonal informality like handshakes, hugs, or holding hands. Attendees at these churches do not want anyone else to touch them while they worship. One man put it this way, "I go to church to be touched by God, not by other people." Congregations like these often use a pew register for people to sign and hand down the pew so they can get to know one another better. This replaces "passing the peace" with passing the register, yet has a similar end in mind.

What is the idea behind the ancient kiss, modern handshake, or hug during worship? It is a unity symbol. It says, "We are one in the bond of love." Both the kiss and the handshake communicate the special relationship Christians have with each other through a symbolic physical act. It is the Christian's way of showing connection with other Christian brothers and sisters. It says, "You and I are not accidental attendees at a movie theater or concert—we are members of one body." It signifies Christian unity and fellowship. To the ancient Christians, the kiss said, "We are friends, part of one family, brothers and sisters together." The modern passing the peace, handshake, or even the low-key "friendship register" attempt to do the same thing.

Though the means have morphed over the years, the idea is the same: to provide some symbolic acts through which humans signify their unique relationship to one another—demonstrating we are connected as one body.

To think about . . .

1. What new discovery did you make from reading this chapter about the development of the holy kiss into a greeting handshake?

2. The Apostle Paul was clear in commanding the first-century Christians to "greet one another with a holy kiss." Most Christians believe these writings of Paul were not just written for the Romans or Corinthians but also for us today, thousands of years later. So, what does this command mean today? Since Paul really meant it—kiss each other—are we then required to obey it literally today? Or do we have the freedom to adapt the literal command into accomplishing the objective of that command—by substituting a handshake or other greeting that fits our culture better? How far can we go in adapting specific commands of Scripture to new cultural situations?

3. If the purpose of the kiss of peace was to give a sign of our intimate family relationship with others in the church (that is, something symbolizing a really special relationship), what would we do today in our culture that would be similar? Should we?

4. Some Christians, like Kenneth in the introductory story, resent the interpersonal familiarity of a handshake or passing the peace as a part of a worship service. Is this "just personality"? Is such a person free to refrain from or resist a greeting? Or is it an indication of a refusal to be a full part of the fellowship? Are some Christians free to "hate that part of the service," when it was a regular part of early church worship and seems to have support in Scripture?

101

5. In accounting for the restrictions on the kiss of peace given during the second century and later, what is your theory?

6. What does the kiss of peace or "passing the peace" have to do with Holy Communion? Why was it often placed as a part of the Communion service?

7. If you were writing a letter today like the early church fathers wrote concerning the holy kiss, what would you list as "cautions or abuses" related to this early church greeting time?

8. How does a small church's greetings (kiss, hug, handshake, register) differ from a large church's greetings? What other kinds of symbolic acts do churches do to symbolize our connectedness?

9. If you had the power to redesign this part of the service to exactly match your own personal preferences, how would you design it?

8

Personal Testimony

The house lights dimmed and the spotlight moved to the pastor who spoke in hushed tones. "A wonderful thing happened this week in the life of Jim and Mary Kunkle. I want you to hear the story of what God did." Seated in the front row, the Kunkles were prompted and ready to join Pastor Paul on stage. The interview that followed was interesting, inspiring, and at times humorous. The Kunkles told how they had received Christ that week in a neighborhood Bible study sponsored by one of the church families. The pastor closed the interview moments later by asking, "How many of you will join in prayer this coming week for Jim and Mary?" Almost every person across the thousand-seat auditorium raised a hand as the keyboard player eased into the next song. The Kunkles returned to their seats, the spot dimmed, and the next praise chorus faded in on the duplicate screens to the left and right of the stage. The Kunkles had just given a twenty-first-century rendition of a "testimony."

Worship includes praise. Psalms, readings, litanies, and music have been the most common modes of praise throughout church history. But in the past five hundred years, personal testimony has emerged as a new praise form, though its roots go far back in worship history and include great Old Testament notions such as "let the redeemed of the Lord say so." The New Testament also illustrates the idea of the testimony, as much for healing ("go show yourself to the priests") as for conversion.

The earliest report in Christian history of anything like a testimony comes from Augustine (354-430). In *The City of God*, he relates the miraculous healing of two Christians, Paulus and Palladia, from a curious shaking disease. After the brother was miraculously healed, Augustine carefully recorded the story, then brought the two to stand before the entire congregation while he read their testimony out loud. The congregation could clearly see the difference between the trembling sister and the brother who had been healed of the shaking disease. The congregation then responded with formal praise and thanksgiving to God for this miracle of healing. Following the testimony, the sister went to the same place where her brother had been healed and was also miraculously healed.

Augustine (early 400s)

"Two of them came to Hippo, a brother and a sister, Paulus and Palladia...and the young man was holding the bars of the holy place where the relics [of St. Stephen] were, and praying, suddenly he fell down, and lay precisely as if asleep, but not trembling as he was wont to do even in sleep. All present were astonished. Some were alarmed, some were moved with pity; and while some were for lifting him up, others prevented them, and said they should rather wait and see what would result. And behold! he rose up, and trembled no more, for he was healed, and stood quite well, scanning those who were scanning him. Who then refrained himself from praising God? The whole church was filled with the voices of those who were shouting and congratulating him...Accordingly, on the following day, after delivering my sermon, I promised that next day I would read his narrative to the people. And when I did so, the third day after Easter Sunday, I made the brother and sister both stand on the steps of the raised place from which I used to speak; and while they stood there their pamphlet was read."

The City of God, Book XXII, Chapter 8. Retrieved 7/23/01 from http: //www.ccel.org/fathers2/NPNF1-02/npnf1-02-28.htm

However, it is difficult to call this event the "birth of the testimony." For the next thousand years and more, the notion of individuals giving a "personal testimony" during public worship would have been a strange idea.

Worship during the Middle Ages was impressive, mysterious, and at times breathtaking. It featured carefully honed litanies, Scripture readings, and processions, along with wonderful and inspiring musical productions. Giant cathedrals were awe-inspiring, and great crowds gathered on high holy days to celebrate mass. Worship, however, was considered a group activity and not something that directed the spotlight on an individual (other than the priest as he presided over the Eucharist).

The Middle Ages: Group Worship

During the Middle Ages, people came to corporate worship expecting a *corporate* worship experience, not any sort of focus on a single individual's religious experience. The worshiper in the Middle Ages would probably have considered a personal testimony inappropriate as a part of the mass because it would attract too much attention to the person speaking rather than to God, the Scriptures, or the Eucharist. Corporate worship has almost always included some means of reciting "God's mighty acts" on our collective behalf through history. In a testimony, however, one recites "God's mighty acts" in an individual's personal life to the glory of God and delight of the body. The culture wasn't ready for this means of personal praise yet.

In our present individualistic culture, it would be quite normal for a person to say, "I don't like peas" or "I always vote conservative, although my husband votes differently." In a group culture we would say, "*We* always vote conservative." The "we" would refer to our group: family, clan, town, or nation. However, the idea of an individual self apart from the group association, while gradually gaining acceptance through the Middle Ages, didn't become dominant until after 1500. Of course, today the individual is supreme, we applaud people who are "finding themselves," and we approve ventures that make the individual unique and different from the group. As well, we consider spouses voting differently proof that this couple has not "melted into one another" but has retained individuality despite being married.

105

A group culture tends to praise God for what He has done *for us all*: bringing His people through the Red Sea, giving them land, promising a Messiah, sending His Son to die on the cross, giving us rain for our crops, protecting us from natural disasters, and so forth. However, as culture came to adopt a view elevating individuality (even above the group), a significant effect on worship occurred (along with an influence on evangelism, baptism, and a whole host of other matters). The rising awareness of the individual provided the cultural setting in which personal testimony became popular.

Puritan Roots in the 1600s

The modern personal testimony was an innovation of English Puritans somewhere during the 1630s. The Puritans, a revival-reform group within the Church of England, were bent on stripping any scent of Roman Catholicism from worship in order to introduce a simpler, biblical, "spiritual" worship.

The first personal testimonies started as interviews of prospective Puritan members. Prospects were to tell their personal stories of coming to faith as a prerequisite to admission to the Lord's table. This was a private meeting at first, something like today's interview with a church board or membership committee. Imagine how this private meeting morphed into a public one—as other members heard the testimonies secondhand from the small group who was present at the original interview. These stories were simply too good to hoard among a few board members. Soon, an open meeting was scheduled for these interviews, where everybody could hear the interesting and edifying personal testimonies of how these people came to faith.

The practice lasted almost a hundred years and into the early 1700s before dying out. By the mid-1700s, Jonathan Edwards (1703-1758) probably represented most others by rejecting the testimony and special service for hearing them as unsupported by Scripture (and perhaps because it gave too much emphasis on the individuals and their experiences rather than on God and His work?). However Edwards did encourage keeping a journal and private introspection.

106

Moravians and Wesley in the 1700s

Count Zinzendorf (1700-1760), a loyal German Lutheran, organized an inside-the-church group that came to be called the Moravians. Rooted in earlier German Pietism, the Moravians led a revival movement committed to reforming the Lutheran Church by preaching "heart religion," though they eventually became separatists and then a separate denomination altogether. Zinzendorf reintroduced the ancient agape meal, also called the love feast, so common in the first-century church. This feast was introduced as a means of revival and renewal in 1727. After a token bit of bread and drink, the rest of the service was given over to praise, prayer, fellowship, and personal testimony—sort of a people's service more than a preaching service.

In 1737 or 1738, John Wesley attended one of these Moravian love feasts and adopted the idea for the Methodists. Like the Moravians, Wesley's love feast included warm personal testimonies. Both the love feast and the testimony became common among Methodists in Wesley's time, continuing after his death as a special praise service. Over the following hundred years and into the 1800s, both Methodists and Moravians gradually abandoned the love feast; thus, the personal testimonies that went along with the love feast had no built-in venue. However, the "class meetings" provided a small group place where something like a testimony might be shared.

Revivalists and Camp Meetings in the 1800s

As the Methodists abandoned the love feast and its featured personal testimony, other groups and movements picked up the practice. Practical lawyer-turned-revivalist Charles Finney (1792-1875) employed the personal testimony as a regular feature of his services. Finney, a Presbyterian, was a practicing "method-ist" when it came to revival; he was a man of methods. Finney figured that getting a revival to happen was essentially a matter of using the *right methods*. Learn the methods, use them, and presto: revival will happen and people will be converted and filled with the Holy Spirit.

Like today's TV advertisers, Finney understood the power of the testimonial: the "satisfied customer." Personal testimonies played an important role in his services. They "softened the soil" for his fervent preaching. The lay testimony may also have made the "professional evangelist's" claims more believable. In the testimony, the congregation heard a personal story from a regular person who lived down the street in their town. Finney used the worship service as a tool for converting men and women, not just for worship of God.

107

The camp meeting also used the testimony in worship. These twin movements (Revivalism and camp meetings) sought the personal conversion of individuals and thus naturally used the personal testimony to promote this experience to others. The testimony provided an opportunity for the laity to speak and was especially significant for women at the time.

Remember, women did not yet have a vote in America. However, at camp meetings they were asked to "give a testimony," providing them with a chance to speak. The "ring meeting" was a special feature of the camp meeting. In such a meeting, believers gathered in a circle or "ring," taking turns giving a personal testimony. Just as many Moravians and Methodists were letting the personal testimony fade, the Revivalist and Camp Meeting movements recharged the practice. Baptists, Adventists, and other frontier-revivalist denominations reintroduced it in local churches.

Around the same time as the Revivalist and Camp Meeting movements, a third movement made use of the personal testimony in a special way—the Holiness Movement. Phoebe Palmer (1807-1874), a medical doctor's wife, began "Tuesday Meetings" for women at her home in New York City. These meetings provided an opportunity to share testimonies of how God had been working in the women's lives. Of special interest were testimonies on how the Holy Spirit had "sanctified" these Christians, and how they had experienced new power and purity in their lives. The meetings were popular and eventually were opened up to men.

Phoebe Palmer and her husband were Methodists and began traveling and promoting this deeper life. While many audiences of the time resisted women preachers, they happily accepted a personal testimony from the likes of Phoebe Palmer, Hannah Whitehall Smith, and other women speakers of the day (who sometimes delivered a far better sermon in their testimony than the actual sermon that followed!). The "Holiness Movement," which adopted the camp meeting as its special means of "spreading scriptural Holiness across the lands," adopted the testimony as an important element of its worship form. Followers came to use the term "testimony meeting" to describe the part of the service dedicated to the democratic opportunity for lay speaking.

The Testimony in the 1900s

In the 1900s, camp meetings began to lose steam, as did Revivalism and the Holiness Movement. However, these three related movements deeply imprinted most American denominations and the modern church. All three were experience-oriented movements. Wherever the church's theology shifts from "objective truth to believe" to a "personal experience to receive," the testimony thrives. That is not to say these three movements lacked belief systems, but to say that personal religious experience was at least of equal (and often greater) importance to them. Thus, the testimony flourished.

The Holiness Movement continued using the personal testimony into the mid 1900s, increasingly limiting them to Sunday evening and their midweek prayer meetings (another innovation of Charles Finney and Revivalism). By the 1960s, Holiness churches were more interested in attaining respectability and providing a safe haven for members transferring from mainline churches than in promoting personal testimony. Gradually the testimony services passed away, first in larger churches and, finally, even in rural and smaller congregations.

However, wherever personal religious experience predominates, the testimony will once again emerge. Great modern collegiate revivals (Houghton '51 and Asbury '69) are usually prompted by extended testimony services rather than traditional preaching services. Charismatic churches are today's brand of experience-oriented Christianity. They have an emphasis on the Holy Spirit, spiritual gifts, and egalitarian acceptance of women and men alike in speaking and preaching. Thus, many Pentecostals still use personal testimony.

Personal Testimony Today

Personal testimony seems to burst out during times when emotionalism, revivalism, and personal experience dominate religion and culture. However, for some unknown reason, a church or denomination seldom seems to maintain the practice much longer than a hundred years. Yet, each time a denomination or movement abandons the testimony, another one surfaces and picks it up.

In many of today's churches, the personal testimony has reappeared as a "pastoral interview" with new converts or new members. Other churches expect a public personal testimony at the point of baptism. Still others hear this testimony in a private interview before the baptism. Some media-oriented churches project video testimonies of their members on large auditorium screens. While the original love feast has been largely lost, modern adaptations of it occur in some men's and women's Bible studies (where the format is geared to snacks and chats, encouraging more personal testimony than Bible study or sermon). Sunday school classes frequently begin with a "prayer 'n' care time," which in some churches has been steered away from physical requests to a new kind of personal testimony time. Personal experience has not left our culture and our religion. Indeed, one might argue that we are increasingly aware of the personal and individual aspects of religious experience. So the testimony, as a means of praise to God for His individual "mighty acts," will probably stay with us in one form or another in future church worship.

To think about . . .

1. What new discovery did you make after reading this chapter on the development of the personal testimony?

2. In the modern world we have a fully developed understanding of the *individual self*, thus enabling the greater understanding of *personal* conversion and *personal* testimony we have today. What about the people who had a group culture view of these things? When the Philippian jailer was converted and presented his "whole house" for baptism, were these people really saved just by going along with the father's decision? In some cultures today, a tribal chief will be converted, and the entire tribe lines up to be baptized in one day. Are they really getting saved? Even though they live in a group culture, do they have to possess personal individual faith?

3. What are the dangers of personal testimonies in a worship service? Can they be overemphasized? How?

4. Why is it that elements of worship like Scripture, the Lord's Supper, baptism, preaching, prayer, and music seem to last in worship, while the personal testimony seems to die out after a hundred years or so? What is it about a testimony that seems to make it a self-destructing device in worship? Are there other such devices?

5. If your church were to reintroduce the personal testimony in a way fitted for your congregation and culture, how would it best be introduced?

6. In what way would a personal testimony be different if done in the context of a love feast service, as was promoted by Wesley and the Moravians? How would the tone be different?

7. What is the difference between a personal testimony of praise that glorifies God and one that attracts too much attention to the individual? How can we tell them apart—what are the "danger signs"?

8. In what way can a personal testimony be used for the cause of evangelism, as Finney did? Is this OK, or is it somehow an abuse of true worship of God?

9. Tell about the most recent "testimony" you've heard and the situation in which you heard it. Can you recall the story?

10. If you were concerned about avoiding abuses and errors in public use of personal testimonies, and you were making a list of "rules" everyone ought to follow in giving a testimony, list what they might be.

11. A popular style of Christian books today is the personal experience approach rather than teaching. "Narrative" is a primary means of influencing the current generation. Indeed, each chapter in this book begins with a "narrative approach" that is a variant of "testimony." What is it about modern learning that makes many more open to a story than systematic factual teaching?

111

9
Ecstatic Expression

*Rebecca left her home in Syracuse, New York, to attend college in
California because she "always wanted to study near the ocean."
Her college roommate Jodi attended Faith Tabernacle Fellowship,
a new church of about three hundred that was meeting in a converted shopping center. Jodi badgered Rebecca every week to come
along. "It's exciting!" she promised. Rebecca demurred and instead
attended the predictable Covenant Presbyterian Church that was so
much like her church in Syracuse.*

*Finally after months of politely refusing, she bargained, "You go to
my church this week and I'll go with you next week." Jodi agreed
and accompanied Rebecca the following Sunday. "That was nice,"
she remarked afterward. "Sorta' relaxing."*

*Rebecca was totally unprepared, however, for what she saw the next
week at Faith Tabernacle. After about a half hour of singing, people
started getting up and dancing in the aisles. Some would shout out,
punctuating the air with their "Hallelujahs," while others seemed
to fall into a trance and speak some sort of gibberish that nobody
(least of all Rebecca) seemed to understand. Then one large woman
shrieked at the top of her lungs and promptly fell to the floor, shaking as if she were suffering from epilepsy. This seemed to delight the
rest of the attendees and they raised the level of their singing, shouting, and dancing.*

*Rebecca was rattled. She felt a "strange spirit" here and just
wanted to escape this weird meeting. When the service finally did
end (three hours later), she walked swiftly to Jodi's car and got
in, relieved to be out of that place. Jodi got behind the steering
wheel and remarked excitedly, "Now wasn't that incredible? What
an outpouring of the Holy Spirit—aren't you glad you came now?"*

Religious ecstasy is not just a Christian phenomenon. Indeed, it appears in many ancient and modern religions. Humans *are* emotional creatures—God made us that way. We get emotional about the things we care about—love of family, patriotism, death, victory, and sports. Is it any wonder that humans would get emotional about their religion?

Ancient Religions

Among ancient religions, all kinds of ecstatic experiences were blended with worship, including dancing, spinning, falling prostrate, falling into trances, crying out, shouting, "being filled" or "possessed" by the god, eating magical food, uttering prophecies, singing repetitively, and speaking in tongues. Some religions, of course, were relatively sober and temperate, but many others specialized in offering ecstatic experiences to the worshipers.

Many Christians have heard of India's *Shiva*, the mad lord of the dance. The Greeks renamed this god *Dionysius* (*Bacchus* to the Romans). During the early church period, Dionysian worship involved frenzied rituals of drinking, dancing, uttering prophecies, and clashing cymbals that led to an altered state, emotional ecstasy, and eventually a nightlong orgy. The worshipers of Dionysius were at first exclusively women, though men were admitted later. Eventually, such ecstatic worship extravaganzas got so far out of hand that the Roman Senate restricted the religion.

Ecstatic experiences are a means of worship in many religions because they are a *human* way of responding to a god. Just like sacrifice, offerings, and prayer are common to many religions, so is ecstatic expression. It is one way humans respond to a higher power.

The Old Testament

Of course, ecstatic expression was not alien to Old Testament Judaism either. Immediately after the Exodus, Miriam led a song of celebration that became a procession of dancing women accompanied by tambourines. We also remember David's extravagant dancing before the Ark in celebration of its return to Jerusalem. The Spirit sometimes came over people in the Old Testament, causing them to utter prophecies from God as if they were oracles. The Spirit would sometimes enable them to do a great physical feat (like kill a bunch of people with a bone). Without detailing all the references to ecstatic experiences in the Old Testament, it is enough to say that some people experienced the extraordinary presence of God in such a way that it altered their lives and produced some ecstatic response.

The Corinthian Christians

It is no wonder in an ancient world where ecstatic experiences were common that Christians would have them too. We learn the most about (though not as much as we'd like) the emotional ecstasy experiences of some Christians in Corinth from Paul's attempt to regulate the excesses of their worship. Here there were tongues, interpretation of tongues, prophecies, testing of spirits, speaking out during worship, a great feast, and even drunkenness during the celebration meal. At first glance, Corinthian worship sounds more like a pagan "emotional orgy" than sensible, moderate Christian worship. Perhaps it was! Or at least perhaps the Corinthians were merely developing a Christian worship style based on their past worship patterns.

While Paul restricted the excesses, he did not abolish most of the ecstatic elements of Corinthian worship, even though many modern folk are disappointed that he didn't. Believe it or not, the writer of the cerebral letter to the Romans, the one so loved by sober and thoughtful Christians today, is also the New Testament's best promoter of ecstatic, emotional experiences as a means of worship—both public and private—and some argue he personally spoke in tongues.

The Early Church

115

Ecstatic experiences didn't last long as an important means of worship. Indeed, one might argue that Corinthian worship was even exceptional during the first century. Like a raging wildfire, ecstatic expression has a way of burning itself out in a church or denomination—moderating itself over time.

While the church soon dropped the celebration banquet that led to the Lord's Supper and congregations seemed to sober up and take a more temperate "teaching approach" to worship, ecstatic expression likely lasted several centuries as a part of worship in some regions or communities.

Eusebius (about 300–325)

"…a recent convert, Montanus by name, through his unquenchable desire for leadership, gave the adversary opportunity against him. And he became beside himself, and being suddenly in a sort of frenzy and ecstasy, he raved, and began to babble and utter strange things, prophesying in a manner contrary to the constant custom of the Church handed down by tradition from the beginning."

The Church History of Eusebius. Retrieved 7/21/01 from:
http://www.ccel.org/fathers2/NPNF2-01/Npnf2-01-10.htm#P3144_1454364

Of course, there were periodic outbreaks of ecstatic emotionalism. The most well known and popular occurred in Asia Minor in the late 100s under the leadership of a trio of people: two women prophets named Priscilla and Maximilla and their leader, Montanus. Montanists believed they lived in the age of the Holy Spirit, and one should expect powerful effects from the Spirit. Indeed they believed the Spirit spoke through Montanus. The movement expected the immediate return of Jesus and practiced an ascetic life (including eating only dry foods). Their worship was anything but dry, including extravagant emotional experiences, prophecies, processions, tears, and even frenzy. The movement spread widely and even persuaded church father Tertullian to join. The church eventually condemned the Montanist movement as pagan, effectually stomping it out.

116

The Middle Ages

Ecstatic expression did not disappear completely, however. It merely went underground. During the Middle Ages, ecstatic experience became a personal rather than public means of worship. Monks and private individuals sought to experience God in their private devotions.

These monks and mystics had strange out-of-body experiences and saw visions of God, Jesus, Mary, or some other saint. Ritual repetitive praying sometimes became the doorway to an altered state, allowing the private worshiper to experience new levels of revelation from God. Some even received a literal mark on their bodies resulting from their "union with God." The idea of "Bridal Mysticism" developed, so that nuns and monks took the idea of being the bride of Christ so literally they had all kinds of experiences of union with Christ—sometimes describing them in sexual terms. Medieval ecstatic experiences were mostly confined to private experiences in private worship settings. Even if they were experienced during collective worship, they were kept private and personal, not public and communal.

Ecstatic expression was a part of the religious experience of people like Meister Eckhart, Teresa of Avila, and other mystics, but it would have been easy in the Middle Ages to have pronounced ecstatic expression as a means of public worship dead and gone forever.

Modern Resurgence

It was not gone forever. As a whole the Reformers focused on a rational integration of scripture and the Christian life and discouraged emotional excesses, even when justified by scriptural support. The nineteenth century saw a great resurgence of ecstatic expression in public worship that continues to this day. Protestantism provided for new expressions in worship. The Reformation did not spawn a new denomination—the Protestant Church—separate from Roman Catholicism. It spawned *hundreds* of denominations, each one with its distinctive emphasis. Some of these specialized in ecstatic expression during worship. At least four streams flowed into what would become the modern Charismatic movement and the current expectation for ecstatic experience in worship.

Quakers and Shakers

In the middle of the 1600s, Englishman George Fox, along with various Puritans, believed in a radical reality of the presence of the Holy Spirit. This society of "friends" began to experience "quaking" during the worship service. Quaking was a kind of stand-up shakes. *Quakers* believed the Holy Spirit could give direct messages to the congregation through any person present, not just an ordained pastor, so they simply sat in silent personal worship awaiting such a corporate message. However, don't get the idea it was all about silence and meditation. Quaker services frequently witnessed—along with quaking and shaking—groaning, tears, and all kinds of other emotional experiences in their Spirit-led meetings.

Jonathan Edwards (1742)

"In the month of May, 1741, a sermon was preached to a company, at a private house. Near the conclusion of the discourse, one or two persons, that were professors [of faith], were so greatly affected with a sense of the greatness and glory of divine things, and the infinite importance of the things of eternity, that they were not able to conceal it—the affection of their minds overcoming their strength, and having a very visible effect upon their bodies...and many others at the same time were overcome with distress about their sinful and miserable estate and condition; so that the whole room was full of nothing but outcries, faintings, and the like. Others soon heard of it in several parts of the town, and came to them; and what they saw and heard there was greatly affecting to them, so that many of them were overpowered in like manner, and it continued thus for some hours; the time being spent in prayer, singing, counseling, and conferring."

An Account of the Revival of Religion in Northampton in 1740-42. Published in *The Christian History,* I (Jan. 14, 21, 28, 1743). Retrieved 7/21/01 from: http://www.jonathanedwards.com/text/jeaccnt.htm

The *Shakers* also originated in England and came to America. The Shaker prophet, Mother Lee, led this group in dancing, repetitive singing, stomping, visions, trances, shouting, tongues, revelations, spinning, Spirit-led laughter, possession by departed souls, along with the violent "shaking" from which they derived their nickname. Group dancing was their worship specialty.

The Quakers and Shakers provided an early template for much of what would become the modern Charismatic movement.

Afro-American Worship

Many African slaves in America brought along their cultural history of emotionalism, ritual dance, ecstatic trance, and possession by *good* spirits. Slaves blended this cultural history with their newly adopted Christian worship, so that "shouting," foot-stamping, rhythmic hand-clapping, and "getting blessed" became features of Afro-American worship. As we shall see, they also powerfully influenced the modern Charismatic movement.

Camp Meeting Emotionalism

Though John Wesley himself condemned what was then called "enthusiasm," his Methodist followers in America did not. They enthusiastically went off to camp meetings, where rhythmic hand-clapping, repetitive singing, running the aisles, "getting blessed," and even barking to "tree the devil" were not uncommon. The term "shouting" became a modifier for Methodist, producing a new moniker: "Shouting Methodist." The Camp Meeting movement, though dominated at first by Methodists, became an interdenominational movement. It was not unknown for folk from more somber churches to sneak off to camp meetings—at first just to watch, and once captivated, to taste of these ecstatic goodies for themselves. Camp meeting emotionalism (and the related revivalist emotionalism) fed the cultural expectations that one's religion can produce feelings and responses—even extravagant responses. The current Charismatic movement sprang from this cultural setting.

Charles Finney (1835)

"If you have much of the Spirit of God, it is not unlikely you will be thought deranged, by many...Multitudes have appeared to those who had no spirituality as if they were deranged. Yet they saw good reasons for doing as they did. God was leading their minds to act in such a way that those who were not spiritual could not see the reasons. You must make up your mind to this, and so much the more, as you live more above the world and walk with God."

Lectures of Revivals of Religion, Lecture VII: "On being Filled with the Spirit," 1868 edition. Retrieved 7/21/01 from: http://www.gospeltruth.net/1835Lect_on_Rev_of_Rel/35revlec07.htm

119

The Holiness Movement

The Holiness churches—both black and white—picked up expressive elements from Camp Meeting emotionalism and took them home to their local congregations. They also took over the camp meetings themselves and used them "for the special promotion of holiness." Holiness folk teach a "second blessing" of the Holy Ghost, who brings cleansing and power to the believer. Holiness followers often responded to the Holy Spirit's work by "running the aisles" and shouting. Women with carefully pinned up hair-dos would "shout their hair down" while raising their hands and crying out "Amen" or "Hallelujah." Men and women would walk or run the aisles of the church, waving their hands while crying and shouting praises. Some would run full speed on the tops of the pews through the crowd of people like a halfback running toward the goal line. (I am not making this up.)

Many Holiness services were taken over by the democratic action of the people (or Holy Spirit, depending on one's view) as the people "got blessed," "testified" one after another, and punctuated the service with songs initiated by the people. This had the effect of making the pastor an accompanist or a kind of referee, instead of the worship leader. Holiness folk claimed the Holy Spirit led the meeting, not the pastor or "some formal order of service printed in a bulletin prepared ahead of time." Holiness people excitedly reported a "great outpouring" when ecstatic exuberance continued so long that "the preacher never got to preach." The nineteenth century Holiness Movement wildfires were just beginning to die down near the turn of the twentieth century when another movement surfaced. This new movement adopted many of these ecstatic experiences and incorporated them into its worship patterns.

The Pentecostal–Charismatic Movement

All these strains painted the backdrop for the next act—a revival that broke out in Los Angeles in 1906. That revival, led by Afro-American pastor William Seymour of the Azusa Street Mission, gave birth to the modern Pentecostal and Charismatic movements. White people attended from the very beginning, as this interracial revival of ecstatic expression burst onto the American scene. Perhaps because its roots come from the Afro-American style of worship, the Pentecostal-Charismatic movement has been more effective at integrating races than any other modern Christian movement.

Like the Quakers and Holiness people before them, the Azusa Street Pentecostal believers emphasized the Holy Spirit's direct guidance of the service. The Holy Spirit was the order of service, and so the congregation sought His movement on one or another person to start a song, give a testimony, dance in the aisles, utter a prophecy or interpretation, or speak in tongues. Hymnbooks were abandoned as the congregation sang and prayed spontaneously. The "baptism in the Holy Spirit" was sought, which resulted in ecstatic experiences often described as something like "electricity running from the top of my head to the toes of my feet." People fell prostrate, lying around the altar for hours at a time. Others came to kneel and pray as they sought God's blessing. What had occurred in an occasional and periodic gathering at camp meetings now occurred every week (every *day* at first) in the local church.

Pentecostal fires invariably die down, as they did at the Azusa Mission—but not before a fire was ignited that spread across America and around the world. No longer can we easily divide Christianity into two parts: Catholic (both Roman Catholic and Orthodox) and Protestant. Today somewhere between 25-30% of the world's Christians are Pentecostal-Charismatics, and few denominations have been unmarked by the movement. It is the third branch of Christianity in the current age and includes both Protestants and Catholics

Recent Ecstatic Expression

There are occasional outbreaks of unique expressions like the "Toronto Blessing" today but the American Charismatic movement has calmed down considerably of late. Indeed, the name "Charismatic" itself represents a kinder, gentler, more inclusive form of "Pentecostalism." Roman Catholic Charismatics join Protestants in seeking baptism in the Holy Ghost. There are Charismatic Episcopal, Baptist, Methodist, and Holiness churches. As Charismatic churches become "super-churches," structure invariably is set up to ensure that fringe elements don't "take over the service." The individual speaking of tongues or prophecy by parishioners is often replaced in larger churches by simultaneous tongues speaking or a spoken prophecy from the pastor or another reliable leader. The wildfires are brought under control by "controlled burns" on the part of the leaders. Yet, the entire worship atmosphere remains one of emotional excitement resulting in deep transforming *feelings*. Charismatics expect to "feel God's presence" at church services. They often get what they expect. Perhaps, when it comes to worship, we all do.

121

The greatest modern influence of the Charismatic movement on worship in all churches has been through music. Even staid and sedate churches have adopted some hymnody of the Charismatics: simple praise choruses sung in unison, projected for all to see, repeated at least a few times.

Today, thanks to this movement (and other cultural factors), the average person attends a church service expecting to "feel something" or to "sense God's presence." When this happens, it is most often during the singing part of the service. The "song service" that Revivalism originally intended as a warm-up to prepare the crowd for the message is no longer preliminary but the main event in many churches. Indeed, in some churches the term "worship" has come to mean the singing part of the service.

Yet, there are strong opponents of this feelings-based emotionalism. As one might expect, many Reformed and mainline churches reject such tendencies. Churches concerned with their respectability have also rejected any tinge of emotionalism. Denominations oriented to pedagogical worship—where worship focuses more on the mind than heart—have usually rejected any "Charismatic leanings." But the surprising development is how many denominations with deep roots in ecstatic emotionalism have also rejected the modern Charismatic movement. Many Holiness churches are among the opposition—rejecting not just tongues, but any element smacking of spiritual ecstasy or emotionalism. Perhaps those denominations that shun the excesses of emotional ecstasy are overly sensitive to their own history, quickly rejecting anything that might be tinged with the memory of previous worship styles—or the preferences of their predecessors.

Few stories are as interesting (and entertaining) as those detailing the history of ecstatic experience in worship. This worship style was driven underground in the first few centuries of Christianity, remaining there for most of history, only to pop to the surface again in the twentieth century and embracing fully a third of Christianity. Pentecostal-Charismatics say this is simply the work of God, who promised to pour out His Spirit on all men and women in the Last Days. The resisters say the movement is not the work of the Spirit at all, but the work of the Devil at worst and the work of manipulating evangelists and pastors at best. Whatever you

choose to believe, there is no denying the fact that the twentieth century
has returned ecstatic expression to worship—for good or bad.

To think about . . .

1. What new discovery did you make from reading this chapter about
    ecstatic expression in worship?

2. Anthropologists who have researched "ecstatic expression" in reli-
    gion have observed a greater tendency toward this sort of expression
    by women and oppressed minorities than men and people in power.
    If this is true, why do you think this would be so?

3. Churches and denominations tend to move upward socio-economi-
    cally. That is, what may start out as a "mission church" or "church
    of the poor" drifts upward over time to become a more professional,
    upper-class church. This factor is sometimes called "redemption and
    lift"—that is, a person is redeemed, straightens up his or her life
    with God and the church's help, gets serious about work, family,
    and civic duties and becomes a respectable citizen. Soon, the former
    drunk is a solid citizen, and the children go on for advanced
    degrees, becoming a part of the upper social class in the city. If
    "redemption and lift" does indeed occur, what implications does this
    concept have for changes in worship patterns of a church's attendees
    over the years?

4. What sort of history does your church have with ecstatic expression?
    Has its stance changed? How? Why?

5. What kind of standard do you think a church should set for
    allowing various forms of ecstatic expression in public services?
    What blessings/problems do you foresee with unlimited expression?
    What "rules" would you set down if you were "king" of your
    church?

6. Can ecstatic expression enrich someone's relationship with God?
    Why is it so sought after, sometimes to the exclusion of other spiri-
    tual disciplines?

7. On a scale of one to ten (ten being highly emotional and feelings-oriented and one being formal, distant, and cerebral), where would you rate your own church? Where would you prefer it to be?

8. Have you ever observed some of the things mentioned in this chapter (running the aisles, speaking in tongues, shouting, etc.)? If so, tell your story to another, especially to someone who has never witnessed such occurrences.

9. What is the biggest loss in making worship something you feel? What is the biggest gain? Do you think the gains offset the losses, or is the opposite true?

10. Has God called some denominations to practice a certain style of worship and others to practice a totally different style—insuring a variety of choices in every community? That is, would it be a good thing for all the churches in one community to worship alike? What are some implications of your answers to these questions?

Part III
Time as a Means of Worship

Most of us think too narrowly when we approach worship. We probably think of worship first as praise—especially singing praise in a public worship service. However, worship is not just limited to singing or involvement in a public service; it is intended to be more of a lifestyle that pervades every aspect of our lives. One of the ways we express this broader view of worship is by using the calendar—days, weeks, and months—as a means of ordering worship. One key aspect of worship is remembering what God has done in the past. The best way for humans to remember is by setting up anniversary celebrations—special days set apart to remember some past event. This is how we get a whole list of holy days. In this section we will look at the use of time in organizing worship and will treat the three most important special days:

> - **Using Time as a Means of Organizing Worship**
>
> - **Sunday and the "Christian Week"**
>
> - **Easter**
>
> - **Christmas**

10
Using Time as a Means of Organizing Worship

Wade and Jamie had not gone to church since they were children. Instead, they had poured themselves into developing their careers. That's why they moved so often. They just didn't have time for religious things. They lived such busy lives that they seldom got to know their neighbors well before they moved again for the next promotion. In their latest move, they had bought a house catty-corner from Eric and Stacey. Before they ever met their new neighbors, they knew Eric and his wife were "religious people." How? They assumed as much. Every Sunday morning, while Jamie was catching up on her business magazines and Wade was loading his golf clubs into the trunk, they saw their neighbor family all dressed up and piling into their van. Wade assumed they were "church folk."

How Christians treat *time* (weekly, monthly, annually) is often their first witness to non-Christians. However, the unique way Christians use time is not primarily a means of witnessing, but a means of worship. Christians have a theological and philosophical reason for treating time differently.

Some religions see time as cyclical: an endlessly repeated or "recycled" pattern of events. Christianity doesn't see time working that way. Christians see time as linear. Linear time issues from the fixed point of creation, continues to the point where I live right now, and goes on somewhere significant in the future—toward the final judgment, consummation, and a time when there will be no time. While some religions "bypass" time, operate above time, or disconnect themselves from time and the temporal realm, Christianity is a time-based religion—rooted in the past, nurtured in the present, and growing toward the future.

Time in the Past

The Bible starts with the creation story: God caused the creation to appear out of nothing. Matter came from no matter and time from no time. In fact, the story presents God as working in time—"seven days." Even the long-ago act of creation is presented as days, demonstrating that God worked within the confines of a week. We even see His schedule—"on the seventh day He rested"!

Christian worship focuses on God—what He has done and who He is. But how will we know what God has done unless we look to His past "mighty acts"? How will we ever understand who He is without knowing the history of His dealings with human beings? Worship that is not rooted in history is not worship of the True God at all, but merely experiential expression to "the God within us." It is worship of a god created in our own image. Christians look to the past to see what God has done so we can praise Him for it. We look to the past to see *who God is*, so that we may worship the True God—knowing His character accurately.

This is why the Bible is important in worship. The Bible is not simply "useful" in teaching and instructing us how to live. Sure, the Bible is useful for discipleship and evangelism, but its role in worship is different. For worship, the Bible's role is primarily to teach us about God—what He has done and who He is—the acts and character of God. When we fully understand what God has done for us in the Incarnation, on the cross, at the tomb, and on the day of Pentecost, we can respond through worship in praise and thanksgiving to Him. It is only when we understand how God dealt with Adam, Noah, Abraham, Jacob, Joseph, Israel, Peter, the Samaritan woman, and Paul that we come to understand who God really is—and thus can worship the True God, not a god we conjure up in our imagination.

Knowing God's mighty acts in history enables us to know whom we really worship. It is not a vague idea or universal principle we gather to venerate. It is a real God we worship—One who accomplished real acts in real time in a real historical past. Worship that is not tied to the past drifts into New Age subjectivism. It offers experience-centered worship "to the unknown God," very much like the ancient residents of Athens to whom Paul proclaimed a real God who acted in history. (See Acts 17:23.)

Christianity is not some mystical religion above time, constructed on universal truths and myths completely disconnected from time. Its foundation is on real historical events that actually took place on definite historical dates in the past. Jesus was born in the "days [of] Caesar Augustus . . . while Quirinius was governor of Syria" (Luke 2:1-2 NIV). Christianity is not based on some wonderful, made-up story—it is historical, rooted in actual events, with great truths that apply to all people in all ages. Thus, when Christians display a cross in their worship centers, it is not merely to symbolize a theological truth, but to remind us of an actual historical event that occurred at Golgotha on Passover weekend in the springtime of 30.

This means that Christians and Jews share a common worship tradition—*remembering* God's past works on our behalf. The primary event Israel remembered was the Passover, when God rescued His people from Egyptian bondage and led them to freedom. For Christians, the primary event remembered is the Crucifixion and Resurrection of Jesus Christ, when God rescued His people from spiritual bondage and gave us freedom in Christ. While both Jews and Christians remember other events as well, Passover and the Crucifixion/Resurrection are the primary events.

So how do Christians remember these events? We use *time*. We commemorate the Resurrection by coming together every Sunday morning to celebrate. We set aside a whole week to recall the events of the final week of Christ's life—from Palm Sunday through Maundy Thursday, Good Friday to Easter Sunday. We recall the coming of the Holy Spirit on Pentecost Sunday. We remember the Incarnation at Christmas. Further, we even stretch these days of remembrance to include entire seasons: preparing for Christmas with Advent and for Easter with Lent. We prolong the Resurrection celebration an additional fifty days to mark Pentecost. In these special days and seasons, we remember what God has done in the past; thus, we respond in praise for His acts on our behalf.

While we have good reason to use time to commemorate God's past

129

work on our behalf, there are more than theological and practical reasons for doing so. Frankly, it is a very *human* thing to do. We have a natural human inclination to commemorate past events through "anniversary celebrations." That is, regardless of one's religion or lack of it, human beings tend to establish days and seasons to remember past events. For instance, even a nonreligious person is likely to celebrate birthdays or wedding anniversaries.

Non-Christian religions do this too with their own set of holy days and seasons. Nations offer a kind of competing "civil religion" to their citizens based on past events in their national history—independence days, thanksgiving days, memorial days for this or that war, and other holidays supporting civil religion. Secularism even offers a competing secular calendar, including a fully secular Christmas and Easter complete with corresponding myths like Santa Claus and the Easter Bunny.

Using the anniversary cycles to celebrate past events is a human trait Christians believe is God-inspired. Thus, it should not surprise us that Christians would remember God's acts of the past on our behalf, especially the central events of the Gospel—the Incarnation, death, burial, Resurrection and Ascension of Jesus, the coming of the Holy Spirit, and the birth of the church.

Time in the Present

However, Christian worship is not stuck looking through the rearview window of history. It is a present-day celebration as well. While it is rooted in historical events, it is experienced in the here and now. God's mighty acts in the Bible are mirrored in my own life—in this present age. What God did on the cross at Calvary echoes in my heart, when on some past day God saved me, *even me*. Even if I cannot sing "It was on a Monday," since I do not know the date for sure, I do know that there was a day when that past sacrifice became a present-tense reality for my sins and me. While there is a real past event when Christ was raised from the dead, there is a corresponding recent event when I personally was raised from my trespasses and sins.

So, while we collectively look back to the past arrival of the Holy Spirit and the birth of the church, I can experience the present-tense coming of the Holy Spirit into my life. I can gather today with the church and see how these present-day personal events in my life echo those great events of the past. And there is so much more to celebrate in worship beyond God's forgiving, raising, saving, and filling us. We celebrate IIis *present* enabling, strengthening, presence, guidance, help, and deliverance this week . . . *even today.*

Time in the Future

Worship looks forward as well—it is *eschatological*, looking forward in hope. We gather to anticipate the future "Second Coming" of Christ and God's eventual "balancing of the books"—punishing evil and rewarding good. When we pray, we believe God will act in the future as He has in the past. We implore God to heal, to mend, to bring peace, to unite and guide, believing He will answer these prayers in the future. Knowing how God has acted in the past, and knowing His character, we have confidence to come before His throne asking Him to act in the future. When we worship, we know the future is in His hands. We can be jubilant and joyous because we know God wins in the end. Good triumphs. We know that His side will triumph. His side will prevail. So, in the positive spirit of the Resurrection, we gather each Sunday to worship a God who has been faithful in the past, prevails in the present, and will triumph in the future.

Christian worship is rooted in the past, so we establish days and seasons to recall the real acts of a real God in real history. Remembering these mighty acts helps us discover increasingly who God really is. Thus, when we offer praise, it is to the True God of the Old and New Testaments, not some vague "inner voice" or "higher power" or "god-as-I-know-him." It is praising the True Historical God of the Bible. Christianity is rooted in actual historical acts that demonstrate how God actually worked in real time. Thus, we remember His actions by commemorating them on special days in our real-time calendar.

131

To think about . . .

1. What new discovery did you make from reading this chapter about the reason Christians use time as a means of worship?

2. How could worship services be better organized to help us really focus on who God is and what He has done, so that we may worship Him more truly?

3. We learn who God is by remembering His "mighty acts," especially as revealed in the Bible. His acts, of course, reveal His character, but not completely so. In Jesus Christ we discover best who God is. So how would you plan to ensure that the "message of the whole Bible" would be covered for people attending your church? How could you know they would get a balanced study of Old and New Testaments, the Epistles, the Gospels, etc.? What plan could you invent for this?

4. What are the dangers of worship that is not rooted in God's work in the Bible and history, but rather focuses exclusively on God's present work in my heart?

5. Find examples of hymns and choruses that emphasize each of the three eras of time: past, present, and future.

6. This chapter reminds us that worship includes a heavy emphasis not only on past events, but also on the present and future. If you were to develop a "pie chart" illustrating what you believe to be the best distribution of emphasis between all three of these elements of time, what would it look like? Would each of the three sections be equal, or would you make one bigger? What would such a pie chart representing your present local church services look like?

7. The first way a neighbor often notices a Christian's witness is in how that Christian observes time. Before they ever talked to you, what would new neighbors notice about your use of time that might indicate you were a Christian believer?

11

Sunday and the "Christian Week"

*Eileen had been raised in a family that invariably attended church
every Sunday. The topic of church attendance wasn't even up for
discussion. Her mother liked to say, "We get up, dress up, and show
up." And they almost always did—until Eileen turned sixteen, that
is. In order to make a little extra money, Eileen got a job as a server
at a downtown restaurant that insisted she work every other Sunday.
Eileen protested, "I'll work any shift, and even on Sundays, but
I can't work Sunday mornings—I always go to church then." The
manager shrugged his shoulders and replied, "We don't make special considerations for religion—the job requires Sunday work. Take
it or leave it."*

Why would Eileen treat Sunday in such a special way? Couldn't she
worship on Sunday evenings or Tuesdays just as well as on Sunday
mornings? Where did this almost universal practice of worshiping on
Sunday morning come from?

The Jews of the first century strictly observed Saturday (the seventh
day), not Sunday, as the Sabbath day. On this day, they did no work nor
permitted anyone in their household—even their animals—to work. It
was a day of personal refreshment and restoration, as well as a weekly
sign of their covenant with God.

133

The Jewish Christians and Sundays

Being Jews, the very first Christians simply continued to observe the
Sabbath each Saturday as their weekly holy day. They saw no need
for immediate change. After all, they hoped to convert the rest of the
Jews into believing Jesus was indeed the promised Messiah of the
Jews. Saturday was the holy day of the Jews and Jesus was the Jewish
Messiah. To reach other Jews, they used the normal channels of com-

munication and persuasion. They attended the local synagogues, which were open to discussion and even arguments. Here they attempted to persuade other Jews to believe that Jesus was indeed the promised Christ.

Luke's Account

"Day after day, in the temple courts and from house to house, they never stopped teaching and proclaiming the good news that Jesus is the Christ."

Acts 5:42 NIV

The Christians also attended (*daily* at first) the Temple, where they gathered at "Solomon's Porch." The porch wrapped around the court of the Temple, providing a shaded place to teach and discuss religious questions. It was the first century's equivalent of today's Sunday school classroom or Christian Education wing.

These Jewish Christians (including all of the apostles and first leaders of the church) continued to practice many rites of Judaism, hoping to convert their brothers. Among other rites, they apparently continued to observe the Sabbath with the rest of the Jews. Thus, the first "Sunday" was actually a Saturday.

However, these Jerusalem Christians were not content to confine their worship to a single day. We know from Scripture that they met *daily*, not weekly. They met from house to house and went to the Temple courts every day in order to worship and evangelize. Therefore, it is only partially true to say the first Sunday was actually a Saturday. It is more accurate to say the first Sunday was every day of the week. These first Christians did not limit their worship to one seventh of the week—they were so committed to Christ they gathered seven out of seven days to worship, perhaps even celebrating the Lord's Supper daily, or at least sharing an "agape meal."

Did these first Christians consider Sunday in any way special? We do know it was a regular "work day" for them. Did they observe the first day in any special religious way? The Gentile church certainly did, and there is some evidence of Sunday worship among the Jewish Christians as well.

Sunday Evidence

Paul hints at Sunday observance when he tells the Corinthians to set aside their offerings *"on the first day of every week"* — that is, Sunday. Why Sunday? It wasn't payday. For Paul to select it thus, Sunday must have had some special significance. The Apostle John was *"in the Spirit on the Lord's day"* when he heard the voice behind him (Revelation 1:10 KJV). Which day? *The Lord's day.* Why single out this day if it was not somehow different from other days? These are only hints, of course. Some argue these references to the "Lord's Day" could just as easily mean the Sabbath, and that Paul's use of "first day" was about saving up one's private offering, a kind of "first fruits offering" of sorts, not public worship. But they are hints.

The Apostle Paul

"On the first day of every week, each one of you should set aside a sum of money in keeping with his income, saving it up, so that when I come no collections will have to be made."

The Apostle Paul to the Corinthians (1 Corinthians 16:2 NIV).

"On the first day of the week we came together to break bread. Paul spoke to the people and, because he intended to leave the next day, kept on talking until midnight."

Luke, telling about the all-night service in Troas (Acts 20:7 NIV).

135

In about 112, the Roman governor Pliny said much the same thing in a letter to the Roman emperor Trajan. Pliny, no friend of Christians, reported on the Christians' activities by saying, *"on an appointed day, they had been accustomed to meet before daybreak, and to recite a hymn antiphonally to Christ, as to a god."* All we get here is an "appointed day," which means that Christians had one day they especially observed. One could argue that was the Jewish Sabbath as easily as a Christian Sunday.

The Didache (about 100)

"On every Lord's Day—his special day—come together and break bread and give thanks, first confessing your sins so that your sacrifice may be pure."

The Didache, XIV. Retrieved 7/17/01 from Indiana Wesleyan University server, Marion, Indiana. http://www.indwes.edu/courses/rel435/didache.htm

We have one other source from about the turn of the first century—making it so old that it was probably circulating even while some of our New Testament was still being written. *The Didache* instructs, *"On every Lord's day—his special day—come together and break bread and give thanks, first confessing your sins so that your sacrifice may be pure."*

While Sunday, or the first day, is not directly mentioned in these references, most scholars believe that the "Lord" referenced here is Jesus Christ. (The earliest Christian creed was simply, "Jesus is Lord.") They believe "his special day" was Sunday, the day He rose from the dead, though a few seventh-day denominational scholars think otherwise. At about the same time as *The Didache* (or just a few years later), one of the apostolic fathers in the *Epistle of Barnabas* rejects the "present Sabbaths" and reports celebrating the "eighth day." Since Saturday is obviously the seventh day, the eighth day must be Sunday, the day they worshiped.

Pliny (about 112)

"On an appointed day, they had been accustomed to meet before daybreak, and to recite a hymn antiphonally to Christ, as to a god."

Pliny the Younger, *Letter 10.* Trans. Henry Bettenson, *Documents of the Christian Church* (New York: Oxford University Press, 1963), 3.

Twin Observance of Both Days

One can easily see how this might be confusing. Why would God toss out one of the Ten Commandments or switch the days? It is even mandated in the Ten Commandments. If the Christians started adapting the clear meaning of one of the Ten Commandments so easily, where might this lead eventually? Perhaps this is why there is so much evidence that Jewish Christians celebrated *both* Saturday and Sunday.

The Epistle of Barnabas (about 105)

"The present sabbaths are not acceptable to me, but that which I have made, in which I will give rest to all things and make the beginning of an eighth day, that is the beginning of another world. Wherefore we also celebrate with gladness the eighth day in which Jesus also rose from the dead, and was made manifest, and ascended into Heaven."

The Epistle of Barnabas, XV, 8-9. Trans. Kirsopp Lake, *Apostolic Fathers* (Cambridge: Harvard University Press, 1965), I, 395-396.

The Gentiles celebrated Sunday for sure, but they might have observed Saturday—the Sabbath—as well. One must not dismiss the Sabbath issue too lightly, for more is at stake than a weekly schedule. Sunday celebration was just that—a celebration. Later in the Middle Ages, worship would become more somber and penitential. But for the early church it was a happy celebrating time. In 205, church father Tertullian—believing the kneeling posture inappropriate for the celebratory tone of Sunday—argued that Christians must never kneel on Sunday. While speaking about kneeling on Sunday, he drops an aside: *"Some few who abstain from kneeling on the Sabbath,"* suggesting that kneeling might still be appropriate on the (old, Jewish) Sabbath. This could also suggest that the twin celebration of Saturday and Sunday was still happening 170 years after the Resurrection.

137

By 375, the "Apostolic Constitutions," a later church document somewhat like the earlier *Didache*, directs the Christians to keep only one Sabbath (Saturday) a year—the day when Jesus was in the grave, the day before Easter. Therefore, the twin celebration of the Sabbath and the Lord's Day must have melted away by then.

Justin Martyr (about 155)

"We all hold this common gathering on Sunday since it is the first day, on which God transforming darkness and matter made the universe, and Jesus Christ our Saviour rose from the dead on the same day. For they crucified him on the day before Saturday, and on the day after Saturday, he appeared to his apostles and disciples and taught them these things which I have passed on to you also for your serious consideration."

First Apology, LXVII. Trans. Edward Rochie Hardy, LCC, I, 287-288.

Sunday as a Day of Rest

Sunday was not a day of rest at first. This is completely in line with the general tenor of the early church and its resurrection-celebration mood. It would be three hundred years before the notion of treating Sunday like the Sabbath/Saturday would take hold. The idea was established by imperial decree of the Roman Emperor Constantine in 321. Even in this decree, country farmers were exempt if they needed to work on their land.

Emperor Constantine (321)

"Constantine to Elpidius. All judges, city-people and craftsmen shall rest on the venerable day of the Sun. But countrymen may without hindrance attend to agriculture, since it often happens that this is the most suitable day for sowing grain or planting vines, so that the opportunity afforded by divine providence may not be lost, for the right season is of short duration. 7 March 321."

Codex Justinianus, III, xii, 3. Trans. Henry Bettenson, *Documents of the Christian Church* (New York: Oxford University Press, 1963), 18.

Weekly Fast Days

Jesus never said, "If you fast, do not fast as the hypocrites." What He said was, "*Whenever* you fast . . ." Fasting was an assumed habit for both the Jews and the early Christians. Like the Pharisee in Luke's Gospel, a good Jew fasted twice a week, on Mondays and Thursdays. The Christians only slightly adapted the twice-weekly fast days by jogging the days forward to Wednesdays and Fridays. Why fast on Wednesdays? We're not sure. At least the "reason" is not articulated (*invented?*) until later. Like many worship traditions, the act precedes the rationale. We do know (from *The Didache*) that within fifty years of the Resurrection, the reason given for a Friday fast was as a "day of preparation." Preparation for what? Sunday? Then why make Friday the day of preparation? Or does the "day of preparation" refer to starting the Friday fast in the evening—the beginning of Saturday?

The Didache (about 100)

"Your fasts must not be identical with those of the hypocrites. They fast on Mondays and Thursdays; but you should fast on Wednesdays and Fridays."

The Didache, VIII. Retrieved 7/17/01 from Indiana Wesleyan University server, Marion, Indiana. http://www.indwes.edu/courses/rel435/didache.htm

In fact, *The Didache* may reveal a second, more fascinating motivation for changing the Jewish fast days from Monday and Thursday to Wednesday and Friday—simply to be *different* from the [Jewish] "hypocrites." By the turn of the first century, having different days than the Jews must have been important. If that was indeed a reason for the shift, it will not be the last time a church changed worship patterns just to be different.

Sunday Summary

Thus, the Jewish Christians and maybe even the Gentiles probably celebrated the Sabbath and the "Lord's Day" side by side at first. As the church spread, Sunday became the more prominent day and eventually crowded out the Saturday/Sabbath. In due course, even the term "Sabbath" would come to be applied to a different day—Sunday. Most modern Christians tip their hats to the fourth commandment, believing it is still binding in some ways, but that the rule's applications have been jogged forward one day. Though Saturday was observed along with Sunday at first, Sunday was so fully established over the first few hundred years that eventually the only Saturday/Sabbath observed in the entire year was the dark day remembering Christ's day in the tomb.

As for the "Christian week," the first believers adopted the Jewish practice of fasting two days, with the only adaptation being the selection of two different days. Except for a small group of seventh-day Christians, the vast majority of Christians through history and around the world today observe Sunday as their special day of worship. However, the early Christians' habit of fasting two days a week has been largely abandoned by modern evangelicals; that is, unless dieting counts.

To think about . . .

1. What new discovery did you make from reading this chapter about the origin of Sunday worship and weekly fast days?

2. In what ways do you think the fourth commandment (Sabbath day) applies or doesn't apply to Sunday observance today?

3. If a Jewish person converted to Christianity today but wanted to continue observing Saturday/Sabbath along with Sunday, would that be appropriate in your mind? Why or why not?

4. Of the two weekly observances—fasting and Sunday worship—why is it that modern Christians cling to one but seem to have easily disposed of the other? If fasting is no longer a "means of grace" to the modern person, is something else more effective today?

5. Beyond attending church, what other ways do you personally observe Sunday differently from other days?

6.   What remnants of Sunday observance does the secular culture still exhibit—at your workplace and in your community?

7.   To what extent are all Christians obligated to observe Sunday? That is, how do you believe all committed Christians should at the least observe Sunday?

12
Easter

Amanda lay in bed the night before Easter, remembering the Easter celebrations of her childhood. Her mom had always bought new dresses for all three daughters. They started the day off by searching for their Easter baskets, followed by their once-a-year pilgrimage to church services. She couldn't remember if they went at Christmas, but she clearly remembered attending church every year at Easter. "I wonder why?" she thought to herself. "Why would Mom insist on going to church this one day of the year?" She closed her eyes and thought to herself, "Who knows, Mom was such an enigma anyway." Then she began to wonder if she was making a mistake by not taking her daughter Julie to church—at least once a year like her mother had. "Is Julie missing something important? I'm so faithful to take her to ballet and soccer—maybe I should get her up tomorrow and take her to church." These thoughts flashed through Amanda's mind as she fell to sleep the Saturday night before Easter Sunday.

Why would Amanda, a totally secular person, think of taking her daughter to church on Easter Sunday? Why does the church make such a "big deal" about this Sunday over all others, even Christmas? When did we start celebrating Easter?

The First Easter

The first celebration of Easter was not an annual event but a weekly one. To the early church, every Sunday was a mini-Easter. Our English term "Easter" comes from the name of a pagan feast in England, but the celebration itself has no pagan roots. Sure, most every culture and religion has some sort of special day in the springtime, but the Christian Easter is rooted in a specific, datable event in history: the Resurrection of Jesus Christ after Passover probably in 30.

Imagine yourself as a first-century Jewish Christian when Passover 31 rolled around. Your Jewish friends and neighbors are preparing for their most sacred Passover feast. Would you be joining them in these Passover celebrations? To what extent? Would you be thinking about the Exodus event of your forefathers? Or rather remembering what God had done just last year—when God raised Jesus Christ from the dead?

Who was the first Jewish Christian to make this suggestion: "Shouldn't we somehow celebrate the Passover differently?" Did someone argue, "Can we ignore at this season of the year the suffering, Crucifixion, burial, and Resurrection of Jesus Christ?" We do not know which Jewish Christian first challenged the notion of business-as-usual for Passover. We can suspect—people being what they were and are—it was not long until the Christians breathed new meaning into the old Passover celebration, giving birth to the first "Easter."

The Christianization of Passover into Easter probably happened at the first anniversary of Christ's death in Jerusalem. After all, these Jewish Christians had to face the issue in a year—celebrate Passover or breathe resurrection meaning into the old celebration. Usually even Gentile churches outside Palestine had a Jewish core. So early on, the Christians had to face the issue of what to do during Passover. In fact, Paul purposefully established a new attitude toward the Passover (unleavened bread) feast when writing to the Corinthian Christians. This Pauline comment provides us with the best hint for a possible Easter celebration even as early as New Testament times.

The Apostle Paul

"Get rid of the old yeast that you may be a new batch without yeast—as you really are. For Christ, our Passover lamb, has been sacrificed. Therefore let us keep the Festival, not with the old yeast, the yeast of malice and wickedness, but with bread without yeast, the bread of sincerity and truth."

1 Corinthians 5:7-8 NIV

For the next couple of hundred years, the Easter season was not a season at all but a single day. Until about 300, the Christian *Pascha* (a term representing either or both the Passover and Christian Easter) wrapped up the commemoration of the passion/suffering, the death, and the Resurrection of Jesus. Just as the Jewish Pascha had remembered the escape from Egyptian bondage, so the Christian Pascha was a commemoration of the believer's escape from death to life through Christ. After 300, the day expanded into a season, as we shall see.

The Date of Easter

So, when did the early Christians celebrate the Resurrection of Christ? They knew that He had risen on the first day of the week, Sunday, immediately following the Passover in 30. So when should they celebrate Easter: on the actual *date*, or on the *day*? Some Christians (*Quartodecimans*) insisted they should celebrate Easter on the actual *date* of Passover, the very day when the Jews were sacrificing their Paschal lamb. This is how you probably celebrate your birthday. If you were born on the first Tuesday in June, the 9th, you probably celebrate your birthday on June 9th each year, whether it is a Tuesday or not. The date is more important than the day.

Eusebius (323)

"Never on any day other than the Lord's Day should the mystery of the Lord's resurrection from the dead be celebrated...on that day alone we should observe the Paschal fast."

Retrieved 7/17/01 from CCEL http://www.ccel.org/fathers2/NPNF2-01/ Npnf2-01-10.htm#P2729_1313445

145

Other Christians insisted that Easter should always be celebrated on Sunday—the *day* of Christ's Resurrection. This group celebrated Easter on the first *Sunday* after the Jewish Passover, reinforcing the weekly Sunday as a mini-Easter. Which group was right? The date-of-Passover people (*Quartodecimans*) were more "accurate," but the Sunday people probably had better roots in theology. The Sunday side won. Ever since the Western church has celebrated Easter on a Sunday, and every Sunday is a mini-celebration of the Resurrection.

However, there are still differences between the Eastern (Orthodox)
and Western (Roman Catholic and Protestant) dates of Easter. The West
sets the date based on the first full moon after the Spring equinox. The
Eastern Orthodox churches set the date based on the Jewish Passover
date. This differential means the West and East sometimes celebrate
Easter more than a month apart and the Western date can even fall
before Passover! As in other things the East is more accurate and the
West more practical.

Easter Day Becomes Easter WEEK

One of the most fascinating accounts of worship in the ancient church
comes from a woman traveler named Egeria. She was a nun from Spain
who took a pilgrimage to the Holy Land and observed the Christian
services in Jerusalem in 384. Apparently she intended to report on her
trip when she returned, so she kept a detailed journal of what she saw
and heard. Her journal, *Egeria's Travels*,[8] provides a firsthand account
of the ancient church's worship style in Jerusalem during the late 300s.
Egeria reported an entire week of celebration, not just a single day for
remembering the passion/suffering, death, burial, and Resurrection of
Jesus. Every day included something to do and something to remember
from Christ's last week on earth.

It could be argued that the Jerusalem Christians developed these separate
days of "Holy Week" simply to give the pilgrims something to do
on their visits. It is more likely—or at least a more reasonable explanation—that separate days were developed as a teaching tool to emphasize
the various events. It also reinforced these events by moving the faithful
around the town in a manner similar to the "Stations of the Cross"
observed today in some churches.

For whatever reason, Easter Day came to be celebrated all week. Egeria
described the Jerusalem events as beginning on *Palm Sunday*, with the
Christians reenacting the march from the Mount of Olives, waving palm

146

[8] *Egeria's Travels*. Translated by John Wilkinson (Warminster, England: Aris & Phillips Ltd., 1999). ISBN 0-85668-710-3

branches and singing as they entered the city. On *Monday and Tuesday*, they sang hymns and read specific Scriptures. On *Wednesday*, they recalled the story of Judas conspiring with the Jewish leaders to betray Jesus. On Thursday evening (*Maundy Thursday*), they celebrated the Lord's Supper in memory of the Last Supper, followed by an all-night vigil. Early Friday morning (*Good Friday*), after the all-night service, they remembered the arrest of Jesus by reading the scriptural account and hearing the words of Pilate. They then went home to meditate several hours before returning to pass by "the wood of the cross," which had been lain on a table. On *Saturday* they held two worship services and, at dark, all the Christians gathered for another all-night vigil to await the celebration the next morning. On *Easter Sunday* morning a glorious celebration occurred, including Scripture, antiphony, preaching, and Holy Communion.

Tertullian (about 205)

"After that [Easter], Pentecost is a most joyous space for conferring baptisms..."

On Baptism, XIX. Trans. S. Thewall, ANF, III, 678.

Egeria reports the celebrations did not end after the Easter service but continued for the next eight days with daily celebrations of joy. Egeria's travel diary gives us an early account of the development of *Holy Week*, which she called the "Great Week." It is true that the earliest Christians remembered the events of Palm Sunday, the betrayal, passion, Crucifixion, death, burial, and Resurrection of our Lord on a single day. But it is also true that before long, they had multiplied the single day celebration into an entire week of focus.

147

Easter Week Becomes Easter SEASON

At about the same time as Easter Day was developing into Easter Week, the week was becoming an entire *season*. Ancient Christians were so committed to having the gospel story pervade their entire lives that they were not satisfied remembering events for a few days of the year or even for a week. Easter was so important to these ancient Christians that the week was extended in both directions—before and after Easter day. The Easter week celebration stressed an enormous shift in emotions—from the mourning, pain, and agony of the week preceding Jesus' death and Resurrection, to the celebration, joy, and elation on Easter Sunday morning and through the next eight days.

Council of Nicaea (325)

"And let these synods be held, the one before Lent (that the pure Gift may be offered to God after all bitterness has been put away), and let the second be held about autumn."

Canon V. Trans. Henry R. Percival, NPNF, 2nd series, XIV, 13.

These Christians were not content with a single week to celebrate this central event in their theology. The prelude of mourning was soon stretched to a period of forty days before Easter (not counting Sundays) to be called *Lent*. The ancient Christians observed forty days of preparation for Easter so that they could fully develop the emotion of mourning and identify with Christ's pain, suffering, agony, and betrayal. The theory is that after this period of mourning, the joyous celebration of the Resurrection would have that much more dramatic, emotional punch. The kickoff day for Lent came to be called *Ash Wednesday* sometime around 1000. This was preceded by "Fat Tuesday" and the Mardi Gras celebration (which, of course, totally missed the point).

148

In addition to stretching backward, Easter also went forward, extending the joyous side of the celebration fifty more days to *Pentecost Sunday.* Pentecost was already established as a Jewish feast that celebrated the giving of the Law. Jews who made the pilgrimage to Jerusalem for Passover often stayed the additional fifty days until Pentecost before they returned home. (All these seasons are technically now "their own" seasons, though they still are related to one another.)

For the Christians, Pentecost commemorated the coming of the Holy Spirit and the birth of the church. Thus, it was natural for the Christians to extend the celebration side of Easter for the next fifty days to

Pentecost. At first the Christians celebrated both Jesus' Ascension and the coming of the Holy Spirit at Pentecost. Later, these events were divided so that the Ascension was remembered forty days after Easter and the coming of the Holy Spirit on Pentecost ten days later.

The fifty days *after* Easter were more important to the ancient church then the forty days before. The tenor of the ancient church was upbeat, positive, and celebratory. Not until the Middle Ages (and modern times), did the "prelude" mourning side of Lent overshadow the "postlude" celebratory side of the Easter season.

Augustine (about 400)

"The forty-day fast of Lent draws its authority from the Old Testament, from the fasts of Moses and Elias, and from the Gospel, because the Lord fasted that many days, showing that the Gospel is not at variance with the Law and the Prophets..."

Letter 55: to Januarius. Trans. Wilfrid Parsons, FC, XII, 283-284.

Thus, by the end of the 300s, Easter Week was Easter *season*, including the preceding forty days of Lent and the subsequent fifty days until Pentecost. The three-month season of Easter included Lent, Palm Sunday, Maundy Thursday, Good Friday, Easter Sunday, Ascension, and Pentecost—still celebrated by most Christians to this day.

149

Indeed, the "History of Easter" is pretty well wrapped up by 300. While the Roman Catholic Church added a plethora of holy days to the church calendar throughout the Middle Ages, it left Easter pretty much alone. The Reformers let Easter celebrations stand as well, though Protestants have tended to downplay the Catholic notion of additional special or holy days. Thus, Lent and Maundy Thursday observances gradually fell out of favor. The "Free Church movement" and American Camp Meeting Revivalism tended to simplify the number of special days as well. Protestants like to put all their special celebrations on Sunday;

thus, Maundy Thursday, Good Friday or Ash Wednesday services were attended sparsely until they evaporated altogether. While other holy days are stripped out of the Protestant calendar, Easter has been a regular celebration of the Christian church since the year after Christ rose from the dead. It should be — it represents the central theological truth of our Christianity.

Easter and Other Holy Days Since the Reformation

What about all the other holy days? The Middle Ages had turned almost every single day of the calendar into a holy day. While the theology of this is sound (every day *should* be a holy day), the practice produced a jumbled calendar where more was less. When every day is holy, it is too easy to make no day holy.

Church of Scotland (1560)

"Lent, Palm Sunday, and Holy Week shall be retained, not to force anyone to fast, but to preserve the Passion history and the Gospels appointed for that season. This, however, does not include the Lenten veil, throwing of palms, veiling of pictures, and whatever else there is of such tomfoolery...Holy Week shall be like any other week save that the Passion history [shall] be explained every day for an hour...and that the sacrament [shall] be given to everyone who desires it."

"The Book of Discipline" in John Knox's *History of the Reformation in Scotland* (London: Thomas Nelson & Sons, 1949), II, 281.

Protestants were divided on what to do with the "church year" calendar of the Roman Catholics. Luther kept the holy days, including Easter, dropping most of the days dedicated to saints. The Church of England kept all the holy days and those dedicated to Bible saints (Andrew, Peter, etc.), dropping most extra-biblical saints' days. In a radical reform movement, the Church of Scotland (1560) tossed out just about every-thing, including Christmas, perhaps with the same theological notion as the Catholics — every day is a holy day! John Wesley retained just about all holy days, including "All Saints' Day," which seemed to have special meaning for him.

So, what of today? Most "mainline" churches celebrate much of the church year, having dropped the minor saints' days. Modern evangelicals are grandchildren of the Free Church tradition—the movement that tried to simplify and strip out complexity and "extras" from worship. They are also children of Camp Meeting Revivalism that made the complex simple and abandoned "irrelevant" past traditions, inventing new ones as needed. Evangelical minimalists celebrate Christmas, Palm Sunday, Easter, and little else when it comes to the church year. They are more likely to celebrate national and secular holidays, including Mother's Day, Thanksgiving, Independence Day, Memorial Day, or Super Bowl Sunday than Pentecost or Maundy Thursday. Nevertheless, an increasing number of evangelical churches are adding sacred days to their church year calendar, which may be a hopeful trend.

To think about . . .

1. What new discovery did you make from reading this chapter on the development of Easter worship and traditions?

2. To what extent does your own church or denomination customarily celebrate these days of the Easter season:
   - Ash Wednesday
   - Palm Sunday
   - Good Friday
   - Ascension Sunday
   - Lent
   - Maundy Thursday
   - Easter Sunday
   - Pentecost

3. In your opinion, was the expansion of Easter from a single day into a multi-day season a good decision or a bad one? What was gained? Lost?

151

4. What difference would it have made in our present-day Easter celebrations if the "date group" had won and the setting of Easter day was not automatically on Sunday?

5. Why do you think many Christians focus more on the passion and suffering of Christ in Lent leading up to Easter, than the joyous celebration of Pentecost season following that day? What theological emphasis does this reflect? Is it accurate?

6. In what ways could the Easter celebration in your own church be made more meaningful and tied to the actual historical events related in the Gospels?

7. How would you compare the Christmas and Easter celebrations in your local church to those of the secular culture?

8. How can a completely secular person celebrate both Christmas and Easter without using any religious symbolism or stories, yet still have great stories to tell?

9. To what extent should the Christian church be free to celebrate and Christianize secular, political, and pagan days like Thanksgiving, Father's Day, and national independence days? Where would you personally draw the line?

13
Christmas

Sayaghi had never been to the United States and was excited when his company sent him to Chicago on business last December. He wanted to see snow— something he had not seen in his tropical Buddhist country. He arrived December 22nd and was impressed by the city's decorations. Every store window, all the streets, and even many individual houses were strung with festive lights for Christmas. His business meeting on the 24th went well, except that everyone was in such a festive mood they got very little accomplished. Everyone then left the offices a little after lunch and told him they wouldn't be back until the 27th. Sayaghi spent the next two days in an almost closed-down Chicago. He didn't know Americans were so religious. At the convenience store down the street from his hotel, he asked the clerk, "Does this whole nation celebrate the birth of Jesus?"

Why did Sayaghi find Chicago "closed down" over Christmas? Why Christmas—a *Christian* holy day? What started this celebration that became so dominant in our culture? Where did it originate? Did the first Christians celebrate Christmas?

The Christmas season probably receives the most attention in the modern annual calendar—for Christians and secular people alike. It is the supreme Christian holiday. An outsider visiting our culture would assume that this holy day represented the most important and central truth of our religion. However, Christmas got off to a rocky start among the early Christians. In fact, they did not celebrate it at all.

When Christmas Started
The early Christians were more interested in the Resurrection than the birth of Jesus. Therefore, Easter was their central holy day. Over the next hundred years or so, the eastern part of the Roman Empire (Turkey,

Syria, Palestine, etc.) developed a new Christian feast, *Epiphany*, celebrated on January 6. This feast remembered more than Jesus' birth, also including His circumcision, the visit of the Magi, His baptism, and all the events up to His first miracle at Cana. Epiphany wrapped all these events into one celebration of "appearance" or "manifestation." That is, Jesus was made manifest—shown forth—at such events as His birth, circumcision, and at Cana: to the Gentiles when the Magi came, to Simeon and Anna in the Temple, and to His disciples when He performed the water-to-wine miracle.

John Chrysostom (380)

"And moreover it is not yet the tenth year since this day has become clearly known to us...And so this day too, which has been known from of old to the inhabitants of the West and has now been brought to us, not many years ago, has developed so quickly and has manifestly proved so fruitful...And the star brought the Magi from the East."

Sermon Preached at Antioch, December 25, 380. Trans. Albert D. Alexander, cited by White in DCW, 30.

What we call an "epiphany" is a sudden illuminating insight or instantaneous grasping of something's meaning. The pre-Christmas feast of Epiphany was about grasping the total significance of who Jesus was and what His Incarnation meant. The later "Christmas" narrowed the focus to His birth. Thus, the first Christmas was on January 6th and commemorated all of Jesus' life up to His first miracle.

Somewhere in the early 300s at the other end of the Roman Empire—the western end, which included Rome—the feast of Christmas emerged as separate from Epiphany. The first actual mention of "December 25" as Christmas was in 354 in Rome, though that probably reflects practice as early as 336.

Historically, Epiphany (January 6th) spread from the East to Rome and the rest of the West, while Christmas (December 25th) spread from western Rome to the East, resulting eventually in both days being celebrated — Christmas and Epiphany — with the "twelve days of Christmas" in between.

Why December 25?

Jesus was probably not actually born in December. The "shepherds in the fields" indicates another season. So, why did Christians select December 25 as the day they would celebrate His birth? There are two theories: (1) the Christians calculated the date through complex figuring, or (2) the Christians simply adapted a pagan feast day and sanctified it.

The calculation theory comes up with December 25 by assuming Jesus died on March 25. Then by a complex set of calculations, the theory figured that Jesus was also conceived on March 25 and was born nine months later on December 25. The Jews had been known for such fanciful theories, and so were some early Christians, so this is at least a possible theory for the December 25th date.

The second and far more plausible theory is that the Roman Christians simply set their feast to remember Christ's birth on a day that would intentionally compete with (and eventually defeat) a pagan feast. In 272, the Emperor Aurelian had established a feast for the "Commemoration of Emesa," dedicated to the Syrian sun god. It was on this day — the winter solstice — that the sun was at its lowest point on the horizon, from which it would be "reborn" to return throughout spring. (The Julian calendar by this time was four days off the actual winter solstice, thus explaining the December 25 date.) The Christians may have decided to simply "overprint" the pagan feast of the sun's return. Perhaps they even used this competing feast for evangelistic purposes, claiming the Lord Jesus as the True Sun who was truly resurrected and would someday truly return. Whatever actually happened, Christmas won the competition. The pagan feast disappeared, while we continue to celebrate the birth of Jesus on December 25th.

155

The Christmas SEASON

What started as a single day (January 6, Epiphany), split into two days (Christmas and Epiphany), then finally developed into a full-blown season. The advent of Advent was recorded by law in 380, requiring attendance during the three-week Advent season from December 17 through January 6. The three weeks would come to include special days to remember and celebrate God's work.

Apostolic Constitutions (about 375)

"Let them [slaves] rest on the festival of His birth, because on it the unexpected favour was granted to men, that Jesus Christ, the Logos of God, should be born of the Virgin Mary, for the salvation of the world."

Apostolic Constitutions, VIII, 33. Trans. James Donaldson, ANF, VII, 495.

Many of the first Christians accepted the Jewish notion that a new day started the evening before. This tended to make the night before a holy day also a celebration; hence, the significance of Christmas Eve. Christmas Day was followed by the "first Sunday after Christmas," then by New Year's Day (which eventually would come to have its own vigil or "watch-night" service, complete with Charles Wesley's "covenant renewal service"). Finally, the season finished up with Epiphany, recalling Christ's presentation at the Temple, the visitation of the Magi, Jesus' baptism, and His miracle at Cana. The season would come to be a time of celebration, rejoicing, gift-giving, elaborate crèches, musicals, processions, children's programs, cantatas, pageants, and plays. It became the most widely celebrated Christian holy day and eventually spawned a completely parallel secular holiday (with its own stories and heroes) for irreligious folk to celebrate. It's ironic, isn't it? Christmas most likely started out as a pagan holiday that became a Christian feast only to become pagan again.

To think about . . .

1. What new discovery did you make from reading this chapter about the development of Christmas worship and traditions—something you didn't know before reading this chapter?

2. If the Christians did indeed adopt December 25 to purposely compete with a pagan feast, was that wrong or OK? Can you think of other secular or national holidays the church observes and adapts to Christian purposes today?

3. How do Christians go about "sanctifying" secular, national, or pagan feast days? What do we do to accomplish this?

4. What are the "competing myths" of a totally secular Christmas today? If the Christians tell stories about the Incarnation, Jesus' birth, and the Magi, what stories do secular people tell their children?

5. If Christmas was not celebrated by the apostles or early church, does that mean we shouldn't celebrate it? Are we obligated to set aside only those days which the apostles and early church observed, or do we have the freedom to adopt Christian feasts which came later? Do you lean to being a "strict constructionist" in worship traditions, or are you more "progressive" in your interpretation of church traditions?

6. Forgetting the matter of pagan dates, which way do you lean on the question of including pagan elements in a Christian holiday—things like Christmas trees as part of a Christian Christmas celebration?

7. Does it matter that December 25 is not likely the actual date of Christ's birth? If we actually found out somehow that the birth was, say, October 15th, what would you suggest we do?

Part IV
Space and Objects:
Aids to Worship

Jesus Christ was not merely a ghost who appeared to be human but wasn't. He actually came to us in human flesh and walked on actual soil and ate real food. Christians do not reject the physical world as if only "spiritual" worship is good. Along with His "still small voice," God used tangible means of communicating with humans in the Old Testament—fire, a cloud, an elaborate Tabernacle and Temple, and commandments written on actual stone. He still does this. In worship, we now use literal, physical elements like bread and wine, real water in baptism, and a physical book we call the Bible to communicate with God. We do not worship these things—for that is idolatry. But we use them as aids to worship. Thus, we build tangible church buildings. And we fill them with useful objects, which provide the basis for the chapters in this section:

- **Church Buildings**
- **Furnishings in Worship**

159

14
Church Buildings

When the Simon family joined Trinity Church, the church was grow-
ing so fast that a third service had just been added to accommodate
the new people. Within three months, this third service also packed
the building. Last Sunday's service kicked off a "capital campaign"
to raise funds for a new church building. Taking his text from 2
Kings 4:1-6, Pastor McIntyre had challenged the people to "provide
more vessels for the Lord's blessing," like the widow did for Elijah's
miracle. Tim and Sherri Simon attended the banquet the following
Tuesday evening. Under a banner proclaiming "Equal Sacrifice, Not
Equal Giving," all were challenged to sacrifice something of great
value for the next three years. The Simons whispered together only
a moment before deciding to keep both of their cars for three more
years and pledge the cost of a new car to the capital campaign.
"We've got to have a new building, or we could lose God's bless-
ing," Sherri said. "He multiplies the oil; we've got to provide the
vessels."

Why do Christians need special buildings for worshiping God? If we
want to be like the early church, shouldn't we copy its style of meeting
in homes and using all the money saved to help widows and orphans?
When we build gigantic temples, aren't we acting more like pagans
than the humble followers that Jesus intended? Why do Christians need
buildings?

The Patriarchs

Noah, Abraham, and Jacob had no temple in which to worship. That
does not mean they were without "sacred space," however. They created sacred space in commemoration of God's intervention in their lives.
Jacob, for instance, had a special dream in an ordinary place. Once
the extraordinary event occurred, the ordinary place had new meaning—Jacob set up a pillar and called it the "House of God." The mount

on which Abraham offered his son Isaac was an ordinary mountain, but it became a sacred mountain after God intervened to save the boy. While the patriarchs had no temple, they set aside and sanctified sacred space for worship even before the development of the portable Tabernacle or permanent Temple in Jerusalem.

Jewish and Pagan Temples

The early Christian church was made up primarily of people who were already religious, not converted atheists. These first Christians were either converted Jews or converted pagans. The Jews had the impressive "Herod's Temple," which was the third edition of the Jerusalem Temple, although usually considered part of the "second" temple period up to the year 70. While impressive to the Jews, it was not particularly prominent in the first-century world. That culture was full of majestic temples to Apollo, Zeus, and Aphrodite, along with gigantic temples for the cult of emperor worship. Such temples were common in the ancient world.

Both Jews and pagans understood worship as something to be done in a temple or synagogue. Indeed, any god worth considering in ancient days had a temple. The faithful came to these temples to hear their god speak, to show their loyalty to the god, and to offer prayers, sacrifices, and other gifts.

Frequently, the massive size and the extent to which the temple dominated its city signified that particular god's power and effectiveness. This is not unlike passing a gigantic church building today and saying, "Something must really be happening at that church!"

162

The First Christians

Being a collection of Jews and pagans, the early Christians might have been expected to immediately build temples or synagogue-like structures to "compete" with the other religions. They didn't. Why not? They were expecting Christ to return right away. Besides, Christianity was not an authorized and approved Roman religion as is would become later. The Romans had not yet approved Christianity as an accepted religion. Thus, the Christians had to meet surreptitiously and illegally, although in Palestine they were still considered a sect of Judaism and thus escaped punishment. Most early Christian churches could easily fit in a room of a house—one more reason the churches were small. At least, this was true at first.

While it is possible to be a Christian without a pulpit, pews, or a pastor, it is unlikely that Christians will ever be Christians without *meeting together.* The assembly of believers has always been a central part of Christianity. Early Christians were willing to meet, despite the authorities and regardless of threats, punishment, and even execution. Christians *have* to meet together—it is what Christians do.

So, where did they meet? The first Jewish Christians continued to worship in the Temple and synagogues for a while. However, within a decade after Christ's Resurrection, Christians were being expelled from the synagogues. Within forty years, the Jerusalem temple had been destroyed (A.D. 70). That left the Christians with homes or rented buildings for their meeting sites.

In Caesarea, a Gentile congregation met in the home of Cornelius. The infant church in Philippi started out beside the river at a "place of [Jewish] prayer," then moved to the home of Lydia. Perhaps the church in Corinth met at the home of Jason or maybe the home of Priscilla, or both. The Romans met in Priscilla's home when she later moved there. The Colossian church may have met in the home of Philemon, the owner of the runaway slave Onesimus. In Ephesus, Paul left the synagogue and rented out the "lecture hall of Tyrannus" for his meetings, even though the Christians were probably still considered a sect of Judaism at that time. Later, there is less evidence of using public meeting halls. The early Christians met in a variety of places, usually a house, but never a "temple." They were an underground movement.

163

This lack of a permanent building enabled radical changes in worship styles for the first-century Christians—Jewish or pagan. Both the Jews and pagans were "temple people." Worship for them was specifically defined by gathering in an imposing building that was designed for worship—a "sacred space." These massive temples projected impressive architecture and elaborate trappings, and they offered memorable sensory elements like incense, fire, oil lamps, and burning sacrifices. Early Christian worship, on the other hand, was mostly a small gathering of folk in an ordinary home. It is little wonder that some of the new Gentile converts kept one foot in both worlds, attending both the Christian house-church while still slipping off for the dramatic razzmatazz offered by the pagan temples.

Romans sometimes accused the first Christians of being atheists because they "didn't go to church"—at least not in the first-century sense. Christians had no temple and, moreover, refused to attend any other temple.

The First Church Buildings

The early church may have been an underground movement of sorts, but it had a hard time staying underground. It kept growing. When a congregation grew, it needed a larger home, so when a wealthy person with a large home was baptized, there was much about which to rejoice besides the saved soul! A congregation was limited to the size of a home, perhaps forty to seventy-five people. When they ran out of space, they would spin off another congregation in town. (Indeed, that idea is still around in the small groups movement.)

Eusebius (300s)

The Honors conferred upon Bishops, and the Building of Churches. "The emperor [Constantine] also personally inviting the society of God's ministers, distinguished them with the highest possible respect and honor...Besides this, he gave from his own private resources costly benefactions to the churches of God, both enlarging and heightening the sacred edifices, and embellishing the august sanctuaries of the church with abundant offerings."

From *The Life of the Blessed Emperor Constantine*, Book I, Chapter XLII. Retrieved 7/22/01 from http://www.newadvent.org/fathers/25021.htm

However, splitting a small, intimate fellowship often meant an uphill sociological battle: groups become a "fictive family" and don't like to divide. That was as true then as it is now. Growing groups often seek first to accommodate their growth. Who was the first to suggest,

"Let's tear out a wall for all this growth?" We don't know who might have suggested the idea, but that is exactly what happened in the earliest Christian church building excavated archaeologically. The building is located on the Euphrates River in the little town of Dura Europas. A well-preserved home that was adapted for Christian worship in the 200s, it was finally destroyed by fire in 256. In this house-church, a wall had been torn out to make room for the Christian assembly of 65-75 believers. One end of the room featured a raised platform, presumably for the bishop-pastor's chair, and a communion table. A separate room contained a font for a canopy-covered baptistery. The walls still exhibit frescoes of biblical scenes.

Were there thousands of these kinds of adapted houses all across the Roman Empire? We don't know. Maybe. Perhaps the exploding Christian movement, to avoid attracting too much attention, disguised its churches by adapting the interiors of homes, leaving the exteriors to look like other houses. (Other small religious sects also adapted homes, so the Christians were not alone in this practice.) We know that the believers in this town had modified a home to make a "church building," and that they did this a long time before the persecution ended and Christianity became an approved religion.

The Basilica

At the beginning of the 300s, Christianity was legalized as a Roman religion. Before the end of the century, it was specially favored and eventually became the Roman Empire's official religion. The persecuted underground church had become supreme, helped by Emperor Constantine and later emperors. Constantine alone built nine new churches in Rome and many others across the empire for his Christian subjects.

165

These churches needed no "capital campaigns" to raise money. The Emperor's architects designed them and the Empire paid the bill. The architects designed Christian churches like they were used to designing for the empire. They adopted the *basilica* design or Roman courthouse plan. This design featured a long open area for the people, with a semicircular *apse* at one end. The judge's throne would be placed in the apse, with spaces for scribes on either side. The open area became the *nave* for the people, and the *apse* became the front of the *chancel*. The bishop-pastor sat on the adapted judge's throne.

The Roman basilica was an impressive and imposing building. No longer did the church need to cram into private homes to worship, and no longer were the gatherings intimate and limited by the size of a home. The church now assembled in large, imposing buildings that projected power and authority. In short, the Christians now had their own temples.

Catholic Bishop (1500s)

"The people in the church took small heed what the priests and clerks did in the chancel...it was never meant that the people should indeed hear the Matins or hear the Mass, but be present there and pray themselves in silence."

Bard, Thomas, ed. *Liturgies of the Western Church* (Cleveland: World Publishing, 1961), 123-137, quoting a Catholic bishop of the 16th century.

As the empire became a Christian nation, the old religions crumbled away. What could they do with all the old temples to these now defunct gods? You guessed it; they sometimes recycled them by retrofitting the temples for use as Christian churches. At times, they even retained earlier artifacts and the burial chambers of local "saints" of the previous religion. And, of course, the growing Christian church could now also afford to build its own basilicas.

Christianity had conquered the Empire! It had eliminated the competition and no longer needed to "compete." In the short span of four hundred years, Christianity had been so successful at church growth that the little band of frightened Jewish disciples had grown into a mighty and dominant religion. Christianity had effectively snuffed out all the competing religions (or at least pushed them underground, where the Christians had been for so long). Christianity reigned supreme and the basilica dominated the cityscape.

Martin Luther (1500s)

"The Mass vestments, altars, and lights may be retained till such time as they shall all change of themselves, or it shall please us to change them: though, if any will take a different course in this matter, we shall not interfere. But in the true Mass, among sincere Christians, the altar should not be retained, and the priest should always turn himself towards the people as, without doubt, Christ did at the Last Supper."

The German Mass and Order of Divine Service. Retrieved 7/21/01 from: http://www.iclnet.org/pub/resources/text/ wittenberg/luther/germnmass-order.txt

The Middle Ages

Christianity reigned for more than a thousand years, constantly manipulating political alliances with various nations in order to improve its position of supremacy and to maintain its ministry to the people. Gigantic cathedrals rose up in large communities, and the parish church was invariably the most imposing structure in every town. Increasingly, official worship happened in the *chancel*, but the people who populated the nave were oblivious to what was happening. Churches became a wonderful place to have personal devotions while the priests were "doing their thing" in a strange language (Latin) up in the front. But few churches built after the Middle Ages rivaled the beauty of these Christian temples.

167

Protestant Churches

Protestants loosened the restraints in constructing church buildings and tried all kinds of arrangements in their buildings. Most of the changes involved interior furnishings, rather than the exterior designs. Some copied the Catholic cathedrals, while others developed the simple pattern of the Quaker meetinghouse. In America, some city churches tried to mimic the style of the European cathedrals, but many rural churches adopted the simple structure Americans so often picture on their Christmas cards. This country church was of wood frame construction with a wooden steeple, including (eventually, though often not at first) a bell. The one-room church, along with the one-room schoolhouse, provided small communities with the only two public meeting places besides the tavern.

Modern Church Construction

Modern churches come in all types of architectural styles and quality of construction. Assuming downtown or town square areas would forever retain dominance in American society, many mainline churches constructed awe-inspiring, cathedral-like stone structures in downtown areas in the early twentieth century. These wonderful church buildings, like many downtown stores, eventually found themselves half full of loyal older members, while the rest of the city moved to the suburbs to live and to worship. Suburbanites often expect their churches to be more like shopping malls, with airy space, a modern feel, and vast parking lots.

Evangelical churches are especially prone to locate in the suburbs, and the church growth movement in the late twentieth century has ignited the construction of hundreds of enormous evangelical temples that dominate the four-lane highways around larger cities. These massive structures are often not so much architectural masterpieces as useful utilitarian space—a sort of magnified "little brown church in the wildwood." They provide lots of parking, a simple place for worship, lots of multipurpose space, and a growing full-week schedule of "programs" for the family—including racquetball, weight rooms, day care, and Christian schools. Some are just souped-up pole barns. While they may not project beauty, inspire awe, or induce a hushed response, they are eminently *useful* to the congregation.

168

Downtown churches, like downtown stores, have sometimes survived by repositioning their "worship product," targeting a smaller "market share"—those who want a particular kind of worship style or those older members who "just couldn't leave this church."

Yet, not all American Christians meet in church buildings. While it is difficult to get solid data, there is a significant house-church movement under way in the twenty-first century. Certainly the home-schooling movement has fed the home-churching movement. The leaders of this movement are sometimes accused of wildly exaggerating their numbers, so it is not completely clear how big this movement actually is. We also do not know the extent to which these house-church members may participate in a "regular" church. Nevertheless, there may be a significant house-church movement emerging once again. We have yet to see if it will last, as it does not face the external pressures of persecution that the first church faced.

While Christians do not believe that God dwells in temples built by human hands, we do tend to construct places to meet. To be a Christian is to meet with other Christians. As worship scholar James F. White sometimes puts it, "It can be anywhere but it has to be somewhere."

To think about . . .

1. What new discovery did you make from reading this chapter about the development of Christian church buildings?

2. Christianity was so effective at evangelism that in three hundred years it turned the Roman Empire into a Christian empire. What was good about this? What was bad? In what ways does it relate to today's church?

3. If you had been in one of those early church assemblies that had grown too big for its house-church, what arguments might you have heard for splitting into two assemblies? What arguments might have been offered for taking out a wall and staying together as one church? In what way do these relate to today's church?

4. In what ways does the history of a church relate to the kind of building it builds for worship? That is, if a denomination is four hundred years old, how might it tend to build differently than a brand-new denomination or independent church might build?

5. How might a church's *eschatology* (its view of the future, the rapture, the end times) relate to its style of construction?

6. In the last fifty years, "the action" has moved from downtown to the suburbs, mall areas, and ring roads in many cities. This chapter observed that many downtown churches assumed that downtown

culture would prevail forever and built their church buildings accordingly. Are some suburban churches now doing the same thing? What cultural and sociological shifts could occur in the next fifty years that might leave the gigantic suburban churches behind?

7. Until modern times, the local church building always dominated the landscape (and skyline) of every town. What did this announce? With the development of the safety elevator by Elisha Otis in 1853 came the possibility of "sky-scrapers" much taller than any church or cathedral. In 1913, F. W. Woolworth determined to build a "temple to commerce" as his headquarters in New York, which spurred an industrial rush that "reached for the sky." These buildings eventually dwarfed church spires—even those of the largest cathedrals. Is there anything to the notion that *the size of a culture's largest buildings will reflect that culture's dominant values?* If that notion has some truth in it, what would be your culture's great values?

8. In what ways could the Internet and the cyber culture relate to church buildings in the future?

9. Thinking only of worship, what was gained and lost when the early Christians moved from small house-churches to large basilicas?

10. How can a church offer the advantages of *both* the large gathering/ assembly and the small church in its programming?

15

Furnishings in Worship

*Until recently, Stephen J. Camden had been a lawyer in
Connecticut, where he attended the local Community Christian
Fellowship. Stephen always thought of himself as a "low-church
evangelical"—until he moved to Chicago, that is. As a new arrival
in this Midwestern city, he searched out a similar church and
found a "Community Christian Fellowship" just six miles from his
suburban home. On the first Sunday after moving, Stephen took
his family to this new church, assuming that it would be somewhat
similar to his old one in Connecticut.*

*Glancing around, he immediately saw several things that were quite
different from his semiformal Connecticut church. More than a thousand attendees sat theater-style in a semicircle, facing a hardwood
stage that included a band pit. The drawn curtains opened, and a
video on a lowered screen began running announcements for events
at the church. These were interspersed with advertisements from
area businesses, especially local realtors.*

*However, what made Stephen J. Camden decide he could never
attend this church was not the **presence** of anything; it was the
absence of a few things. "How can they call this a church when
they don't even have a cross?" he muttered, not completely under
his breath. His wife Cynthia poked him with her elbow, to which he
responded, "I want to go to church, not a concert. And this just isn't
a church—not a real one at least."*

171

What are the "things" that Christians ought to have in their worship
space? Should Christian worship always have a cross somewhere, or
is worship so essentially "spiritual" in nature that it needs none of the
traditional objects as worship aids or symbols? Can we worship in a
completely neutral building, just as well as we can in a place that "looks

like a church"? Should a church have a Communion table up front every week, even if they only serve actual Communion several times a year? How about a pulpit? Since most modern communicators like to work in the open, do we even need a pulpit anymore? Should a church have stained glass windows or art on the walls? Is it OK for a church to display the national flag or symbol of a political party, or should the Christian church always be politically neutral? All these questions concern the use of furnishings in worship.

Worship: The Spiritual and Material

It is easy to say that we worship God "spiritually" and, thus, need nothing material to aid our worship. Yet Christian worship is both spiritual and material. Some non-Christian religions seek a totally spiritual worship and consider anything material to be evil. They seek to escape the (evil) material world in order to achieve true spiritual worship as an out-of-body experience. However, Christians do not reject the material, the physical, or the tangible, but rather *use* objects as aids to worship.

Perhaps this is due to our Christian theology. Christians believe God actually came to earth and was incarnate in a physical body—in Jesus Christ. Jesus was not a ghost of God that possessed or borrowed some human's body for a time, then departed. He was actually God incarnate—God truly resident in a human physical body.

Some ancient people (including some early Christians) were troubled at the notion of God-becoming-flesh. Their argument might have gone something like this: "We all know that material is evil, including human flesh; so how could God inhabit evil flesh and still be a sinless God?" These Christians (like some today) have concluded that the purely "spiritual" is superior.

Sound Christian theology takes a different view. Christianity accepts both the spiritual and material world and does not consider material things essentially evil in and of themselves. Thus, in worship, Christians *use* the material as an avenue to spiritual worship. We gather in physical space: homes, simple meetinghouses, or elaborate cathedrals, but we will always gather in some space. When we gather, that space will have a special use, even if it is dual purpose and is also used as a gym for the youth group. We will *arrange* that space for the special uses of worship. Even if we are planting a new church in a high school auditorium, we will start out by "setting up"—arranging worship space. A church plant may have to do this every week, while a permanent church congrega tion may make an arrangement decision that will last decades. But both arrange their worship space. As we create and arrange space, we have to *furnish* that space. That is, we'll put something inside the building— even if our furnishings are as simple as rough board benches lined up in rows facing a camp meeting "platform." These are the elements of litur- gical architecture—creating, arranging, and furnishing worship space.

Furnishings of Worship

Few Christian communities have been satisfied with an empty building for worshiping any more than they'd be happy with an empty home for living. The early church was no different. Though they met in homes at first, they needed some furnishings for their worship. For instance, since they served Communion every time they met, where would they place the bread before taking it? From what would the people drink the wine? Since they read the Scriptures at each meeting, where would they rest the sacred writings while they were being read? And once they moved baptism indoors, where would they have enough water to baptize their new converts? All the practical needs in worship led to furnishing the worship center.

Some people furnish their homes with a few simple pieces of furniture, leaving lots of open space and very few personal items around. They like simplicity and uniformity. Visitors to these homes might criticize the home as "feeling sterile" or "like a hotel room." Other people go for lavish decorating, with plenty of personal mementos filling space on the walls and tables. These folk can tell you a story about every object and piece of furniture. "My great-grandmother moved that stand out here from Ohio on an ox cart back in 1847." "I brought that bottle of water back from the Pacific Ocean on our honeymoon back in '67."

173

Furnishing a church is not unlike furnishing a home. Some worshipers prefer simple neutral space with few mementos on the walls. Others like their church packed with meaningful objects and furnishings that have powerful and historic meanings. However, both types of people will have *some* kind of furnishings. Even the most radical advocates of stripping out all hard-to-explain objects will wind up with a new set of meaningful objects—they'll talk about how their theater seating or orchestral pit "communicates" a message to unbelievers. A church cannot escape communicating through its atmosphere and objects. The decision is *what* to communicate. So, what are some of the most common furnishings in the church today, and where did they come from?

Communion Table

As soon as the Lord's Supper quit being the concluding rite of a common meal and moved toward being a stand-alone ritual concluding the entire service, some sort of table was needed. Taking the Eucharist is a sacred act. It is easy to see how the bread and wine used in Communion would come to be treated with special respect. Sure, the bread could be placed on any old plate and the wine/juice in any old ordinary goblet for drinking. And today we could take Communion out of a box of Saltines and drink directly from the Welch's grape juice bottle. But we don't. We want to treat the elements more distinctly. Why? Because Communion is a sacred act, and sacred acts usually bring us sacred objects.

Hezekiah's Reign

"In the third year of Hoshea son of Elah king of Israel, Hezekiah son of Ahaz king of Judah began to reign. He was twenty-five years old when he became king, and he reigned in Jerusalem twenty-nine years. His mother's name was Abijah daughter of Zechariah. He did what was right in the eyes of the LORD, just as his father David had done. He removed the high places, smashed the sacred stones and cut down the Asherah poles. He broke into pieces the bronze snake Moses had made, for up to that time the Israelites had been burning incense to it. (It was called Nehushtan.)"

2 Kings 18:1-4 NIV

Thus, Christians set apart a special table from which Communion would be served. On that table we came to set apart a special chalice for the wine and a special plate for the bread. We came to "set apart" (sanctify) these objects for exclusive use in the Lord's Supper. So, very soon the church furnished its space with a Communion table, chalice, and plate (paten) for the weekly Lord's Supper.

By the Middle Ages, the table was an "altar" for the "sacrifice" which was reenacted each week. All kinds of additional paraphernalia appeared, most performing a practical purpose. For instance, imagine how inappropriate it might have been to leave the wine chalice open for any length of time. All kinds of things might fall or fly into the goblet of "the blood of our Lord." Thus the *pall* originated—a stiffened square of linen draped over the chalice. The medieval altar was the central furnishing—the entire medieval church was constructed around the altar-table.

The Reformation brought changes in the use of the altar-table, but not immediately. The Reformers' emphasis on Scripture-preaching (as compared to the Eucharist) would invariably influence the centrality of the altar-table. The pulpit increased in importance and the altar-table diminished. The altar-table was moved by Luther to the front of the chancel nearer the people—or even down on the level of the laity. Finney and other Revivalists finished off the task by simply moving the Communion table off to the side and placing the pulpit in the center (some would argue placing *himself* in the center).

For churches serving Communion every week, the table tended to be used only for its traditional purpose—as a table for the Lord's Supper. Elaborate altar-tables were often carved of a combination of wood and stone. "This Do in Remembrance of Me" was carved into the table. For a long time churches have had a permanently lit "sanctuary lamp" to symbolize the constant presence of God through the ages. But when candles appeared, two of them found their way to the Communion table to represent the two natures of Christ.

175

As for the churches serving the Lord's Supper quarterly or once a month, the table has been useful for other purposes. It came to be a handy place for the offering plates, since the first offering was the collection of the Communion elements brought from the homes. Some children of the Reformation placed a large open Bible on the table, making the Scripture symbolically trump the Eucharist. Evangelicals today who infrequently take Communion often use the Communion table as a flower stand, while others have done away with the table completely to gain space for the worship band's set-up. These churches clean off the furnace room dust and bring the table back into the sanctuary for their quarterly service of Communion.

Whatever can be said of the Communion table, it is one of the oldest, longest standing sacred objects dedicated to worship. Attend a Christian worship service almost anywhere in the world in any denomination, and you'll invariably see a Communion altar-table.

Chancel Chairs

Perhaps as old as the Communion table and as deeply rooted in ancient culture are special chairs for those officiating during worship. The Roman basilicas (before some became churches) all had a raised area in the front with an impressive throne set aside for the local representative of Rome, sometimes with two attending (lower) thrones on either side for his aides. It represented the seat of Roman power. When the Christians got their own basilicas, they kept the throne for the pastor-bishop, though it eventually came to be placed on the floor near the altar. The people were given no seats, of course; for well over a thousand years, standing was the posture for congregational worship. The bishop, however, got a seat—not because he needed a rest, but because it denot-

John of the Cross (1500s)

"Wherefore, although churches and pleasant places are set apart and furnished for prayer...yet, for a matter as intimate as converse held with God, one should choose that place which gives sense the least occupation and the least encouragement...it is good to choose a place that is solitary, and even wild, so that the spirit may resolutely and directly soar upward to God, and not be hindered or detained by visible things."

The Ascent of Mt. Carmel, Chapter XXXVIII. Retrieved 7/21/01 from *Christian Classics Ethereal Library;* Calvin College, Grand Rapids http://www.ccel.org/j/john_cross/ascent/ascent_of_mt_carmel0.9.htm

ed authority. The throne-like seat represented the authority of God, and perhaps also was meant to rival the other power in Rome.

Today, one can walk into most any fifty-year-old country church in America and see the echo of this early church chair arrangement: one large impressive chair-throne for the pastor in the center, with a smaller throne-chair on either side. Even modern churches often have such chairs, though largely subduing their throne-like appearance in democratic America. Like ornate pulpits or liturgical vestments, special chairs denote authority.

Of course, many evangelical pastors do not want to appear to be seen as "lording over" their laity. Reverend Smith became Pastor Smith, who became "Pastor Chad." Pastor Chad prefers to sit down with the people, not "up there like I was a king or something," so the chairs have disappeared in many modern churches.

Yet another change contributed to this shift. The church at first had a "chancel"—the part of the church up front where the Communion table and monk's choir sat facing the altar-table. A chancel is a sacred place for hallowed rites like the Eucharist. In Revivalism, the chancel became the platform—a place for preaching and persuasion. But the chancel-become-platform has recently experienced another name change. Many contemporary churches (and most all younger students) call the chancel-platform the "stage." Pastors in these churches are more likely to be sitting on a cheap steel folding chair "backstage" before they "go on," following a variety of other parts of the service. But in many older churches one can still see the 2,000-year-old chair arrangement trying to communicate something about authority.

177

Baptistery

Though the early church preferred cold running water for baptism, in less than two hundred years, baptism had moved inside. As we have seen, in the oldest archaeological excavation of a church (dated pre-256), a separate room contained a full canopy-covered baptistery with frescoes of biblical baptism scenes on the walls. Many of the earliest church ruins still accessible in present-day Turkey located their baptistery in separate rooms. These often had four alcoves surrounding a cross-shaped pool (a bit less than waist deep) large enough for two persons.

Once Christianity became the dominant (and finally exclusive) religion of the Roman Empire, baptism was primarily for babies, and thus only a smaller font was required. Very early fonts of "holy water" were placed near the entrance to the church—as a reminder at every service of the person's baptism.

Pre-Reformation Anabaptists gathered by the river to publicly baptize adults in running water, as the camp meetings would do centuries later. Modern churches have variously placed their baptisteries, often hidden under the platform or stage with easily removable coverings. Others place the baptistery centrally on the back wall of the chancel, sometimes with related artwork as a backdrop. Others cling to the habit of baptizing converts outside in running water like the early church, especially youth groups at the end of many evangelical camps. A small font is sometimes placed on the chancel-platform in churches practicing infant baptism. If a religion is going to put water on people (or put people under the water) as an induction rite, it is likely to develop some sort of furnishing to do so. The baptismal pool or font is the furnishing of choice for most modern churches. While it is less common than a Communion table, it is still a common furnishing of worship.

Art

Humans can worship without art, but they seldom do. At the ancient archaeological excavation mentioned above, the baptismal room is decorated with frescoes depicting biblical baptism scenes. This means Christians were already using art during the first half of the third century as an aid in worship.

Frescoes and stained glass windows were the best tools of Christian education for more than a thousand years. Here one could see the entire Bible visually—or at least the important parts. Attendees did not even have to read to learn. *Icons* eventually emerged—flat depictions of people and events. *Statues* and other carvings also emerged as three-dimensional depictions. In fact, one of the great historical church fights was the "iconoclastic controversy"—Christians trying to decide if such representations were idolatry or not. (The Orthodox church accepted only the

John of the Cross (1500s)

"The use of images has been ordained by the Church for two principal ends—namely, that we may reverence the saints in them, and that the will may be moved and devotion to the saints awakened by them. When they serve this purpose they are beneficial and the use of them is necessary; and therefore we must choose those that are most true and lifelike, and that most move the will to devotion, and our eyes must ever be fixed upon this motive rather than upon the value and cunning of their workmanship and decoration. For, as I say, there are some who pay more attention to the cunning with which an image is made, and to its value, than to what it represents; and that interior devotion which they ought to direct spiritually to the saint whom they see not, forgetting the image at once, since it serves only as a motive, they squander upon the cunning and the decoration of its outward workmanship."

The Ascent of Mt. Carmel, Chapter XXXV. Retrieved 7/21/01
Christian Classics Ethereal Library; Calvin College, Grand
Rapids   http://www.ccel.org/j/john_cross/ascent/ascent_of_mt_
carmel0.9.htm

flat icons, while the Western church accepted both flat and three-dimensional representations.)

Modern evangelical churches make scant use of art in the traditional sense. Their walls are neutral and even their windows are simple, single-color glass. However, many contemporary churches have made extensive use of the "portable arts"—art not fixed to the walls or windows. These churches use live drama, including professionally done Easter pageants and Christmas plays, but they especially use film clips and projected art to create an atmosphere. To illustrate a message, the pastor in these churches might step aside for a moment while a film clip of a song or Bible story runs. While these churches might not display a cross on the walls, they project what seems to be a live portrayal of the Crucifixion made by a Hollywood producer. This, of course, is nothing new for art. Churches have always employed professional artists to "do art" for them. The difference is in the portability. As styles and artistic preferences change, these churches do not have to paint over older styles—they simply get a new video clip.

Pulpit

If Christians are going to hear Scripture read, there will emerge a place upon which to set the Scriptures while reading. And if we are going to hear preaching and instruction from our priest, pastor, or preacher, there will need to be a place for the preaching notes. These two practical needs brought two furnishings into the church: the lectern and the pulpit.

The *lectern* was located at the front edge of the chancel to the right of the congregation. The lectern is a kind of lesser pulpit for reading Scripture, leading songs, making announcements, and sometimes preaching on lesser days. The Old Testament reading and the reading from the Epistles were often presented from the lectern. The Gospel reading was often given from the *pulpit,* to the left of the congregation. Thus, the medieval church was divided into the "Gospel side" (the left from the congregation's perspective) and the "Epistle side" (on the congregation's right). The symbolism produced a Bible hermeneutic of sorts: the Gospels taking precedence over the Old Testament and the Epistles, principally because of the locations from which they were read.

The Latin term *pulpit* simply means "raised platform." But pulpits became elaborate and elevated places of authority. Located on the Gospel side of the church, the pulpit was often carved of stone with winding steps to a high point, where a congregation of a thousand could see and hear the speaker. Pulpits in the Middle Ages were especially imposing places of authority.

Modern churches brought the pulpit down a peg or two, partly due to the democratization of the church and partly due to electronic amplification. Many Protestant churches combine the lectern and pulpit into a single-purpose pulpit centrally located on the platform. Many recent churches have raised the entire stage area so that speakers and all musicians can move about freely while communicating with body language, not just with their voices. The merged lectern-pulpit eventually shrank in size along with the pastor-thrones. Plexiglas see-through pulpits tried to replace the old wooden ones for a time, but failed to last. In many mod-

ern churches, the pulpit has been moved into storage. The communica-
tor-pastor moves all over the stage, using memorized notes or large-print
notes that are taped to the sound monitor. While the pulpit has been used
for several centuries, it is fast disappearing in many newer evangelical
churches. Some say this is a depreciation of Scripture and preaching.
Others say it is a necessary change to increase effective communication
of truth to the people.

A Cross

For many years the church did not so much *have* a cross; it *was* a cross.
The floor plan of the cruciform church was constructed in the shape of
the cross, with the *nave* (where the people stood) as the long part of
the cross, the two *transepts* providing the "arms" of the cross, and the
head being the *chancel*.

That is not to say they were without crosses. From the outset the cross
was the dominant symbol of Christianity. The *pectoral* cross was worn
around the neck of a bishop (and later all clergy). A *processional* cross
was attached to a staff that led the procession of the clerics at the beginning and end of the service. The *rood* cross was located in the center of
the beam, dividing the nave from the chancel. Of course, every Christian
church wanted to have a *spire* cross on its roof. An *altar* cross was sometimes located on the altar-table. Old churches had plenty of crosses and,
of course, there was a cross in at least one stained glass window, in several paintings, and perhaps on icons and statues. The *crucifix* was a cross
that depicted Christ's body still hanging and suffering.

Modern churches, especially evangelical churches, have reduced the
number of crosses in the sanctuary. Post-Reformation Protestant architecture eventually abandoned the cruciform design, and stained glass
took a back seat to more contemporary construction preferences. Usually
a single large cross is placed on the front wall in evangelical churches,
along with one on the spire (if the church has one that survived the construction committee's budget cut). Seeker-friendly churches sometimes
remove all crosses and other symbols that unbelievers might not understand, leaving a building devoid of religious symbolism (but packed with
plenty of symbolism just the same). But the cross is hard to get rid of.
Progressive churches (and pastors) have survived removing pulpits and

181

even Communion tables, but they seldom survive removing the cross
from an existing building.

Instruments

For most of a thousand years, Christian worship made music with human
voices. By the turn of the first millennium, however, the organ had found
its place in church, and space was made for it. While it was accepted with
considerable controversy, the organ paved the way for later instruments,
including a full orchestra, the piano, guitar, electric keyboard, and drums.
The set-up in some modern churches includes a dozen instruments and
an elaborate array of sound equipment and monitors. What started out as
an organ that could represent the sounds of all other instruments wound
up being all other instruments that can represent the sound of an organ!
The organ won the battle to be included in worship and eventually lost
the war to newer and more modern inventions that replaced it for worship
use. Musical instruments in modern worship are here for the long haul.
While individually they are far more compact than the massive organs of
yesteryear, they actually use more space due to the multiplied number of
musicians needed to play the instruments.

The Altar

The first Christian altar was the Communion table, as mentioned above.
This is not what evangelicals in the Revivalist tradition mean when they
talk about the altar. They mean the low wood railing that divides the
chancel-platform from the nave-congregational seating.

The church from early times set apart the chancel from the nave, at
least by raising it above floor level. However, during the Middle Ages,
a *rood screen* developed which almost totally blocked the worshipers
from seeing what was happening in the chancel where the Eucharistic
"sacrifice" was being offered. The rood screen was an elaborately carved
lattice-type screen made of wood or iron that rose from the front of the
chancel, floor to ceiling — or at least to the "rood beam."

In England during the 1500s, Queen Elizabeth reformed the churches
and made them Protestant. The altars (used for the "sacrifice" Eucharist)
were turned into tables and set tablewise. The actual communion rail

was introduced in the 1800s. The Church of England and most American Episcopal churches serve the Lord's Supper at this altar.

It was at the frontier camp meetings in the early 1800s that the "mourner's bench" was introduced. Here in a section of benches up front, those "under conviction" sat as they sought God's mercy. Later, these benches were placed crossways, strung across the front of the meeting place where people could kneel and pray. Still later in the 1800s, Charles Finney developed and honed the "altar call" as a method of inviting people to accept Christ at the conclusion of the service. Local Revivalist churches put the remnant Anglican altar to a new use as a mourner's bench, and began inviting people forward to kneel at this altar—the same altar where Communion was served—to receive Christ.

Many modern churches still have an altar, though fewer use it as a mourner's bench than in the nineteenth century. The altar is still a place to receive Communion for smaller churches (though seldom in super-churches). The altar is still a place of dedication, ritual, and sending out— it is where ordination prayers are offered, where babies are dedicated, weddings take place, and where mission teams are consecrated. Many evangelical churches still use the "altar call" in a traditional way as well. Newer churches are often designed with removable or portable altars, bringing them back to the camp meeting *ad hoc* mourner's bench again.[9]

Flags

National flags are a more recent addition to the array of sacred objects used in worship. An argument can be made that Christianity has always mixed a generous amount of nationalism into its worship since 300. Medieval paintings and stained glass windows often featured local war heroes right alongside Bible saints, and national flags and banners were commonly worked into the stained glass. Flags often find their place in worship during times of national emergency and war. Many American churches display both the American flag and a Christian flag, though there is often disagreement on which should have the place of prominence as they are displayed.

183

---

[9] See chapter 6 on the altar call for more on this subject.

The old pagan religions of northern Europe were a threat to Christianity as it spread. The missionaries found they could compete better if they incorporated bits of the pagan religion into their Christian worship, figuring Christianity would eventually overprint the pagan elements. Church leaders have at times done the same with civil religion. "Civil religion" is often a kind of nationalism that acts like a religion, complete with holy text, heroes of the faith, and great stories of deliverance. Church leaders have sometimes incorporated elements of civil religion into Christian worship to "compete" and thus survive. Perhaps national flags, Independence Day pageants, veneration of national heroes, and other such celebrations eventually will minimize the competition. Melding two great passions—nationalism and religion—produces an alloy hard to beat in spite of the theological problems doing so has brought the church. Other churches display dozens of flags from around the world to give a worldwide flavor to the atmosphere and thus diminish the seemingly narrow nationalism of displaying only one flag.

Some modern Christians resist any nationalistic blending with Christian worship, notably those with Anabaptist traditions. These would even reject adding a national flag to the sanctuary to share space with other objects and symbols. They like to remind the rest of the church how some German churches demonstrated their national loyalty—by draping the Nazi flag over the Communion table.

Conclusion

Humans are symbolic people. We are also practical folk. Our symbolic nature causes us to use objects to recall important truths, like a cross or a picture of the final judgment. Our practical side causes us to find ways to use objects for worship, like a special plate for the bread at the Eucharist. Sacred rites like Communion or baptism (or going to the altar to get saved) tend to share their hallowedness with the object itself. The hallowedness of preaching gets invested into the pulpit. The reverence of the Eucharist can carry over into the Communion table or chalice. Objects thus become holy—set apart for sacred use.

However, if the objects themselves become objects of worship, we become guilty of idolatry. Furnishings aid our worship experience and speak more loudly than any words we say. Indeed, a worship service that

184

tries to have no Christian symbolism or sacred objects at all is quite as symbolic as one with a thousand images. The only difference is what the symbolism of each says to those attending.

To think about . . .

1. What new discovery did you make after reading this chapter on furnishings in worship?

2. Are there *required* furnishings for worship? That is, do you believe all furnishings in worship are optional and, thus, we are free to dispose of past furnishings and add new ones any time we want?

3. In order to become seeker friendly, some churches seek to remove anything that may be confusing or too symbolic for the unchurched. Some of these churches remove all symbols or Christian objects from the physical setting. What do you think of this plan? Is it a good idea or not? Why do you think so?

4. What connection can you see between the status of a priest-pastor-minister in the culture and the chancel chairs? Any? If so, how has your church adapted to the changing role of a pastor in our culture in your lifetime?

5. Do you prefer a visible baptistery or a hidden one? A baptistery at a public river or a private one in church? Why? Compare the advantages of each.

6. What do you think of the notion that modern churches portray their art by drama and video more than by paintings on the walls? Is this an equivalent use of art or somehow different? How would you prefer to see the use of the arts upgraded in your church? What are the dangers of too little art in churches? Too much art?

7. What is your opinion on displaying national flags, banners, or emblems of political parties in churches? Is it OK for some countries and not others? Where would you draw the line?

8. When does the simple setting apart of an object or furnishing become idolatry? That is, when does a person (or a denomination, local church) cross the line in venerating an object to a degree that it becomes idolatry?

9. Can you identify with Stephen's feelings of discomfort in the beginning story? What kinds of furnishings make you feel at home?

186

Part V
Special Occasions

It is not surprising that Christians would try to bring their religion into the ordinary passages of life—births, weddings, graduations, 50th wedding anniversary celebrations, and funerals. After all, being a Christian is a full-time occupation, not something we relegate to Sunday mornings. While we might wonder if these are truly "worship" in the narrow sense of the word, they often act like it—gathering in the church building, a sense of solemnity, a minister or priest presiding, with some sort of vow or litany recited in public. With the recent emphasis on worship renewal have come increasing attempts to turn such occasions into actual worship services, especially weddings. This is a good trend, considering the alternative. Thus, this section addresses two primary special occasions in the church:

- **Church Weddings**

- **Christian Funerals**

16
Church Weddings

*Jennie had always dreamed of having a church wedding. Finally,
the day had arrived! Here she was at the front of the church, having been escorted there by her father. The minister had just asked,
"Who gives this woman to be married to this man?" Her father had
responded, "Her mother and I." She felt a lump in her throat and
tears welling up in her eyes as her dad returned to his pew. Jennie
knew that within fifteen minutes she and Jeff would be pronounced
"man and wife." As the minister's words droned on in the background, she thought, "This was always my dream—a big church
wedding . . . now here I am living out my dream!"*

Jennie's "church wedding" was a late addition to the Christian church's
list of possible worship services. The early church had nothing to do with
wedding ceremonies. The matter was left to families, and the wedding
ceremony took place at home. Even when the church got into the wedding business, the bulk of the ceremony was held outside the front door
(where other civil contracts were often established). It took 1,500 years
for the entire wedding ceremony to take place inside the church building.
And even though there are occasional attempts to make the wedding
ceremony a true "worship service," it has never been completely at home
in the church.

189

Weddings in the Early Church: 70–500

The wedding feast at Cana (John 2:1-11) was, of course, not a "Christian
wedding," but a Jewish wedding reception. We know little about this
feast except that the wine flowed generously. So we cannot derive any
argument for a Christian wedding worship service from this passage—

other than that Jesus attended (and improved the quality of wine) and thus presumably approved of weddings such as these.

During the first 1,000 years of Christian history, the church adopted and adapted wedding customs from the Jews and the pagans, eliminating idolatrous elements of the pagan practices or (more often) breathing new meaning into them. Since the church itself was not involved with weddings for hundreds of years, the wedding customs of Christians reflected the local customs of whatever culture the Christian lived in. Christians (and everybody else) considered marriage to be family business, not church business.

The Christian Jews most likely continued the wedding practices of their Jewish tradition. Gentile Christians in Corinth, Athens, or Philippi probably continued the Roman customs of their culture. Christians would have dropped the most blatant pagan practices, like the soothsayer or sacrifices to the Roman gods, but undoubtedly kept less objectionable elements.

In the Greco-Roman world, men were considered to be most "marriageable" at age thirty, and women at age sixteen. The Christian bride may have met her "intended" for the first time at their betrothal (*engyesis*), where the wedding contract was made and the vows were exchanged. However, the vows were not between the bride and groom, but between the bride's father and the groom. The bride was silent. Refusing to marry the suitor was out of the question, not just because of obedience, but because everyone else was married in this way. Our modern notion of romantic marriage between two people who have fallen in love and chosen each other would have been totally foreign to the early Christians. Witnesses were present at the betrothal, and the father paid a handsome dowry to the groom to guarantee that his daughter would not have to be put to work. The betrothal was also the time to set the date for the next stage—the "handing over of the bride" *(ekosis)*.

The day before the "handing over of the bride," the bride would take a ceremonial purification bath in a spring and the groom in a river. Pagans added a series of sacrifices to the family gods, but the Christians likely replaced that with some sort of family prayers or home-based religious ceremony. At an impressive wedding feast the next day, the bride would be accompanied by her *nymphettria*, a best friend who would hold her veil. Wearing a wreath, the groom would be accompanied by his best man of sorts, the *parochos*. After dinner, the nymphettria performed the "unveiling ceremony" (*lyptera*), a practice still common today. Then the guests offered presents.

After they had received the presents, the bride and groom entered a carriage for a procession to the groom's home (they walked if they were poor). The couple was sprinkled with dried figs and walnuts as they entered the home. After a walk around the hearth, they entered the nuptial chambers to consummate the marriage, while the "best man" stood guard outside the door and the "maid of honor" sang songs. This is a picture of the kind of wedding the Gentile Corinthians, Ephesians, or Colossians would have expected.

Christian Weddings: 500–1500

Through the Middle Ages, Christians developed the rites of marriage and gradually moved the ceremony inside the church. As local secular or pagan marriage customs were adopted or adapted, the wedding moved progressively from home, to the church doorway, and finally to the altar. The Roman idea of marriage as a contract gained increasing acceptance. Marriage was a legal matter that involved issues of legitimacy and inheritance, and thus it required written legal records. Who would write down this record? The priest was often the only person in a village who could read and write, and so the church was a natural place to record marriages legally. Perhaps there was a spiritual reason as well. Did the couple want to start off marriage with a spiritual boost by having a church wedding instead of a wedding at home? Or, as the wedding became a more important transaction, was the church pulled into the service to upgrade the splendor and sacredness of the ceremony? Who knows? All these theories and others we have not mentioned may be the reason.

Marriage Vow (1300s)

"Here I take you [name] to my wedded wife, to hold and to have, at bed and board, for fairer for [fouler], for better for worse, in sickness and in health, till death do us part, if Holy Church it will ordain, and thereto I plight you my troth."

Manual of York Use manuscript, University Library, Cambridge, p. 25 B, quoted by James F. White in *A Brief History of Christian Worship*, 96.

Over time the wedding ceremony came to include joining the couple's right hands, giving and receiving a ring, veiling the bride, serving Communion to the couple, and placing crowns on their heads. Pope Nicholas I (866) gives the first detailed description of a formal wedding ceremony. His account includes the giving of a ring and the execution of a "marriage deed" as part of the betrothal (*espousals*), which was followed at a later date by the ceremony (*nuptials*) at the church door. The nuptials involved veiling the woman, crowning the couple, and moving inside the church to the altar for a nuptial mass, where the couple received Holy Communion.

192

Banns were read in three public services, announcing the intended wedding of the couple. This announcement provided an opportunity for someone to "speak now or forever hold your peace," a quote which lasted into the twentieth century in many churches.

Espousals occurred outside the church door, where vows were made and the rings were blessed with holy water. The ring was placed in turn on the first, second, and third finger, representing the Father, Son, and Holy Ghost, then moved to the fourth finger as a final resting place. Following the ceremony at the church door, the couple followed the priest inside to the altar for the mass and Holy Communion. Not until the late fourteenth century did the woman's vow come to include a promise to obey her husband. Throughout the Middle Ages, weddings moved increasingly closer to the church and altar. By the end of the 1500s, the at-the-door ceremony had been moved inside and the complete "church wedding" as we know it was born.

Canon X (1563)

"If anyone saith, that the marriage state is to be placed above the state of virginity, or of celibacy, and that is it not better and more blessed to remain in virginity, or in celibacy, than to be united in matrimony: let him be anathema."

Council of Trent, *Canons and Decrees of the Council of Trent*. Twenty-Fourth Session, held November 11, 1563. Trans. Philip Schaff, *The Creeds of Christendom* (Grand Rapids: Baker Book House, 1983), II, 197.

Protestant Weddings: 1500–

Since weddings are perhaps the most conservative of all ceremonies, the Reformers did not toss overboard all of the wedding practices of the Roman Catholic Church. The Reformers agreed theologically that marriage was not a sacrament as Catholics had listed it. (However, even for Catholics marriage barely made the list of seven sacraments. When it did, it was listed last and its inclusion came by a misunderstanding of a Greek term in Ephesians 5:32.) Dropping only the Holy Communion in the wedding and the blessing of the rings, the Reformers sustained most other elements of the Catholic wedding ceremony.

193

Luther provided a marriage ceremony in the common language of the people, as did Calvin. After banns were read, Calvin held the wedding ceremony in a regular worship service just before the preaching on any day the church was meeting. Eventually weddings were moved away from Sunday services for reasons you might guess. Small changes took place that cannot be attributed to theology or Protestantism. Among these was the placement of the ring, shifting it from the right hand to the left hand.

Wedding ceremony (1549)

"Dearly beloved friends, we are gathered together here in the sight of God, and in the face of his congregation, to join together this man and this woman in holy matrimony, which is an honorable estate instituted of God in paradise, in the time of man's innocency, signifying unto us the mystical union that is betwixt Christ and his Church: which holy estate, Christ adorned and beautified with his presence, and first miracle that he wrought in Cana of Galilee, and is commended of Saint Paul to be honorable among all men; and therefore is not to be enterprised, nor taken in hand inadvisedly, lightly, or wantonly, to satisfy men's carnal lusts and appetites, like brute beasts that have no understanding: but reverently, discreetly, advisedly, soberly, and in the fear of God."

The Booke of the Common Prayer, "The Forme of Solemnizacion of Matrimonie" (1549). *The First and Second Prayer Books of Edward VI* (London: J.M. Dent & Sons, 1910), 252.

Speaking of rings, the Puritans discarded the ring ceremony as superfluous, as later did John Wesley (though his Methodist followers put it back in the ceremony). Quaker couples, in their quest for simplicity, simply recited their public vows in a regular meeting. Wesley also eliminated the "giving away of the bride" by the father, but who knows why? Generally, weddings among Protestants were relatively faithful to Catholic traditions.

Weddings Today

Which brings us to today. After taking more than a thousand years to get inside the church, today many weddings are moving back out of the church. Many couples now insist on writing their own wedding vows, keeping a positive spin with such phrases as, "for better or best; in sickness and health, so long as we both shall *love*."

It took the wedding 1,500 years to move completely inside the church. Given the most recent "creative" requests to perform weddings underwater in masks and snorkels, or while skydiving from an airplane, some ministers wonder if it is time to move it back out. After all, worship, the church, and the minister are minor factors in many weddings.

John Calvin (1559)

"The last one [sacrament] is marriage. All men admit that it was instituted by God [Gen. 2:21, Matt. 19:4ff.]; but no man ever saw it administered as a sacrament until the time of Gregory [VIII]. And what sober man would ever have thought it such? Marriage is a good and holy ordinance of God; and farming, building, cobbling, and barbering are lawful ordinances of God, and yet are not sacraments."

Institutes of the Christian Religion, IV. Trans. Ford Lewis Battles, LC, XXI, 1480-1483.

Yet, at the same time, there is a significant countertrend. An increasing number of couples want a "traditional wedding," steeped in the customs of the last few thousand years. Couples are realizing that a wedding vow is a sacred act that should be performed before God and the people. Many Christian weddings now offer Holy Communion to the entire congregation as part of the service and make the joining of the couple and the unity of the church a connected theme. An increasing number of young people ask the pastor to say, "This is a worship service for all and our bride and groom want each of us to worship God today, not just watch a ceremony." These weddings sometimes feature a full song service of praise choruses and hymns, along with elongated prayer and

195

praise times. In a day of no-fault divorce, when marriage vows are easily broken, young people want to make their vows more sacred, not less. And that means a "church wedding" is likely here to stay. For where else would you go for sacred things?

To think about . . .

1. What new discovery did you make from reading this chapter about the history of weddings?

2. Is a wedding ceremony "worship"? Should it be?

3. Wedding ceremonies are perhaps the most conservative of all ceremonies—with many elements surviving for more than a thousand years. Why is that? What do we learn from this?

4. Why do many young people want a "traditional wedding," yet do not want "traditional worship"? What are the implications of this?

5. Was the early church mistaken by not seeing the importance of a "church wedding" for all those years? Why did it take so long for this idea to develop?

6. When performing a wedding, does a pastor act as an agent of the state, the local church, or the denomination? In what ways? What does your answer imply?

7. What limiting policies do you think a church should have on hosting weddings? Can anyone be married in your church?

8. In your opinion, what limiting policies should a pastor have on performing wedding ceremonies? Can a pastor refuse to perform a wedding he or she thinks is a bad idea—not an unbiblical marriage, just one that seems to be inadvisable?

9. Where is the wedding ceremony headed in the future?

10. If you have been married, did you consider your wedding to be an act of worship? How was this so or not so?

17
Christian Funerals

Michael was a New York stockbroker with little time for church or religion. When the subject came up—which it occasionally did—he dismissed religion as "superstition, like believing in witches, goblins, and the tooth fairy." Michael and Julie's lifestyle was totally secular. Thus, their little daughter Jessica never heard of God or religion except for what she sometimes caught on TV (before Michael quickly changed channels).

His perspective changed last spring when Jessica suddenly contracted a staph infection. Her little body swelled up hideously, and within two days she was dead.

Michael and Julie were shattered. Before they headed off to the funeral consultation, Michael sat thumbing through the yellow pages. "What ya lookin' for?" Julie asked. Michael responded sharply, "Gotta find a priest to do the funeral—we can't let Jessica be buried without a priest, a minister, or someone religious officiating."

While a totally secular person might find a way to have a totally secular wedding, when it comes to burial of a loved one, secular people often turn to the church. Why is this? Why is a religious burial so important to people—even to unbelievers? Is a funeral a worship service? Should it always have a somber tone, even when the deceased is a believer and according to our doctrine has been received by Christ in the afterlife? Can it ever be a happy occasion? How should a funeral for a Christian man differ from one for an unsaved, agnostic man (who has a Christian spouse and children)? How did we get the burial customs we have today?

Nobody likes to talk about funerals. Most modern Christians face death with denial or fear, not unlike their secular neighbors. But it did not start out that way.

Death and dying bring out serious questions of life. It is only natural that humans would want their religion involved in their burials, especially if that religion teaches the existence of an afterlife. Few experiences get a person thinking about the afterlife more than the death of a friend or loved one.

Tertullian (late 100s)

"We take also, in congregations before daybreak, and from the hand of none but the presidents, the sacrament of the Eucharist, which the Lord both commanded to be eaten at meal-times, and enjoined to be taken by all alike. As often as the anniversary comes round, we make offerings for the dead as birthday honours."

The Chaplet or *Of the Crowns*, chapter III. Retrieved from New Advent Church Fathers 7/18/01 http://www.newadvent.org/fathers/0304.htm

A Christian funeral provides a sort of right-hand bookend to life, emphasizing that our religion is a birth-to-afterlife affair. The church's special occasions for worship are usually happy affairs like the birth or dedication of a child, baptism ceremonies, graduation celebrations, commissionings, ordinations, weddings, or even recognizing the 50th anniversary of a faithful couple in the church. However, the worship service for the burial of a person—even of a committed Christian—is often not such a happy affair. We think mostly of our loss. This was not so in the early church.

200

The New Testament is silent on Christian funerals. We do hear of the burial of Lazarus and the shocking burial of Ananias when he had deceived the Lord in the property-pledge fiasco. However, these glimpses do not give us knowledge of Christian burial customs, but of Jewish ones. We do know about Roman funeral customs, and they can provide insight into what early Christians may have done.

Roman Funeral Practices

Many of our current funeral practices date to the Romans. When a person died, the Romans closed the eyes, then washed and prepared the body. The body laid in state for several days (sometimes up to a week) in the atrium of the home. Women were hired as mourners to establish an atmosphere of sorrow.

The body was then carried by pallbearers outside the town, where it was either buried or cremated on a tall pyre (wood for burning). When cremated, the person's ashes were often placed in an urn or full-size burial sarcophagus. Grave markers were used, a practice that would disappear for a long time. A funeral meal may have occurred at this time. Such a meal certainly happened later, as the family gathered to eat and commemorate the dead person's memory, often annually.

Early Church Funerals

What we know of early Christian funerals comes from our knowledge of Roman and Jewish burial customs and the writings of the early church fathers.

Augustine (early 400s)

"Wherefore all these last offices and ceremonies that concern the dead, the careful funeral arrangements, and the equipment of the tomb, and the pomp of obsequies, are rather the solace of the living than the comfort of the dead. If a costly burial does any good to a wicked man, a squalid burial, or none at all, may harm the godly...For the body is not an extraneous ornament or aid, but a part of man's very nature...And the Gospel speaks with commendation of those who were careful to take down His body from the cross, and wrap it lovingly in costly cerements, and see to its burial. These instances certainly do not prove that corpses have any feeling; but they show that God's providence extends even to the bodies of the dead, and that such pious offices are pleasing to Him, as cherishing faith in the resurrection."

Nicene and Post-Nicene Fathers, Series I, Vol. II, chapters 12, 13. Retrieved 7/18/01 from CCEL
http://www.ccel.org/fathers2/NPNF1-02/npnf1-02-07.htm

201

The early church's burial custom had four parts. First, the body was prepared, most likely in the home. This involved the washing, anointing with oil, and wrapping of the body. Second, there was a procession to the burial grounds. The Roman notion of a family burial ground probably prevailed for the early Christian as well. The Christians proceeded to the burial grounds in broad daylight, a countermove to the burial practices of many pagan religions that buried their dead at night. Third, at the burial site, there was a funeral service. While one might be tempted to think this was a simple service, it was actually more elaborate than we might think. Prayers were offered, and the final kiss of peace was given the departed. The body was buried with feet pointing east to the sunrise. The early church burial service included the celebration of the Lord's Supper, something unusual for many funerals today. However, the idea gains merit when understood in the context of the communion of the saints, both alive and departed, which is implied by the Lord's Supper. Finally, there was likely some sort of fellowship meal following the actual burial. Some Roman religions held a great feast at the burial site, and some Christians may have followed suit with an "agape feast." Others may have returned to the home or a regular meeting place at another home and eaten an agape meal together.

Early funerals were not filled with sorrow and fear. The entire tenor of early Christian burials leaned toward celebrating the dead person's victory, not mourning their loss. Remember, "keeping the faith" was an early

Augustine (of his mother Monica) (about 400)

"So, when the body was carried forth, we both went and returned without tears. For neither in those prayers which we poured forth unto Thee when the sacrifice of our redemption was offered up unto Thee for her, the dead body being now placed by the side of the grave, as the custom there is, prior to its being laid therein, neither in their prayers did I shed tears; yet was I most grievously sad in secret all the day, and with a troubled mind entreated Thee, as I was able, to heal my sorrow..."

Confessions, IX, 32. Retrieved 7/19/01 CCEL
http://www.ccel.org/fathers2/NPNF1-01/npnf1-01-
17.htm#P1302_551946

theme for Christians. When one "kept the faith" to the very end, there was a sense of triumph. Death was considered birth—birth to new life. In fact, Christians sometimes celebrated the anniversaries of martyrs' heavenly birthdays, often at the gravesite.

The locations involved in these early funerals were the home (where preparation was made), the burial grounds (where prayers were offered and the Lord's Supper was taken), and perhaps again at a home (where an agape meal may have followed in some cases). The whole affair was one of celebrating the victor who had finished the course successfully and was born anew into his heavenly life.

Middle Ages

As the Christians acquired church buildings, it is no wonder that they would relocate the funeral service inside. They served the Lord's Supper at these indoor services, which led to the development of the requiem mass. The biggest change in burial customs during the next thousand years was the atmosphere. The tenor of funerals changed through the Middle Ages to acquire a superstitious, fearsome atmosphere of denial and retribution. Celebrating the person's victory of faithfulness diminished. Purgatory was certainly on the minds of the attendees at a funeral service—how long might the departed suffer before being released into heaven? Church art didn't help either, for many pieces graphically depicted the torments of hell better than they portrayed the joys of heaven.

In the Middle Ages, the body was prepared at home, then brought to the church for the mass, which, of course, included the Eucharist. Incense was offered, holy water was sprinkled over the body, and the dead person was granted final absolution for his sins. Indeed, absolution may be the best representation of the significant changes that occurred in the Middle Ages—from triumph for "finishing the course" to the somber business of dealing with sin.

The body was then taken by procession to the burial site, where the priest again presided. The actual burial for the average person was in a temporary site. The location would be recycled for another body in another generation or less.

> ## Eulogy, circa 1730
>
> "Yesterday were Buried here the Remains of that truly honourable & Devout Gentlewoman, Mrs. Sarah Byfield, amidst the affectionate Respects & Lamentations of a numerous Concourse. Before carrying out the Corpse, a Funeral Prayer was made, by one of the Pastors of the Old Church, to whose Communion she belonged: Which tho' a Custom in the country towns, is a singular Instance in this place, but it's wish'd may prove a leading Example to the general Practice of so Christian & decent a Custom."
>
> "The Boston Weekly News Letter," December 31, 1730. From Groton Historical Series by Dr. Samuel A. Green, Vol. III, 1893, 123. Retrieved 7/18/01 from http://www.usgennet.org/usa/ma/state/main/funeral.html

The Reformation

Martin Luther tried to restore the early church's victory atmosphere to Christian burial, but he largely failed, as have most others who have tried to do so since. The radical Reformers and minimalists also tried to strip down the funeral to its simple skeleton. The "Westminster Directory" of 1645 instructs the people to take the body "without any ceremony" directly to the burial site. Many Puritans considered burial rites too secular or high church, and the early Pilgrim settlers of America simply took the body to the burial site and interred it without ritual. The addition of prayers to the rite caused enough interest in 1730 to warrant mention in the Boston newspaper.

However, many Reformers did more than the radical minimalists allowed. They sang Psalms, prayed, read Scriptures (as one would expect of the Reformers), and heard a sermon as part of the funeral. Anglicans made the Lord's Supper optional for a funeral service in the mid-1500s.

In the 1600s, tombstones emerged, and even the common people wanted them. Like a mansion or fancy house might illustrate a person's importance in life, that person's tombstone could now continually communicate the same in death. The body was wrapped in a shroud and placed directly in the ground.

Caskets did not emerge until the 1800s. (They actually reemerged, since they were an ancient custom.) Also, embalming the deceased became common in the late 1800s.

Modern Funerals

Funerals today reflect the fast-paced, mobile culture we have created. The body is taken directly to the funeral parlor, where a professional does the preparation. A "viewing" may occur, offering friends and family the opportunity to come and pay their respects and comfort the mourners. The actual funeral service may take place at a church or at the funeral chapel with a minister presiding. The service generally fails to attain the victorious atmosphere of the early church, except in the case of a very old Christian. The sermon usually focuses on comfort for those grieving. Following this service, there is still a procession, now with automobiles and a hearse. In smaller towns, all other cars on the road pull over in respect. At the burial plot, there is a separate simple service of interment or committal to the ground. Finally, following the ancient four-fold pattern, there may be a dinner or meal, at least for the family and those who have traveled from a distance.

As in wedding ceremonies, some contemporary families have come down with a case of extreme creativity when planning a funeral, including projecting videos of the deceased, playing recordings of the dead person's joke-telling in life, or celebrating his life while spreading his ashes during skydiving. Funeral directors and ministers, used to adapting to the desires of people in weddings, often resist the most radical of these ideas during funerals.

205

The recent worship movement has affected funerals as well as weddings, with increasing attempts to make the actual funeral service a worship service. Few evangelical churches have restored the Lord's Supper to the funeral service, though at least some families have requested it (and been told by their ministers that it is "out of place" at a funeral).

Christians believe that their religion is not something that is practiced an hour a week at a temple, but is a "24-7" way of living. Believing that our faith (and our worship) is pervasive, it is not surprising that we would want religious rites for the various passages of life—from birth to death. The life of a person who has lived in faith and faithfulness, dependably attending worship through his life, ought to finish its course at church—with a Christian funeral. And the friends and family of the deceased ought to attend that service to remember his life, honor his memory, receive comfort from the Lord, and prepare for their own departure. For the departed shall never return again to us. We shall join the departed.

To think about . . .

1. What new discovery did you make from reading this chapter about Christian funerals?

2. Should a funeral service be worship? Why or why not? How?

3. How should a funeral service be different for a Christian and an unbeliever? What are the factors influencing this?

4. Due to mobility and to other factors, cremation is on the rise in America—rising from 7% in 1970 to nearly 25% of all funerals today. Is cremation "just as good" as burial in the ground? Is it OK for Christians to be cremated, or are there traditional and theological reasons not to cremate?

5. Should the church hold funerals for stillborn babies? Why or why not?

6. How has the arrival of a mobile society changed funeral practices?

7. Some funerals provide for embarrassingly extravagant praise for the departed person, describing them as something a bit less than angelic. The Puritans and other minimalists sought to escape this with simple rites. What are some guidelines you think a church or pastor today ought to have to avoid the extreme flattery of the dead?

8. What do you think of the various "creative ideas" some families invent for their funeral plans? Is the funeral "their service and they can do what they want with it," or is it a "local church worship service and thus the pastor/church has a right to insist on some things"?

9. Why is it that even avowed agnostics often seek out a church funeral?

10. Is using a funeral to present the Gospel to unsaved family members in bad taste or acceptable in your opinion?

11. What kind of funeral would you prefer for yourself? Do you want a worship-oriented service, an upbeat celebration of your life, a solemn grieving service, or does it "depend"? On what does it depend?

Part VI
Background and Study Resources

In this section you'll find lots of helps in understanding the background of worship. If you're interested in how Old Testament worship affected Christian worship, this section is just for you. Or perhaps you wonder where some of today's denominational streams of worship originated—like Lutheran or Methodist or Camp Meeting Revivalist churches. This section includes a chapter on recent streams of worship as well. You'll certainly want to read through the reviews of other excellent worship books to decide which one you might read next. If you are especially interested in "finding out for myself" what really happened in early church worship, we've included a guided study of Bible passages and several ancient documents of worship. In addition, we've included two reference chapters. One is a complete worship time line to give you an idea of the context and flow of worship history. The other reference chapter is a complete glossary of terms. Few folk actually ever sit down and read a list of definitions—but you might find yourself doing exactly that with this easy-to-read glossary!

- **Four OT Streams of Worship**
- **Jewish Feasts and Festivals**
- **Recent American Streams of Worship**
- **Books to Read Next**
- **A Study of Worship Sources**
- **Worship Time Line**
- **Glossary of Worship Terms**

18

Four Old Testament Streams of Worship

Four streams of worship in the Old Testament flowed into Christian worship. While one or another of these streams seemed to dominate during certain periods of history, all four streams continue to flow into today's contemporary worship patterns.

1. Personal/Family Worship

The first worship in the Bible was personal and individual, not corporate. Adam, Noah, Abraham, Isaac, Jacob, and Joseph had no synagogue or temple to attend, nor even the Ten Commandments to follow. Their religion was a direct, personal, one-on-one experience with God. Adam and Eve worshiped as they were "walking [with God] in the garden in the cool of the day." Enoch and Noah experienced a similar devotional intimacy as they "walked in the presence of God." Jacob was bold enough to claim, after spending the night wrestling with the Lord, "I have seen God face to face." Worship was a personal activity for the patriarchs before it became a family activity and eventually a group activity.

In fact, for more than two thousand years—more than half of the Old Testament—there were no temples or synagogues, and the worship was more like "personal devotions" or "family worship." The patriarchs' worship included sacrifice and prayers, hearing God speak, and living in obedience to His words.

The personal/family worship stream flowed into the early church and included daily prayers and "blessings" before meals. Later it emerged again in monasticism and German pietism. It continues today in personal devotions and family worship traditions.

2. Temple Worship

Temple worship is quite another story. Visiting the Temple (or the Tabernacle that preceded it) was not a private matter, but public. It was not typified by peace and quiet; instead the teeming crowds provided a virtual flood of sensory experiences. The Temple may have been the Old Testament's sensory equivalent of today's laser-pyrotechnics show at a Christian concert!

We do not know for sure when the Hebrews started to gather for corporate worship. Maybe this occurred at about the same time they began developing a collective identity as *Hebrews* during their Egyptian slavery. Imagine them serving as slaves in Egypt, where their children could have been attracted to the powerful and impressive Egyptian religions. What could these parents do to make sure their children remembered and valued their religious heritage? Did they start to gather in clans to worship and pass on the faith to their children? We do not know. We do know the Hebrews said they had to leave Egypt to offer sacrifices to their God. Were they sacrificing in Egypt, too? Perhaps they were gathering to worship but wanted to leave to sacrifice. Nevertheless, not long after their exodus from Egypt, they constructed the Tabernacle and initiated the elaborate Jewish worship system. This Tabernacle, or those that replaced it, would be the Hebrews' prime corporate worship space for the next 500 years (from about 1500 B.C. to 1000 B.C.). A bit after 1000 B.C., the tabernacles were replaced by a permanent structure patterned after the Tabernacle, "Solomon's Temple" in Jerusalem.

Tabernacle and Temple worship was impressive, exciting, and moving. The worshiper would experience all kinds of astonishing sights, sounds, and smells. Instead of talking with God alone on a mountain, hundreds and even thousands of people jammed into the courts. Travelers from distant lands spoke strange languages. Thousands of animals were sold, bathed, slaughtered, and had parts of their carcasses burned as sacrifices in a roaring fire. Imagine the mingled scent of wood smoke, burning flesh, and the sweet fragrance from the altar of incense. Temple worship (and its foreshadowing Tabernacle worship) was rich with symbolism and sacred objects: the altar of burnt offerings, table of showbread, lights, altar of incense, laver, etc. It was full of the pageantry of sacred actions.

The Temple stream of worship was not prevalent for the first few centuries of the Christian church, but elaborate pageantry and celebration worship reemerged after a few hundred years. It rose to a peak in the Middle Ages and even today appears in the dramatic and gigantic gatherings at conferences, praise gatherings, conventions, rallies, and concerts.

3. Festivals and Holy Days

Old Testament worship was not just about sacrificing animals for the sins of the people. It was also about *remembering God's mighty acts.* Indeed, one might argue that Old Testament worship was *primarily* about recalling God's past faithfulness. The most common way we humans tend to remember the past is through anniversary memorial celebrations—that is, celebrating each year at the same time what God did in the past at that time. Holy days are a means of *remembering* and memorializing what God has done in the past. Besides these feast days, the Jews observed a Sabbath every week. Thus, both their annual calendar and the weekly calendar provided a means of worship.

This "festivals stream" flowed into the early church. What did first-century Christian Jews think when Passover rolled around the year following the Resurrection? Did they recall that at this very time a year ago Jesus had been crucified and then had risen from the dead? They likely did.

The stream of Old Testament festivals and holy days not only flowed into the early church, it did so quickly. The early Christians adopted the first day of the week as their day of worship—remembering the Resurrection. Before long, Christians developed a full calendar of holy days to remember what God had done for them, just as He had acted in history for the Jews. Eventually, the church crammed the calendar with so many holy days that they began to lose their specialness and drowned in a flood of saints' and martyrs' days. Nevertheless, almost all Christians everywhere in the world still use the stream of special days as a means of worship. Christians still gather to remember the birth of Jesus at Christmas (perhaps even getting ready for His birth in Advent), recall His passion on Palm Sunday, commemorate His Crucifixion on Good Friday, and celebrate His Resurrection on Easter Sunday (and on every Sunday). Many Christians even celebrate Pentecost Sunday, Maundy Thursday, or Ash Wednesday. Besides these services of the

213

church year, many churches celebrate a whole set of national and secular holidays that they adapt, adopt, or otherwise sanctify. These include Thanksgiving, Mother's Day, Father's Day, Independence Day, Memorial Day, and others. The stream of feasts and festivals that started flowing in the Old Testament continues to flow in the present.

4. Synagogue Worship

We're not positive when the Jews invented synagogue worship, but the best bet is that it came into being when they were in Babylonian captivity. Why invent the synagogue? Perhaps to preserve and pass on the faith to their children while they were far from Jerusalem and its temple site. The Jews probably brought this Babylonian innovation back to Israel with them when they returned under Ezra and Nehemiah. By the time of Jesus, there appears to have been a synagogue in every village of Palestine. If the Jews could collect together the required core group, a synagogue would be organized anywhere in the Gentile world. Synagogue worship was all about Bible study focused on the Torah, the first five books of the Old Testament. A synagogue service in the time of Jesus began with a quotation from Deuteronomy, then included the *tefilah*, a series of prayers of praise, petition, and thanksgiving. The rest of the synagogue service focused on the word of God—the Torah. The Torah was read with reverence and then explained, the ancient equivalent of an expositional sermon.

While temple worship was extravagant, sensory, experiential, and packed with pageantry, synagogue worship was more simple, cerebral, and teaching-oriented. Synagogue worship had a massive influence on early Christian worship, where praying and expounding the Scriptures became the first half of the Christian worship service (with Communion the second half of the two-part service). The synagogue service is an Old Testament prayer-and-Scripture stream running directly into early Christian worship. Most churches today would not consider having worship without Scripture-preaching or prayer playing an important part. We thank the synagogue for this.

Four Streams of OT Worship

OT WORSHIP STREAM	FOCUS	LATER APPEARANCES
1. Private or family worship	*Intimacy*	Daily prayers, monasticism, family worship, home schooling, devotions
2. Tabernacle-Temple worship	*Celebration*	Easter pageants, conferences, conventions, concerts, praise gatherings
3. Feasts and Holy Days	*Remembering*	Church days and seasons like Advent, Christmas, Lent, Easter, Pentecost; secular days like Thanksgiving, Memorial Day, Mother's Day
4. Synagogue worship	*Teaching*	"Pedagogical worship," teaching-preaching, seminars, Sunday school, some small groups

To think about . . .

1. What new discovery did you make from reading this chapter about Old Testament streams of worship?

2. In your own local church, where do the modern equivalents of these four Old Testament streams of worship appear today? How does your own local church focus on intimacy? Celebration? Remembering? Teaching?

3. Do these four streams of Old Testament worship represent a kind of "balanced approach" to worship that we might consider today? What is missing? What is unnecessary?

4. If the four streams do indeed represent some sort of "balanced approach," which is the strongest stream in your current church? The weakest? Why?

5. Why do you think the Temple-Tabernacle stream went "underground" during the first few hundred years of Christian history?

6. Throughout history, the church has adopted or adapted secular, pagan, and national special days, often breathing Christian meaning into them. In what way is this good? Dangerous?

7. Which of the four streams is most easily adapted to evangelism? Discipleship? Fellowship?

8. What would an "order of service" for a first-century synagogue service look like if they had used a printed "worship folder" or "bulletin" in those days?

9. List the elements of continuity that Christian worship and Old Testament worship share—that is, what elements of worship do both have in common (e.g., prayer)?

10. List the elements of variation between Christian worship and Old Testament worship—that is, what elements of worship do Christians have that do not stem from the Old Testament? Conversely, what elements did Jewish worship include that Christians have not kept?

11. Forty years after Christ's Resurrection, Jerusalem was destroyed. The Jewish Temple has never been rebuilt, because Jerusalem is the only "holy mount" upon which the Temple may stand. Can you think of other Old Testament examples of "holy places" or "memorials" where place is pivotal for remembering? Are there any equivalent pilgrimage-type places today?

19
Jewish Feasts and Festivals

Jacob and Anna had been Jews all their lives. Their parents were Jews too. In fact, they could trace their lineage all the way back to Abraham. Relatively wealthy, they didn't let that keep them from being fully observant Jews, finding instead that their wealth sometimes helped. This year, for instance, they had taken a long journey to celebrate the Passover in Jerusalem. They planned on staying until the week after Pentecost before returning to their home in Ephesus.

But God had other plans. Jacob and Anna were swept into the new Christian movement, coming to believe that Jesus was indeed the Promised One of Israel. They were so convinced of this that they never went home, but decided instead to set up a small shop in Jerusalem where they were full witnesses to the events of 30-35. When they fled the persecution that broke out in connection with Stephen's martyrdom, they finally returned to Ephesus, connecting with other Jewish Christians (and eventually Gentiles).

*Over the next several decades, Jacob and Anna went through the gradual transition from Jewish practices to Christian ones. While they never believed they "quit being Jewish," they rather saw themselves adapting their Jewish practices to reflect who Jesus was and what He had done. With this came the realization that many of their Jewish rites could be kept, but needed to be adapted. For instance, they immediately felt awkward celebrating the Passover in the old way. But over the years they felt there was plenty of continuity with their old Jewish practices. After all, the practices weren't **that** much different.*

How much of the Christian use of time—festivals and feast days—comes from Judaism? To what extent did Jews have to change their practices or adapt them? What Old Testament roots use time as a means of organizing worship?

Jewish Christians

The first Christians were Jews. At least for the first five years all the Christians were Jews. The first clearly Gentile convert is recorded in Acts 10. Thus, these Jewish Christians were familiar with the notion of using time as a mode for worship. To the Jews, worship was *event-oriented.* That is, they looked back and remembered the mighty acts of God in the past, which reminded them of His ongoing faithfulness. Since one of the primary ways human beings remember past events is through "anniversary celebrations," it is natural that the Jews would use their calendar to remember God's past acts and to schedule other important days to emphasize the beliefs and sacred actions of their religion.

The Old Testament established five required feasts, but by the time of Jesus, the list had been expanded to include several others. The first Christians adapted several of these feasts, remembering God's mighty acts through Jesus Christ. So, understanding the Jewish calendar gives us more insight into how the Christian church established its own "Church Year" over time. Jesus, His disciples, and all those saved on the day of Pentecost would have been familiar with the following eight feasts.

1. The Weekly Sabbath

Like most ancient peoples, the Jews followed a lunar calendar—that is, their months began with each new moon, every 28 days.[10] The Jewish Sabbath, or seventh day, then neatly divided the lunar month into four equal weeks. The Sabbath is modeled after creation, when God rested—or caused all of creation to rest on the seventh day. God commanded the observance of the Sabbath to Moses and the Israelites when they left Egypt. It was to be a day of rest, even for slaves and animals. The purpose was refreshment, but it also served as a sign of God's covenant with Israel. Israel's observance of the Sabbath is often taken as a primary indicator of its loyalty to the covenant with God.

---

[10] The lunar calendar produces a year of only $354^1/4$ days, eleven days short of the required $365^1/4$. The Jews repaired this gradual but cumulative error by periodically adding the extra month of Adar. However, all Jews did not follow the lunar calendar. The Essenes followed a solar calendar—in fact, this was one of their "beefs" with the Jerusalem temple leaders.

Every week—on the Sabbath—Israel stopped working and remembered God's covenant with the nation and its people. The Sabbath became somewhat of a model for the Christian's "Lord's Day," though not totally so.

> ## On Passover
> "The LORD'S Passover begins at twilight on the fourteenth day of the first month."
>
> Leviticus 23:5 NIV

2. Passover/Feast of Unleavened Bread

Each year during (our months of) March-April, the Jews celebrated Passover. Like our Easter, Passover is a "movable feast." The date moves around based on the arrival of the spring equinox and the related full moon.

This feast (technically two feasts) remembered God's deliverance of Israel out of Egyptian bondage, including saving their firstborn and engineering the Exodus. It occurred during the barley harvest, and thus the first fruits of that harvest were given as offerings. Bitter herbs were eaten to remind them of the suffering of their ancestors as slaves in Egypt. Unleavened bread was eaten to remind the Jews of the haste with which their fathers escaped— without time to let the bread rise. A lamb was slain and eaten. For the Christians, the Passover was to become Easter. While some elements were retained, other elements (like slaying a lamb) were dropped, though perhaps not immediately for some Jews.

221

3. Pentecost/Feast of Weeks

Fifty days after Passover (in late May of our calendar), the Jews celebrated Pentecost. This was also called the "Feast of Weeks" since it represented a "week of weeks"—seven weeks. On this day, the Jews remembered God's faithfulness in giving them the law on Mt. Sinai. It came during the wheat harvest, so the first fruits of wheat were given as offerings. Pilgrims visiting Jerusalem for Passover celebrations would often stay until Pentecost before returning to their homes. This explains why so many Jews from all around the world were present for the Pentecost recorded in Acts 2. The Jewish Pentecost feast eventually became the Christian Pentecost, remembering the "birthday of the church" and coming of the Holy Spirit.

On The Day of Atonement

"The LORD said to Moses, 'The tenth day of this seventh month is the Day of Atonement. Hold a sacred assembly and deny yourselves, and present an offering made to the LORD by fire.'"

Leviticus 23:26-27 NIV

4. Rosh Hashanah/Feast of Trumpets

Rosh Hashanah, or the "Day of Blowing Trumpets," occurred on the new moon of the seventh month (our month of September). Rosh Hashanah was the beginning of the Jewish civil calendar and was celebrated by the blowing of trumpets, a "New Year's Day" of sorts.

5. Yom Kippur/Day of Atonement

Yom Kippur (in late September) was a somber day of fasting and repentance. On this single day each year, the high priest made atonement for the people's sins by sacrifice. The Christians did not adopt or adapt this feast, believing Christ to have made one sacrifice for all. However, the season of Lent later picked up the tone of mourning.

6. Sukkot/Feast of Tabernacles

222

Once a year (late in our month of September), the Jews moved out of their homes and into homemade booths to recall how God had cared for Israel during the forty years of wandering. The booths/tabernacles symbolized their temporary housing when they had no permanent place to live. While the early Christians did not adopt the festival, 1,800 years later the "Camp Meeting movement" adapted the idea of a once-a-year outdoor living experience. Many camps even followed the Old Testament setup, organizing their tents and cabins around what they called a "tabernacle."

7. Hanukkah/Feast of Lights

About 150 years before the birth of Christ, the Syrians subjugated Palestine. Their king, Antiochus IV, attempted to stamp out Judaism by persecuting Jews, destroying Torahs, and even sacrificing a pig on the holy altar in Jerusalem. In 164 B.C., under the leadership of Judas Maccabaeus, Israel regained its "independence." What could they do with the desecrated Temple? They couldn't just walk back in and begin sacrificing after its desecration. So, they held a "cleansing of the Temple" and rededicated it. As part of this rededication, they relit the holy "menorah" or lights; hence the name "feast of lights." Of all the Jewish feasts, this was the newest one Jesus and the disciples would have observed. It is actually a minor feast in Judaism. However, since the feast falls in mid-December, Jews today who live in "Christian countries" often upgrade the celebration nearer the level of the competing Christian Christmas.

8. Purim/Feast of Esther

Also a minor feast, Purim was celebrated during our month of February. The Jews remembered how God delivered the Jews from execution, which had been engineered by Haman, advisor to the king of Persia. Of significance was how Esther had come to her position as queen of the Persian kingdom for "such a time as this." In modern Israel, children often dress up as one or another of the characters in Esther's story, looking much like North American "trick-or-treaters."

These are eight ways the Jews in Jesus' day used the weekly and annual calendar to worship/remember God's mighty works in the past. While worship is not exclusively about remembering, no worship can avoid remembering what God has done for His people in the past. The early Christians, familiar with the notion of using the calendar as a means of organizing their worship, adopted and adapted this habit. And Christians have continued to observe holy days and holidays ever since.

To think about . . .

1. What new discovery did you make after reading this chapter on Jewish feasts and festivals?

2. How would you summarize the influence of the Jewish festival calendar on the Christian calendar?

3. Make a chart of the Jewish feasts, then list Christian or secular equivalents or parallels.

4. What brand-new feasts did the Christians come up with that did not involve adapting Jewish festivals?

5. If you had been a first-century Jewish Christian, one that had always had a Passover celebration with the family—how would you have revised your observance of Passover after the Resurrection? How would you have revised the celebration of Pentecost? The Day of Atonement?

6. Since many Jewish feasts were both national and religious holidays, is it then acceptable for modern countries to celebrate national holidays as religious days? Which secular or national holidays do you think are *not* appropriate for Christians to celebrate?

7. How does *remembering* play a part in Christian festivals and holi-days?

20

Recent American
Streams of Worship

Jason and Cindy had always been dyed-in-the-wool Presbyterians until they moved to Arizona. There they "dropped in for a day" at Sunnyside Community Church. "We just felt so at home here we decided to stay," they said. Sunnyside was not a denominational church but attempted to provide worship experiences that drew from all traditions. Sunnyside offered Jason and Cindy seven different services, four of them meeting simultaneously. The "Mystery Service" that met in the stone chapel on the property was advertised as "worship in ancient forms." A simultaneous service that seemed more like a rally or Charismatic worship met in the modern auditorium. The "Teaching Service" at 11 a.m. seemed to promote sober preaching and intellectual stimulation. Sunnyside offered still another service called "Gospel Worship." Cindy said this one seemed a lot like the old Billy Graham rallies. There were three other worship services as well, each with a particular style. After visiting several services, Cindy and Jason settled on the "Teaching Service," but occasionally visited one of the other services as well. In the membership class, Pastor Frank explained it this way: "We have people from all streams of worship history at Sunnyside, so we offer a variety of worship styles. In a way we're like a shopping mall—all kinds of choices under one roof."

Where did all these traditions and styles of worship come from and what makes them different from one another?

Since 1500, worship styles have multiplied. While the two Catholic traditions (Roman Catholic and Eastern Orthodox) continued with less or little change, the Protestant Reformation ushered in a wild array of worship styles. In America, innovation and competition are consistently rewarded—in business or worship styles. We offer a bewildering variety of styles, each one finding its own "market niche" of satisfied parishioners.

This chapter examines the primary streams of worship since 1500, with a special eye toward how those streams have influenced American worship.[11] The streams will be dealt with from the most traditional to the most radical and innovative, as they related to ancient patterns of worship. That is, the first stream is the most "conservative" in sticking with ancient worship styles, while the last is the most progressive or liberal in adopting new styles not based on ancient patterns.

Eastern Orthodox

The Reformation had no effect on Orthodox worship, nor has any other movement or event made much significant difference in Orthodox worship style. Eastern Orthodox worship is not about change and innovation; it is about consistently continuing patterns of worship unchanged from ancient times. Attending a modern Orthodox service is probably the best representation of what it would have been like to attend the worship of the Christians around 400.

Orthodox worship planners do not chase fads and trends in worship. They attempt to provide a worship service that is true to the ancient way. In fact, in an odd way, Orthodox worship patterns sometimes become more meaningful to the attendees precisely because they do not attempt to be "relevant" to the temporary whims of culture. Orthodox worship attempts to bring heaven down to earth and lift earth up to heaven. It is rich in liturgy, ritual, sacred actions, and sensory experience. Worshiping in an Orthodox church might feel like you've time-traveled to an ancient worship service. Many evangelicals attending an Orthodox service of worship remark, "That was weird" or "How out of touch!" Of course, that is precisely what these same folk would say if they had time-traveled to Ephesus or Philippi in 300 to experience an ancient worship service.

226

---

[11] I am indebted to the work of James F. White, who writes a superb outline of ten modern worship streams first published in an article in *The New Dictionary of Sacramental Worship* (Collegeville, MN: The Liturgical Press, 1990). The article was edited and revised and now appears in the excellent book, *Christian Worship in North America: A Retrospective, 1955-1995* (Collegeville, MN: The Liturgical Press, 1997), 17-31.

Roman Catholic

The Reformation had little effect on Roman Catholic worship. Catholics held their ground and continued their patterns of worship—until the 1960s, that is. The Vatican II Council of the Catholic Church ushered in radical changes in worship styles. The mass shifted from being spoken in Latin to the popular languages of local cultures. The homily or sermon became more important and moved more toward something like a Protestant message. Even guitars were introduced as Catholic worship was redesigned to be more "relevant" and user-friendly. Just imagine being a Roman Catholic in the 1930s: the mass was in Latin and all other patterns of worship followed ancient forms. Then in just a few decades your priest is delivering a chatty sermon from down front, and choruses led by guitars are projected on a screen. Few Protestants have experienced so much change in so little time as the Catholic worshipers of the last third of the twentieth century.

Yet Catholic worship has retained many of the traditional elements and approaches to worship, including the centerpiece, the Eucharist. Many Protestants attending Catholic mass are totally mystified by the complicated symbolic acts and procedures. However, some Protestant leaders have pointed out that it is just as mystifying for unchurched people who attend a Protestant service. While Roman Catholic worship continues many medieval patterns, it is more open to innovation than Orthodox worship, though perhaps less so than Protestant worship.

Lutheran

Martin Luther (1483-1546) is the senior statesman of the Protestant Reformation and founder of Lutheran churches. Worship for the Lutherans changed little in the Reformation. The Reformation was (initially) more about doctrine than methodology. For instance, the Reformers were not as interested in tossing out the Lord's Supper as revising the doctrine behind it.

227

However, once the split with Catholicism took place, and national, regional, and ethnic denominations emerged, it was inevitable that there would be shifts in worship styles. But these shifts may have had more to do with other matters than doctrinal distinctions.

The former Catholics-now-Lutherans experienced three changes: preaching was upgraded, congregational singing emerged, and Communion was practiced more frequently. Other than these shifts, a person attending a Protestant Lutheran worship service would see great similarities to the Catholic mass. Actually, the Enlightenment brought greater changes to Lutheran worship than the Reformation did. However, many of the modernizations resulting from the Enlightenment were reversed in the nineteenth century as Lutherans returned to many of the former patterns of worship. So today's Lutheran worship may have more in common with Luther than with the style of the 1700s. To a Charismatic or Baptist, Lutheran worship seems very similar to Catholic worship—though a Lutheran would point out the differences immediately.

Anglican

The English Church is Protestant, but in many ways it is not a Reformation church. It is reformed in the sense that it broke away from the Roman Catholic Church, but the reason for that break (the divorce Henry VIII wanted) was not so much about doctrine as it was about control of the church and nationalism. Nevertheless, once the break occurred, worship in Anglican churches (Episcopal in America) drifted away from Catholic practices and was not immune to what was going on among the radical Reformers.

It might be said that worship style is the primary definition of the Anglican Church. This is a church organized more around a means of worship than doctrine. Anglicans seek the "middle way" between the extremes on both sides of the church. The most significant event in Anglican worship was probably the release of Thomas Cranmer's *Book of Common Prayer* in 1549. The *BCP* became the uniting force in Anglican worship, providing a consistency in worship styles anywhere one might travel.

228

Anglicans reintroduced the daily prayer service that had been dormant (except among monks and friars) for so long. Early on, the Anglicans practiced Communion three times a year, but preachers like John Wesley argued for more frequent ("as often as you can") celebration of the Lord's Supper. In the 1800s the "Oxford Movement" was eventually effective at completely restoring weekly Communion among the

Anglicans, which is the practice today.

In worship styles, Anglican and Episcopal worship hold much in common with traditional Catholic worship, yet there is an openness to change. Again, the "middle way" is the core value—neither too traditional nor too innovative.

Reformed

The Reformed tradition is a bit more radical than the Anglican, willing to strip away even more of the "unnecessary" elements of traditional worship. The Reformers rejected "papist practices" and attempted to strip all excesses of Roman Catholicism from worship. The resulting worship included less symbolism and mystery and more preaching and teaching of Scripture. In this attempt to reform worship, some reformers went too far. Zwingli (1484-1531) rejected all music whatsoever. John Calvin (1509-1564) also insisted on no singing at all in worship, but he later relented and returned music to worship. Reformed worship includes a heavy emphasis on Scripture through preaching and preaching-teaching, sometimes called "pedagogical worship."

Methodist

In the 1700s, Anglican worship was about to face a revolution. Two Anglican priests, John Wesley (1703-1791) and his brother Charles Wesley (1707-1788), ignited a spiritual revival that swept across England and eventually imprinted all of American religion. John and Charles Wesley, while never giving up their ordination as Anglican priests, organized "societies" and "class meetings" of people committed to spiritual growth and fervency. What might at first be called a "parachurch organization," later became a denomination—the Methodists. Frequent Communion, fervent preaching, and hearty hymn singing typified Methodist worship. Small groups were organized, the all-night vigil was reintroduced as the "watch-night service," and the Wesley brothers dug up and reintroduced the old "love feast" from the first-century church. The movement evangelized England and swept vast numbers of Anglican people into its societies.

229

When Methodism came to America, Anglican and Congregational churches had largely clustered on the East Coast, leaving the West with few places of worship. The Methodists were quick to adopt circuit-riding methods of spreading Methodism across the West, and the Methodists dominated American Protestantism by the end of the 1800s.

Just as the Methodists in England had absorbed many Anglican people, frontier revivalism swept up an enormous number of Methodists in the 1800s. One might easily argue that if John Wesley were to visit today's American churches, not knowing which denominations they were, he would assume the Episcopal Church was probably Methodist. Methodist worship today often finds the "middle ground" of contemporary worship movements.

Puritan

The Puritans were more radical than the Methodists in departing from medieval forms of worship. Puritans sought "Scriptural worship." That is, if an element of worship was not clearly sanctioned by Scripture, they believed they had no business introducing it into worship. Puritans came to Salem (1629) and to Boston (1630), committed to purifying worship by stripping out all papist elements. They celebrated Communion monthly, sang only psalms, and practiced a stern yet joyful form of worship. Puritans stood firm and refused to bend to frontier revivalism worship. In the process, many of their people were swallowed up by revivalism. The remaining Puritans today are in the Unitarian Church or the Congregational Church (United Church of Christ).

Anabaptist

Even more radical than the Puritans in moving from traditional Catholic worship were the Anabaptists. The Mennonites, Amish, and Brethren churches insisted on adult baptism. Sometimes called "Rebaptisers," they rejected the validity of infant baptism and insisted that Christians be baptized as adults, based on their personal adult confession of faith. Baptism, however, did not always have to be by full immersion; pouring or sprinkling also was accepted. Anabaptists saw the need for a pure church, so the stream includes the Amish home-church strain. Anabaptist worship was traditional and simple.

Camp Meeting Revivalism

The 1800s experienced a revival movement that permanently altered the face of worship, American style. As the American population spread west, many of the East Coast denominations did not immediately follow. "The West" originally meant Pennsylvania, Kentucky, Ohio, Indiana, and the upper Ohio valley. Western settlers were left with little religious training at first. They brought with them their religious opinions and positions, but had little opportunity for worship. Worship became a family affair much like the Old Testament patriarchal period. The western people were spread out, illiterate, and had few chances for collective worship experiences.

Then came the Camp Meeting movement. Here the people gathered for four or more days at a time for religious services outside. They were somewhat similar to "rendezvous" trading gatherings, with which all trappers and hunters were already familiar. However, camp meetings were spiritual revival services, not designed for trading and drinking.

Camp Meeting worship featured lively singing, dramatic preaching, all-day activities, and baptism, with the entire "encampment" crowned off with an all-camp Communion service. The worship style was anti-liturgical—simplicity and excitement were more important than ritual and form. The exciting personality of the speaker dominated, as seen with the variety of eccentric preachers who sometimes were just as adept at fist fighting as they were at preaching. The music—in fact, the entire experience—was quite emotional. It was a moving, life-altering experience from which the attendees returned to the difficult humdrum of pioneer life. Attendance was in no way limited to believers, but open for all sorts of ruffians and unbelievers to attend. It was the most exciting thing happening! One can easily imagine these pioneer families looking forward to the next camp meeting "mountain top experience." Camp Meeting Revivalism is perhaps the only contribution Americans have made to world worship liturgy. It is typically American in culture and approach.

231

The Camp Meeting movement was not to be restricted to the West, however. Charles Finney (1792-1875) brought it east and introduced a similar camp meeting experience in his "protracted meetings." These included that innovation, "the mourner's bench," at which penitent souls could wait on the Lord until they found peace and power. Citywide crusades, local church "revival meetings," and eventually camp meetings now spread across the East along with the West. To invite attendees to his mourner's bench, Finney used the "altar call," an invitation to come forward. "Invitation" is probably too weak a word for what really took place. Actually, the entire service was designed to persuade the spiritually needy to come forward to get right with God at the end of the service. Finney's movement, along with Camp Meeting Revivalism, introduced a new three-part liturgy, which many American churches followed to modern times:

1. High-octane music and testimony
2. Persuasive preaching for decision
3. The harvest of souls—the altar call

Camp Meeting Revivalism swept America, both West and East. Denominations either adopted the style or lost many of their people. Lutheran, Reformed, Methodist, Puritan, and Quaker members were caught up in the new movement. The remaining holdouts circled the wagons against what they believed was a movement of illiterate and shallow emotional excess.

Camp Meeting Revivalism won the battle of worship styles. It became the dominant tradition in America and still prevails today in a pragmatic approach to "reaching the lost" or designing "worship for the unchurched." America's television evangelists, the church growth movement, the Charismatic movement, Christian contemporary music, most mega-churches, and the seeker movement are all grandchildren of Camp Meeting Revivalism.

Pentecostal–Charismatic

In 1906 at the Azusa Street Mission in Los Angeles, a new revival broke out. Rooted in the emphasis on personal experience of Camp Meeting Revivalism and classic Pentecostalism, a fresh revival wind began to blow among the attendees of the mission. Form and plans were tossed out and a new "liturgical democracy" emerged. Worship was delegated to the people—they were welcome to lead worship from the pew—to speak up in services that had no set program. The people delivered prophecies, gave words said to be directly from God, spoke in tongues, and were healed, all with great emphasis on the "baptism of the Holy Spirit."

Diversity prevailed as women, Afro-Americans, Hispanics, and Anglos worshiped together in this new expressive style of worship with no set plan. Leaders still led, but the focus was less on the platform than on the people. The movement spread rapidly along the channels one would expect—among classic Pentecostals, Afro-Americans, and Camp Meeting Revivalists. Like Camp Meeting Revivalism before it, this movement swept up millions of people from other denominations. It crossed oceans to Africa and Latin America and spread around the world.

In the 1960s, some fifty years after Azusa Street, the Pentecostal movement gained a second boost as it morphed into the "Charismatic movement," a softer, more adaptable version of Pentecostalism. It easily leaped across denominational boundaries and influenced worship and religious life in almost every American denomination. Then in the 1970s and 1980s, the movement gave the rest of America the "Praise and Worship movement," which had stripped out the doctrinal aspects of the baptism of the Holy Spirit. This wave presented churches with the option of adopting Charismatic styles of praise without having to accept the rest of Pentecostalism. As a result, some churches came up with a strange liturgy—starting their services with Charismatic, subjective, experience-oriented praise, then moving awkwardly into a more sedate, objective style for the remainder of the service. If the 1800s marked the Methodists' century of growth, then certainly the 1900s can be given to the Pentecostal-Charismatics.

233

Quaker

The Quakers were the most radical of all Protestant groups. All Protestants attempted to strip out elements of Roman Catholicism to some extent, but the Quakers sought a total break from the worship of the Middle Ages. Quakers took the "priesthood of believers" so seriously that they eliminated the clergy altogether, along with sermons and all sacraments. Quakers kept only the "meeting" and simple "meeting houses." They offered everyone direct access to God, and like the Pentecostals would do later, they invited their people to speak a word from God to the congregation. Until then, the congregation sat in silence listening for God's voice and to the "Inner Light." Quakers were as diverse as the Pentecostals would later become, including men, women, and slaves on an equal basis. Social justice was to become a prime concern, and Quakers were prime movers in the movement to abolish slavery in America. Camp Meeting Revivalism and the Holiness movement eventually swallowed up vast numbers of Quakers.

To think about . . .

1. What new discovery did you make from reading this chapter on the streams of worship since the 1500s?

2. What do you think of the idea in the opening story—a church offering differing styles of worship for different worship traditions in the church?

3. If Eastern Orthodox worship is in fact a style of worship most in continuity with the early centuries of the church, does that mean this style is the best way to worship? That is, should the modern church try to worship like the first church did, or not? If not, then how much are we obligated to keep and how much are we free to add to these ancient styles?

4. This chapter is a bird's-eye view of material covered in depth elsewhere in the book. Using this summary, make a chart listing the ten streams of worship and one or more "characteristics" or "contributions" to present-day worship you think these streams of worship made.

5. The Puritans sought to have worship that was "biblical." What do you think of their notion that we should do only those things in worship that are explicitly mandated by Scripture?

6. This chapter lists the Quaker stream as the most "radical" in departing from traditional patterns of worship since the 1500s. While many modern Quakers do not fit into this category (including a host

of evangelical and Holiness Quakers), draw some parallels between the Quaker stream and the Charismatic stream.

7. Considering your present church worship, draw a pie chart including as many of these streams as you see evidenced in worship—that is, if you were making a "recipe" for your present worship, what percentages of several of the above streams would you show?

21
Books to Read Next

This short book was not designed to answer all your questions about the history of worship. Indeed, if the author has been successful, you now have more questions than you had when you first picked up this book. Of course, you may know more than you did before, but you may also know how much you *don't* know—how much more there is to learn. For some (sadly), this will be the last book on the history of worship you will read. Yet, for many others this book will prod you to further and deeper reading on worship history. So as you read this chapter, ask, "Which of these books do I want to read next?"

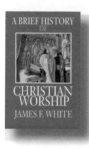

A Brief History of Christian Worship
By James F. White

James White is the best-known liturgy scholar in North America. However, don't let the term "scholar" scare you away from his writing. His books are not difficult to read and any average person can devour them. White, a Methodist, taught for years at Perkins School of Theology before finishing up his teaching career at Notre Dame. Thus, he writes as an alloy of Methodist Camp Meeting heritage and Notre Dame Roman Catholicism. However, don't let his Roman Catholic ties scare you either—after all, most of the history of the church is Catholic—Roman and Orthodox.

This particular book is a 192-page sequential history of worship. The book you have just completed is topical in approach—tracing one element or practice through all history in a single chapter. This book by White is not topical, but sequential. He starts with worship during the New Testament times, then moves through chapters on worship during the early years, the Middle Ages, the Reformation period, and modern times, before ending the book by reflecting on worship in the future.

White peppers his history with generous amounts of the philosophy and theology of worship, though that is not the primary purpose of his book.

James White, *A Brief History of Christian Worship* (Nashville: Abingdon Press, 1993).
ISBN 0-687-03414-0
192 pages

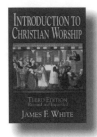

Introduction to Christian Worship
By James F. White

This book, a companion to *A Brief History of Christian Worship* mentioned above, organizes its information differently. Instead of moving through the periods of worship history sequentially, the author covers the territory in this book topically, like the book you now hold in your hand. White's book is the most popular text in American worship classes, and it follows what White himself believes is the best way to teach worship history: topically, not sequentially. The book begins with a delightful chapter defining worship, then traces worship history using the following rubric:

- Time (the Christian year)
- Space (architecture, art)
- Daily Public Prayer (the "People's office")
- Service of the Word (Scripture, preaching)
- The Sacraments (introducing the sacraments)
- Christian Initiation (baptism)
- The Eucharist (Lord's Supper)
- Journeys and Passages (marriage, ordination, burial, reconciliation)

238

Since the book is so widely used as a textbook, White has made it easy for students to study by using boldface type for more than 600 terms throughout the book. A glossary is developed in context with the chapter, rather than requiring a reader to look up terms in the back of the book. While White is no Dave Barry, his dry humor comes through repeatedly in all his books. As for bias, as one would expect of any worship history writer, he tends to favor worship with strong roots in historical patterns, patterns the church has used for millennia, as opposed to last year's pop ideas.

As you read topically, you'll get a half-dozen trips through all of church history, topic by topic, so that by the time you've read several chapters, the overall flavor of each period begins to appear in your background thinking.

James White, *Introduction to Christian Worship* (Nashville: Abingdon Press).
ISBN 0-2000 687 09109-8
317 pages

Protestant Worship—Traditions in Transitions.

By James F. White

Probably White's most unique work, this book traces the history of nine streams of Protestant worship since the reformation: Lutheran, Reformed, Anabaptist, Anglican, Puritan, Quaker, Methodist, and the two streams contributed by Americans, Frontier and Pentecostal worship. Devoting a chapter to each stream he uses a seven-element rubric to give a lively description of each: Piety, Time, Place, Prayer, Preaching, Music and (centrally) the People in the movement. White does a marvelous job describing cultural movements of other forces influencing worship movements in the church. If you are an evangelical, you'll most likely jump to the final two streams so you can have fun reading about the frontier camp meeting-revivals and the Holiness-Pentecostal-Charismatic movements. But once you've read this recent history you'll then be hungry to read farther back into the history of Protestant worship so you'll catch up by reading about the other seven streams. If you can only purchase one of James White's books, this is probably the best one to buy. It is a wonderful book and will captivate your interest.

James White, *Protestant Worship—Traditions in Transitions* (Louisville: Westminster John Knox Press, 1989).
ISBN 0-664-25037-8
251 pages

239

Sacred Games
By Bernhard Lang

This recent (1997) hardback book is not for the faint-hearted. Bernhard Lang (Religion professor, University of Paderborn, Germany) sees worship as a "sacred game." This is not an attempt to dismiss worship as frivolous, but is based on two sources of the "game" concept. The first is by Plato, who referred to worship as playing games. The other is from a 1937 book by Romano Guardini, who argued that worship, art, and children's play share one thing in common—they "have no purpose, but they are full of profound meaning." That is, worship in its most perfect sense is not useful but is profoundly meaningful and is more like celebration than duty or work. Whatever you think of this notion, Lang's book proposes worship as having six "games" to be played: Praise, Prayer, Sermon, Sacrifice, Sacrament, and Spiritual Ecstasy.

Lang's book has several strengths. He is the best current author at helping a reader see the universality of these six "games." These elements are common to all worship, not just to Christianity (though the book is still a history of Christian worship). Second, Lang has one of the finest chapters on "Spiritual Ecstasy" available in any of the books reviewed here. Graphically and with great gusto, Lang tells the story of the Pentecostal-Charismatic experience as rooted in a long history of extravagant experience-oriented worship that most worship scholars would prefer to forget. Lang pulls no punches and addresses his subject with a seemingly unbiased approach. Anyone interested in a broader view of the nature of Christian worship will enjoy this book. As for bias, this author is what some might call a "liberal scholar," and thus he protects or promotes no one style of worship. However, due to his approach to the Bible and history, some evangelicals will need to hold on to their hats while riding through the book.

Bernhard Lang, *Sacred Games – A History of Christian Worship* (New Haven and London: Yale University Press, 1997).
ISBN 0300069324
527 pages

240

Worship Old and New
By Robert E. Webber

In the last few decades Robert Webber has joined James F. White as a leading American worship scholar and author. Webber's journey has been a fascinating one, beginning with his undergraduate studies at Bob Jones University and continuing through his later education at Episcopal, Covenant, and Concordia seminaries. He taught at Wheaton College and then Northern Baptist Seminary. Webber wrote the bombshell book *Evangelicals on the Canterbury Trail* (1989; ISBN 0819214760), explaining why evangelicals are attracted to the liturgical church. The author of more than forty books, he conducts scores of seminars for ministers in every denomination through the Institute in Worship Studies, which he founded in 1995.

This book is not a worship history per se, but rather a summary of the history, philosophy, and practice of worship in a single book. It includes seven chapters on worship and sixteen other topical chapters, including three in which Webber explains his threefold "Biblical Theology of Worship." Webber has written dozens of other books on worship, including the following popular books: *Blended Worship* (1994; ISBN #1565632451), tracing the recent convergence of various streams of worship for the sake of both relevance and substance; *Ancient-Future Faith* (1999; ISBN 080106029X), in which he calls for a rethinking of Evangelicalism for a postmodern world; and *Worship Is a Verb* (1996; ISBN 1565632427), an easy-to-read philosophy of worship that is the source of the widely used "eight principles for transforming worship." Webber is less of a worship historian than a worship activist—he is the foremost leader of worship renewal in America. Thus, he is admittedly "biased." While he attempts to spread worship renewal that is relevant to "this present age," he defends worship that is deeply rooted in historic patterns. Webber is probably the most widely read worship writer among evangelicals, so if you have not read any of his works, plan to start soon.

Robert E. Webber, *Worship Old and New* (Grand Rapids: Zondervan Publishing House, 1994). ISBN 0310479908
287 pages

241

Twenty Centuries of Christian Worship
By Robert Webber, Ed.

This is volume two of the seven-volume set, *Encyclopedia of Christian Worship*. The entire set is designed for pastors and worship leaders and includes lots of practical resources, along with encyclopedic articles on almost every subject one might imagine. This particular volume covers the history of Christian worship, our present subject.

The first 260 pages of this volume lay out worship history, period by period, beginning with the New Testament era and moving through each subsequent era of history. It is particularly strong in providing two sections on Middle Ages worship—a Roman Catholic section and a separate section on Eastern Orthodox tradition. Many worship histories only follow the Western/Roman limb of the family tree, referencing our Eastern cousins only as a footnote in comparison to what was happening in the West. Churches with sympathies to the Eastern branch of tradition (Wesley, Charismatic, post-modern styles of worship) will especially appreciate this attention. Though edited by Robert Webber, a host of writers contributed to the encyclopedia-type writing. Thus the book is especially strong because it includes representatives from various streams outlining their own models of worship. On the other hand, sometimes these writers perform more public relations than reporting, so their accounts of recent trends in their denominations are sometimes as much wishful thinking as they are an accurate treatment of actual trends. Part four in this book includes thirteen separate theologies of worship, from a Reformed view to a Holiness-Pentecostal theology of worship. While beyond our present interest of worship history, it is a very helpful introduction to the philosophy-theology of worship, a much-overlooked field today.

The final section of the book examines current worship movements, then explores the future of worship. While the multiple authorship sometimes produces a herky-jerky style, the entire set is worth the expense and is an excellent resource for any professional worship leader in a local church. Sets like these often go out of print and are unavailable for a decade or more, so get one while you can.

Twenty Centuries of Christian Worship, ed. Robert Webber (Nashville: StarSong Publications, 1994).
ISBN 1562330128
413 pages

They Gathered at the River
By Bernard A. Weisberger

If you were raised in a Revivalist-Camp Meeting tradition, this book is a must-read for you. In an enjoyable reading style, Weisberger tells the stories of the revivals/awakenings in America, including the Camp Meeting movement, and such leaders as Charles Finney, D. L. Moody, Billy Sunday, and others who so influenced American religion to this day. Not directly a worship history but more a revival story, this author constantly orients the story to worship styles. American worship has been powerfully influenced by Camp Meeting Revivalism. Hardly a church has been immune to the movement, even those who rejected it. Once you have read this book, you will understand American worship much better. After all, Camp Meeting Revivalism is the one contribution of this country to the worldwide worship movement, for good or bad. If this book is out of print when you try to purchase it, try one of the many online used bookstores.

Bernard A. Weisberger, *They Gathered at the River — The Story of the Great Revivalists and Their Impact upon Religion in America* (Chicago: Quadrangle Books, 1958).
ISBN 0812960416
345 pages

Egeria's Travels
By John Wilkinson

This is the fascinating travel journal of a Spanish nun who visited the Holy Land just fifty years after Constantine became emperor. Thus, her account is the earliest surviving "pilgrim journal" you can read. Describing worship in Jerusalem in lavish detail, the book supplies a peek at how worship actually occurred in Jerusalem in the late 300s. Egeria writes in such a style that you feel as if you have unearthed a 1,700-year-old journal—which is exactly what it is. If you cannot afford John Wilkinson's translation and notes, there is a version posted free for reading on line.

John Wilkinson, *Egeria's Travels* (Wiltshire, England: Aris & Phillips, 1999).
ISBN: 0856687103
225 pages

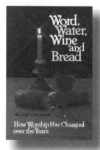

Word, Water, Wine and Bread
By William Willimon

This is a short sequential history of worship that moves through each era and especially highlights the "changes in worship." Willimon was Professor and Dean of the Chapel at Duke University for many years. The title reminds us of three primary elements of worship: Scripture, baptism, and the Lord's Supper.

William Willimon, *Word, Water, Wine and Bread – How Worship Has Changed over the Years* (Valley Forge: Judson Press, 1980).
ISBN 0-8170-0858-6
128 pages

At the Origins of Christian Worship
By Larry W. Hurtado

This recent (1999) book is by Professor Hurtado of New Testament Language, Literature, and Theology at the University of Edinburgh, Scotland. Hurtado does an exceptional job at placing early church worship in the context of first-century culture. He argues for two features of early Christianity: its exclusivity—that is, a Christian could not add Christ to his or her other religions, but swore off all other religions to adopt Christianity, an unusual feature of the day. The second feature is the "binitarian" nature of worship—that is, worship of both the Father and the Son from the very beginning. (Some scholars argue that worship of Jesus Christ as God developed over many years.) A somewhat heady book, it is not that difficult to read if you are interested in the early church.

Larry Hurtado, *At the Origins of Christian Worship* (Grand Rapids: Eerdmans Publishing Co., 1999).
ISBN 0802847498
138 pages

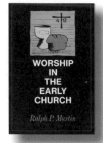

Worship in the Early Church
By Ralph P. Martin

This 1964 book continues in print long after many other worship books have disappeared. Focusing on Christian worship during the first century, this book is essentially a "New Testament Worship" history which one might expect from a New Testament professor—Ralph Martin served as one at Fuller Theological Seminary. The book is easy to read and a popular preaching/teaching resource for pastors. It is a good introduction to the elements of worship in the early church, proceeding one element at a time.

Ralph P. Martin, *Worship in the Early Church* (Grand Rapids: William B. Eerdmans, 1964).
ISBN 0802816134
144 pages

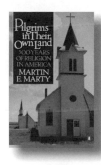

Pilgrims in Their Own Land
By Martin E. Marty

Martin Marty is probably the best writer and authority today on American religion. This book is the captivating story of American religion. In it you will meet Pilgrims, Calvinists, Lutherans, Catholics, Quakers, Jews, Christian Scientists, and Seventh-Day Adventists, along with individuals from Jonathan Edwards to Billy Graham. If reading about the history of worship has piqued your interest in American religious development, then this is probably the next book you'll want to read. This is an eminently readable book that tells the story in such a riveting style that you'll likely stay awake later than you intended once you begin this journey. While not specifically a worship history, Marty's book will familiarize you with the landscape of American religion that is the background for present worship patterns (and differences).

Martin E. Marty, *Pilgrims in Their Own Land: Five Hundred Years of Religion in America*
(Boston: Little Brown & Co., 1984). Penguin paperback edition (1985).
ISBN 0140082689
500 pages

Worship Without Words
By Patricia S. Klein

If you were raised in a "low church" denomination and want to know what in the world they are doing in Roman Catholic worship or in an Episcopal church, this book is for you. Well, it isn't exactly for you. It is probably written more for the people described in Robert Webber's 1989 book, *Evangelicals on the Canterbury Trail*; that is, low-church Revivalists who start attending "high-church" worship. These folk feel stupid and don't even know when to stand or sit or what in the world BCP125 means in the worship folder. Patricia Klein's little manual is for such folk. It is far more than a glossary, for it features a generous number of drawings, so you'll know the difference between a censer and a chalice.

245

Patricia S. Klein, *Worship Without Words* (Brewster, Massachusetts: Paraclete Press, 2000).
ISBN 1557252572
208 pages

A History of Christian Worship
By Oscar Hardman

Before James White and Robert Webber there was Oscar Hardman. This classic work moves sequentially through history, telling the story of worship at each era. It is out of print but can still be secured from used book dealers. Hardman was a professor at the University of London. As you might expect, a Londoner's book on worship is strong on ancient and European worship history and fails to do justice to the North American scene and contribution, as many North American books (including this one) give inadequate attention to worship in Europe. Nevertheless, Hardman's book is a fine reference book.

Oscar Hardman, *A History of Christian Worship* (Nashville: Cokesbury Press, 1937). 263 pages

History of Christian Worship
By Richard Spielmann

This quick-read book that was published in the 1960s provides a simple, nontechnical approach to worship history. In this short, ten-chapter summary history, Spielmann gives half of the chapters to Post-Reformation worship movements, especially related to various prayer books.

Richard Spielmann, *History of Christian Worship* (New York: Seabury Press, 1966). 182 pages

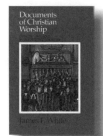

Documents of Christian Worship
– Descriptive and Interpretive Sources
By James F. White

An incredible collection of primary sources in worship, this book is designed to save doctoral students thousands of hours of research time in the primary sources. The book is organized by topic but presented within the topic sequentially. The organizing sections are: time, space, daily public prayer, service of the word, Christian initiation, Eucharist, and occasional services. Although expensive, it is worth the price in time saved. While the work of many early church fathers is posted online, this book includes all kinds of other quotes from writings, journals, and even newspapers. This helps the reader get the flow of worship history by reading the original sources, not just a writer's interpretation of those sources. By reading this book you can "decide for yourself" what really happened.

James White, *Documents of Christian Worship – Descriptive and Interpretive Sources* (Louisville: Westminster John Knox Press, 1992).
ISBN 0-664-25399-7
251 pages

History of the Christian Church
By Henry Sheldon

This is more history that you may want to know; thus, it is more of a reference work, like a commentary. Sheldon's work runs to several thousand pages and includes everything you ever wanted to know about church history, and more. In each of the five exhaustive volumes, Sheldon details the minutiae of church history. Sheldon, once a professor at Boston University, gives the reader a full separate section on worship for each period. The 1895 edition has recently been republished by Hendrickson Publishers. The drawback: Sheldon's work is not based on the discoveries during the 100+ years since he wrote it. Even if you never buy this nineteenth-century work, at least page through it in a library to see what students were expected to read before television and the Internet.

Henry Sheldon, *History of the Christian Church* (Peabody, Massachusetts: Hendrickson Publishers, Inc., 1895, reprinted 1988).
ISBN 0-943575-00-1
5 volumes

247

HELPFUL INTERNET SITES

Christian Classics Ethereal Library
http://www.ccel.org/

The Christian Classics Ethereal Library is a massive (and growing) collection of resources from church history. Its "Church Fathers" section includes many of the full manuscripts quoted in this book. Originally located at the University of Pittsburgh (1993-1995), the CCEL next moved to Wheaton College (1995-1999) and from there to Calvin College in 1999, though the web address is simply www.ccel.org. It is controlled by a board of directors that is part of the structure of Calvin College.

Church Fathers —New Advent Site
http://www.newadvent.org/fathers/

While most Protestants prefer to use the CCEL site above, this is an alternative Catholic site for accessing many writings of the "church fathers," some of which are not included on the CCEL site.

Institute for Worship Studies
http://www.instituteforworshipstudies.org/index.html

Robert Webber's worship site includes a variety of practical helps for worship, including some of his thought-provoking articles along with practical ideas for worship.

Notre Dame Center for Pastoral Liturgy
http://www.nd.edu/~ndcpl/

A collection of very helpful information, but a site that is difficult to navigate. See the excellent worship bibliography on this site.

249

22

A Study of Worship Sources

"Decide for Yourself"

A study in selected primary sources of First-Century Christian Worship

This book is designed as a "reader" for students of Christian worship. The text is based on the writer's own conclusions from reading and research. However, a true thinker is seldom satisfied with someone else's rationale on a subject. So why not "decide for yourself" what some of the sources actually say about worship? In each topical section we have included excerpts from primary sources. We have also provided questions in bold type as a guide to your study of these sources. For the first century, the ultimate "primary source" is the Bible itself. We will also examine two other extra-biblical sources that are from the same time period.

The aim of this book is to ignite an interest among readers, compelling them to start reading the many intriguing primary sources on worship. This section supplies just a sample of the very first sources—from the Bible, from an early Christian document, and even from a Roman governor who was an enemy of the Christians. In reading these primary sources, you can "decide for yourself" what was really happening in the early church. When you have finished this study, perhaps you'll move on to other readings. Who knows? Maybe you'll become your church's local expert on worship history!

The following Scriptures are from the NIV.

A. THE BIBLE AND EARLY WORSHIP

BAPTISM

1. **From the following references list a summary of all the elements apparent in the practice of baptism during New Testament times.**

   Acts 2:38 — Peter replied, "Repent and be baptized, every one of you, in the name of Jesus Christ for the forgiveness of your sins. And you will receive the gift of the Holy Spirit."

   Acts 8:12 — But when they believed Philip as he preached the good news of the kingdom of God and the name of Jesus Christ, they were baptized, both men and women.

   Acts 10:48 — So he ordered that they be baptized in the name of Jesus Christ. Then they asked Peter to stay with them for a few days.

   Acts 8:16 — . . . because the Holy Spirit had not yet come upon any of them; they had simply been baptized into the name of the Lord Jesus.

   Acts 19:5 — On hearing this, they were baptized into the name of the Lord Jesus.

   Acts 22:16 — And now what are you waiting for? Get up, be baptized and wash your sins away, calling on his name.

   Romans 6:3 — Or don't you know that all of us who were baptized into Christ Jesus were baptized into his death?

2. **What difference in nuance do you see between being baptized in and into the name of Jesus Christ?**

THE LORD'S SUPPER AND THE AGAPE FEAST

   Acts 2:46 — Every day they continued to meet together in the temple courts. They broke bread in their homes and ate together with glad and sincere hearts . . .

Acts 20:7 — On the first day of the week we came together to break bread. Paul spoke to the people and, because he intended to leave the next day, kept on talking until midnight.

1. **When did the first Christians in Jerusalem "break bread" together?**

2. **Is "breaking bread" the same thing as the "Lord's Supper," or something different?**

3. **A few have suggested Jesus was not instituting a rite at all but doing something else. Can you figure out what these other interpretations of what Jesus was doing here could be?**
    Luke 22:19 — And he took bread, gave thanks and broke it, and gave it to them, saying, "This is my body given for you; do this in remembrance of me."

    1 Corinthians 11:23-26 — For I received from the Lord what I also passed on to you: The Lord Jesus, on the night he was betrayed, took bread, [24] and when he had given thanks, he broke it and said, "This is my body, which is for you; do this in remembrance of me." [25] In the same way, after supper he took the cup, saying, "This cup is the new covenant in my blood; do this, whenever you drink it, in remembrance of me." [26] For whenever you eat this bread and drink this cup, you proclaim the Lord's death until he comes.

4. **In reading the Apostle Paul's corrections to Corinth, "reverse engineer" the situation—that is, guess from his words what must have been happening at this supper. Was this "Lord's Supper" an agape meal, or some combination of both?**
    1 Corinthians 11:17-22; 27-34 — In the following directives I have no praise for you, for your meetings do more harm than good. [18] In the first place, I hear that when you come together as a church, there are divisions among you, and to some extent I believe it. [19] No doubt there have to be differences among you to show which of you have God's approval. [20] When you come together, it is not the Lord's Supper you eat, [21] for as you eat, each of you goes ahead without waiting for anybody else. One remains hungry, another gets drunk. [22]

253

Don't you have homes to eat and drink in? Or do you despise the church of God and humiliate those who have nothing? What shall I say to you? Shall I praise you for this? Certainly not! . . . [27] Therefore, whoever eats the bread or drinks the cup of the Lord in an unworthy manner will be guilty of sinning against the body and blood of the Lord. [28] A man ought to examine himself before he eats of the bread and drinks of the cup. [29] For anyone who eats and drinks without recognizing the body of the Lord eats and drinks judgment on himself. [30] That is why many among you are weak and sick, and a number of you have fallen asleep. [31] But if we judged ourselves, we would not come under judgment. [32] When we are judged by the Lord, we are being disciplined so that we will not be condemned with the world. [33] So then, my brothers, when you come together to eat, wait for each other. [34] If anyone is hungry, he should eat at home, so that when you meet together it may not result in judgment. And when I come I will give further directions.

5.   **Given all of the references above, plus the one following, describe the operation of the first-century "Lord's Supper" and "love feast."**
     Jude 1:12 — These men are blemishes at your love feasts, eating with you without the slightest qualm—shepherds who feed only themselves. They are clouds without rain, blown along by the wind; autumn trees, without fruit and uprooted—twice dead.

DAILY PRAYERS

1.   **Taken together, how do these Scriptures describe the Old Testament's and the apostles' habit of daily prayer?**
     Psalm 55:17 — Evening, morning and noon I cry out in distress, and he hears my voice.

     Psalm 119:62 — At midnight I rise to give you thanks for your righteous laws.

     Psalm 119:164 — Seven times a day I praise you for your righteous laws.

     Daniel 6:10 — Now when Daniel learned that the decree had been published, he went home to his upstairs room where the windows opened toward Jerusalem. Three times a day he got down on his knees and prayed, giving thanks to his God, just as he had done before.

Acts 3:1 — One day Peter and John were going up to the temple at the time of prayer—at three in the afternoon.

Acts 10:9 — About noon the following day as they were on their journey and approaching the city, Peter went up on the roof to pray.

Acts 16:25 — About midnight Paul and Silas were praying and singing hymns to God, and the other prisoners were listening to them.

1 Thessalonians 5:17 – [Pray] continually . . .

THE LORD'S DAY

1. **Describe the Apostle Paul's habit regarding the Sabbath/Saturday.**
   Acts 13:14 — From Perga they went on to Pisidian Antioch. On the Sabbath they entered the synagogue and sat down.

   Acts 13:42, 44 — As Paul and Barnabas were leaving the synagogue, the people invited them to speak further about these things on the next Sabbath. [44] On the next Sabbath almost the whole city gathered to hear the word of the Lord.

   Acts 16:13 — On the Sabbath we went outside the city gate to the river, where we expected to find a place of prayer. We sat down and began to speak to the women who had gathered there.

   Acts 17:2 — As his custom was, Paul went into the synagogue, and on three Sabbath days he reasoned with them from the Scriptures . . .

   Acts 18:4 — Every Sabbath he reasoned in the synagogue, trying to persuade Jews and Greeks.

2. **Why would Paul in Troas use the First Day/Sunday instead of the Sabbath/Saturday?**
   Acts 20:7 — On the first day of the week we came together to break bread. Paul spoke to the people and, because he intended to leave the next day, kept on talking until midnight.

255

3. **What Christian discipline does Paul connect with the First Day here?**

   1 Corinthians 16:2 — On the first day of every week, each one of you should set aside a sum of money in keeping with his income, saving it up, so that when I come no collections will have to be made.

4. **What new term does the Apostle John introduce in this verse?**

   Revelation 1:10 – I was in the Spirit on the Lord's Day, and I heard behind me a loud voice like a trumpet . . .

5. **What must have been going on in the Colossian church to bring the following admonition from the Apostle Paul?**

   Colossians 2:16 — Therefore do not let anyone judge you by what you eat or drink, or with regard to a religious festival, a New Moon celebration or a Sabbath day.

FAST DAYS

1. **What abuses of fasting were apparently present in Jesus' time?**

   Matthew 6:16-17 – "When you fast, do not look somber as the hypocrites do, for they disfigure their faces to show men they are fasting. I tell you the truth, they have received their reward in full. [17] But when you fast, put oil on your head and wash your face . . ."

2. **Why do you think Jesus exempted His disciples from fasting? What is the meaning of this?**

   Matthew 9:14-15 — Then John's disciples came and asked him, "How is it that we and the Pharisees fast, but your disciples do not fast?" [15] Jesus answered, "How can the guests of the bridegroom mourn while he is with them? The time will come when the bridegroom will be taken from them; then they will fast."

3. **The Pharisee simply confessed to the expected lifestyle of a pious Jew—tithing and fasting. How often and how much?**

   Luke 18:12 – "I fast twice a week and give a tenth of all I get."

SCRIPTURE

1. **To what "Scriptures" are these verses referring?**

   Acts 17:2 — As his custom was, Paul went into the synagogue, and on three Sabbath days he reasoned with them from the Scriptures . . .

Acts 17:11 — Now the Bereans were of more noble character than the Thessalonians, for they received the message with great eagerness and examined the Scriptures every day to see if what Paul said was true.

1 Corinthians 15:3-4 — For what I received I passed on to you as of first importance: that Christ died for our sins according to the Scriptures, [4] that he was buried, that he was raised on the third day according to the Scriptures . . .

2. **How does the Apostle Peter treat Paul's writings? How early was 2 Peter written?**

2 Peter 3:16 — He writes the same way in all his letters, speaking in them of these matters. His letters contain some things that are hard to understand, which ignorant and unstable people distort, as they do the other Scriptures, to their own destruction.

MUSIC

1. **Taking the following Scriptures together, how would you describe Christian music in the first century?**

Acts 16:25 — About midnight Paul and Silas were praying and singing hymns to God, and the other prisoners were listening to them.

Ephesians 5:19 — Speak to one another with psalms, hymns and spiritual songs. Sing and make music in your heart to the Lord . . .

Colossians 3:16 — Let the word of Christ dwell in you richly as you teach and admonish one another with all wisdom, and as you sing psalms, hymns and spiritual songs with gratitude in your hearts to God.

1 Corinthians 14:26 — What then shall we say, brothers? When you come together, everyone has a hymn, or a word of instruction, a revelation, a tongue or an interpretation. All of these must be done for the strengthening of the church.

2. **What hints about early church worship might we find in John's writing as he describes "Heaven worship" in Revelation?**

257

Revelation 5:8-9 — And when he had taken it, the four living creatures and the twenty-four elders fell down before the Lamb. Each one had a harp and they were holding golden bowls full of incense, which are the prayers of the saints. [9] And they sang a new song:

> "You are worthy to take the scroll
> and to open its seals,
>> because you were slain,
> and with your blood you purchased men for God
> from every tribe and language and people and nation."

Revelation 14:3 — And they sang a new song before the throne and before the four living creatures and the elders. No one could learn the song except the 144,000 who had been redeemed from the earth.

Revelation 15:2 — And I saw what looked like a sea of glass mixed with fire and, standing beside the sea, those who had been victorious over the beast and his image and over the number of his name. They held harps given them by God . . .

3. **If the following were indeed Paul's recording of early church hymns or creeds, what observations on their music and/or creeds do you have?**

Romans 11:33-35 — Oh, the depth of the riches of the wisdom and knowledge of God!

>> How unsearchable his judgments,
>> and his paths beyond tracing out!
> [34] "Who has known the mind of the Lord?
>> Or who has been his counselor?"
> [35] "Who has ever given to God,
>> that God should repay him?"

Ephesians 5:14 — [For] it is light that makes everything visible. This is why it is said:

> "Wake up, O sleeper,
> rise from the dead,
> and Christ will shine on you."

Colossians 1:15-20 — He is the image of the invisible God, the firstborn over all creation. [16] For by him all things were created: things in heaven and on earth, visible and invisible, whether thrones or powers or rulers or authorities; all things were created by him and for him. [17] He is before all things, and in him all things hold together. [18] And he is the head of the body, the church; he is the beginning and the firstborn from among the dead, so that in everything he might have the supremacy. [19] For God was pleased to have all his fullness dwell in him, [20] and through him to reconcile to himself all things, whether things on earth or things in heaven, by making peace through his blood, shed on the cross.

4. **Though most of Luke's hymns became sung or chanted hymns, some may have been used as hymns in the first-century church. While they may lose something in translation from the original language (as most poetry and lyrics do), a modern reader can still see the cadence of these hymns. As a learning exercise, read (or sing, if you have the pluck) the following passages to yourself to sense the content and "flow."**

Luke 1:46-55 (Mary's song—the *Magnificat*)

> And Mary said:
>> "My soul glorifies the Lord
> [47] and my spirit rejoices in God my Savior,
> [48] for he has been mindful
>> of the humble state of his servant.
>> From now on all generations will call me blessed,
> [49] for the Mighty One has done great things
>> for me—holy is his name.
> [50] His mercy extends to those who fear him,
>> from generation to generation.
> [51] He has performed mighty deeds with his arm;
>> he has scattered those who are proud in their
>> inmost thoughts.
> [52] He has brought down rulers from their
>> thrones
>> but has lifted up the humble.
> [53] He has filled the hungry with good things
>> but has sent the rich away empty.
> [54] He has helped his servant Israel,
>> remembering to be merciful
> [55] to Abraham and his descendants forever,

259

even as he said to our fathers."

Luke 1:68-79 (Song of Zechariah, the *Benedictus*)

"Praise be to the Lord, the God of Israel,
because he has come and has redeemed his
people.

[69] He has raised up a horn of salvation for us
in the house of his servant David

[70] (as he said through his holy prophets of long
ago),

[71] salvation from our enemies
and from the hand of all who hate us—

[72] to show mercy to our fathers
and to remember his holy covenant,

[73] the oath he swore to our father Abraham:

[74] to rescue us from the hand of our enemies,
and to enable us to serve him without fear

[75] in holiness and righteousness before him all
our days.

[76] And you, my child, will be called a prophet
of the Most High;
for you will go on before the Lord to prepare
the way for him,

[77] to give his people the knowledge of salvation
through the forgiveness of their sins,

[78] because of the tender mercy of our God,
by which the rising sun will come to us from
heaven

[79] to shine on those living in darkness
and in the shadow of death,
to guide our feet into the path of peace."

Luke 2:29-32 (Simeon's song, *Nunc Dimittis*)

"Sovereign Lord, as you have promised,
you now dismiss your servant in peace.

[30] For my eyes have seen your salvation,

[31] which you have prepared in the sight of all
people,

[32] a light for revelation to the Gentiles
and for glory to your people Israel."

5. **Again, as a learning exercise, read the following possible hymns from Revelation as if you were reading the lyrics of a hymn or chant. Sense the tempo as you read or sing to yourself.**

Revelation 4:11

"You are worthy, our Lord and God,
to receive glory and honor and power,
for you created all things,
and by your will they were created
and have their being."

Revelation 5:9-10

And they sang a new song:
"You are worthy to take the scroll
and to open its seals,
because you were slain,
and with your blood you purchased men for God
from every tribe and language and people and nation.
[10] You have made them to be a kingdom and
priests to serve our God,
and they will reign on the earth."

Revelation 11:16-18

And the twenty-four elders, who were seated on their thrones
before God, fell on their faces and worshiped God, [17] saying:
"We give thanks to you, Lord God Almighty,
the One who is and who was,
because you have taken your great power
and have begun to reign.
[18] The nations were angry;
and your wrath has come.
The time has come for judging the dead,
and for rewarding your servants the prophets
and your saints and those who reverence your name,
both small and great —
and for destroying those who destroy the earth."

Revelation 15:3-4

[They] sang the song of Moses the servant of God and the song

261

of the Lamb:

"Great and marvelous are your deeds,
Lord God Almighty.
Just and true are your ways,
King of the ages.
[4] Who will not fear you, O Lord,
and bring glory to your name?
For you alone are holy.
All nations will come
and worship before you,
for your righteous acts have been revealed."

TONGUES

1. **How would you summarize the use of "tongues" in the book of Acts as it relates to worship?**

Acts 2:3-4 — [at Pentecost] They saw what seemed to be tongues of fire that separated and came to rest on each of them. [4] All of them were filled with the Holy Spirit and began to speak in other tongues as the Spirit enabled them.

Acts 2:11 – [the multinational crowd at Pentecost] "[We] hear them declaring the wonders of God in our own tongues!"

Acts 10:46 — [at Cornelius' house] For they heard them speaking in tongues and praising God.

Acts 19:6 — [Paul in Ephesus] When Paul placed his hands on them, the Holy Spirit came on them, and they spoke in tongues and prophesied.

2. **While correcting some problems in the use of tongues as a means of corporate worship, Paul gave us a glimpse into the practice in Corinth. If you were to organize Paul's instructions into a list, how would that list read?**

1 Corinthians 12:10 — . . . to another miraculous powers, to another prophecy, to another distinguishing between spirits, to another speaking in different kinds of tongues, and to still another the interpretation of tongues.

1 Corinthians 12:28, 30 — And in the church God has appointed first of all apostles, second prophets, third teachers, then workers of miracles, also those having gifts of healing, those able to help others, those with gifts of administration, and those speaking in different kinds of tongues. [30] Do all have gifts of healing? Do all speak in tongues? Do all interpret?

1 Corinthians 13:1 — If I speak in the tongues of men and of angels, but have not love, I am only a resounding gong or a clanging cymbal.

1 Corinthians 13:8 — Love never fails. But where there are prophecies, they will cease; where there are tongues, they will be stilled; where there is knowledge, it will pass away.

1 Corinthians 14:5-6 — I would like every one of you to speak in tongues, but I would rather have you prophesy. He who prophesies is greater than one who speaks in tongues, unless he interprets, so that the church may be edified. [6] Now, brothers, if I come to you and speak in tongues, what good will I be to you, unless I bring you some revelation or knowledge or prophecy or word of instruction?

1 Corinthians 14:18 — I thank God that I speak in tongues more than all of you.

1 Corinthians 14:22-23 — Tongues, then, are a sign, not for believers but for unbelievers; prophecy, however, is for believers, not for unbelievers. [23] So if the whole church comes together and everyone speaks in tongues, and some who do not understand or some unbelievers come in, will they not say that you are out of your mind?

263

1 Corinthians 14:39 — Therefore, my brothers, be eager to prophesy, and do not forbid speaking in tongues.

HEALING

1. **If James is here describing an actual first-century healing service (of which we are not sure), what would have been the procedure if it had been written down as a list — a sort of "order of service"?**
   James 5:14-15 — Is any one of you sick? He should call the elders of

the church to pray over him and anoint him with oil in the name of the Lord. [15] And the prayer offered in faith will make the sick person well; the Lord will raise him up. If he has sinned, he will be forgiven.

GREETING KISS

1. **Describe how a kiss was used as a greeting in first-century culture. What might be today's parallel act?**

   Luke 7:45 – "You did not give me a kiss, but this woman, from the time I entered, has not stopped kissing my feet."

   Luke 22:47-48 — While he was still speaking a crowd came up, and the man who was called Judas, one of the Twelve, was leading them. He approached Jesus to kiss him, [48] but Jesus asked him, "Judas, are you betraying the Son of Man with a kiss?"

2. **Imagine how the common kiss became upgraded to a holy kiss and was integrated into worship.**

   Romans 16:16 — Greet one another with a holy kiss. All the churches of Christ send greetings.

   1 Corinthians 16:20 — All the brothers here send you greetings. Greet one another with a holy kiss.

   2 Corinthians 13:12 — Greet one another with a holy kiss.

   1 Thessalonians 5:26 — Greet all the brothers with a holy kiss.

   1 Peter 5:14 — Greet one another with a kiss of love.

264

CONFESSION

1. **What was it about the early church situation that seemed to provide no route back into the church for a member who abandoned the faith and apostatized?** (It may be easier to answer this question after jumping ahead and reading the Roman governor Pliny's letter to Trajan included later in this chapter.)

   1 Corinthians 5:5 – [Hand] this man over to Satan, so that the sinful nature may be destroyed and his spirit saved on the day of the Lord.

2 Corinthians 13:2 — I already gave you a warning when I was with you the second time. I now repeat it while absent: On my return I will not spare those who sinned earlier or any of the others . . .

Hebrews 6:4-6 — It is impossible for those who have once been enlightened, who have tasted the heavenly gift, who have shared in the Holy Spirit, [5] who have tasted the goodness of the word of God and the powers of the coming age, [6] if they fall away, to be brought back to repentance, because to their loss they are crucifying the Son of God all over again and subjecting him to public disgrace.

B. *The Didache* AND EARLY WORSHIP

The Didache is probably the oldest surviving piece of Christian literature not to make it into the canon. Packed with instructions derived directly from the teachings of Jesus, it is a handbook of sorts for the church, especially focused on new Christian converts. It is comprised of three sections. The first six chapters are catechetical lessons most likely used with candidates for baptism. The next four chapters give descriptions of the liturgy at the time, including baptism, fasting, and Communion. The final six chapters outline the church organization.

The Didache claims to have been authored by the twelve apostles; hence, its alternate title is *"The Teaching of the Twelve Apostles."* A few believe this and think *The Didache* might be the result of the first Apostolic Council in about 50 — the one recorded in Acts 15. Though unlikely, if this claim were true, *The Didache* would have been written earlier than most of the rest of the New Testament. Parts of *The Didache* may have been circulating around the church during the time the rest of the New Testament was being written (the last half of the first century). However, we are probably safer dating the book to right around the turn of the first century, though modifications may have taken place well into the third century. The work was never officially rejected by the church, but was eventually excluded from the canon. The complete text of *The Didache* was discovered in the *Codex Hierosolymitanus*, but a number of other fragments exist, most notably in the *Oxyrhynchus Papyri*. It was originally composed in Greek.

265

The Didache is valuable to the student of early church worship because it supplies us with the first glimpse into what the early church really did in worship in the period immediately following the writing of the New Testament.

The Didache on BAPTISM

1. **How does this "in-the-name-of" formula for baptism differ from that recorded in the New Testament?**

2. **What are the three preferred methods of baptism and the alternative to each when the preferred method is not possible?**

3. **What role did fasting play in baptism?**

   Didache 7:1-4 — But concerning baptism, thus shall ye baptize. Having first recited all these things, baptize in the name of the Father and of the Son and of the Holy Spirit in living (running) water. [2] But if thou hast not living water, then baptize in other water; and if thou art not able in cold, then in warm. [3] But if thou hast neither, then pour water on the head thrice in the name of the Father and of the Son and of the Holy Spirit. [4] But before the baptism let him that baptized and him that is baptized fast, and any others also who are able; and thou shalt order him that is baptized to fast a day or two before.

The Didache on THE LORD'S SUPPER

1. **What does "Eucharist" mean?**
2. **What is the "flavor" of the attitude in the prayers for the cup and bread?**

   Didache 9:1-4 — But as touching the eucharistic thanksgiving give ye thanks thus. [2] First, as regards the cup: We give Thee thanks, O our Father, for the holy vine of Thy son David, which Thou madest known unto us through Thy Son Jesus; Thine is the glory for ever and ever. [3] Then as regarding the broken bread: We give Thee thanks, O our Father, for the life and knowledge which Thou didst make known unto us through Thy Son Jesus; Thine is the glory for ever and ever. [4] As this broken bread was scattered upon the mountains and being gathered together became one, so may Thy Church be gathered together from the ends of the earth into Thy kingdom; for Thine is the glory and the power through Jesus Christ for ever and ever.

2. **Whom did *The Didache* ban from the Lord's Supper (and what scriptural support was used)?**

   9:5—But let no one eat or drink of this eucharistic thanksgiving, but they that have been baptized into the name of the Lord; for concerning this also the Lord hath said: Give not that which is holy to the dogs.

3. **Following the cup and bread in the prayer of thanksgiving, what emphases are apparent?**

   10:1-6—And after ye are satisfied thus give ye thanks:

   [2] We give Thee thanks, Holy Father, for Thy holy name, which Thou hast made to tabernacle in our hearts, and for the knowledge and faith and immortality, which Thou hast made known unto us through Thy Son Jesus; Thine is the glory for ever and ever. [3] Thou, Almighty Master, didst create all things for Thy name's sake, and didst give food and drink unto men for enjoyment, that they might render thanks to Thee; but didst bestow upon us spiritual food and drink and eternal life through Thy Son. [4] Before all things we give Thee thanks that Thou art powerful; Thine is the glory for ever and ever. [5] Remember, Lord, Thy Church to deliver it from all evil and to perfect it in Thy love; and gather it together from the four winds— even the Church which has been sanctified— into Thy kingdom which Thou hast prepared for it; for Thine is the power and the glory for ever and ever. [6] May grace come and may this world pass away. Hosanna to the God of David. If any man is holy, let him come; if any man is not, let him repent. Maran Atha. Amen.

4. **Are there repetitive phrases in these prayers? If so, what?**

5. **What general observations concerning the early church practice of the Lord's Supper do you derive from these readings?**

267

The Didache on DAILY PRAYERS

1. **How does "The Lord's Prayer" here in *The Didache* differ from the one in Matthew 6:9-13?**

2. **How frequently were the early Christians to pray this prayer?**

3. **We do not know how they prayed this prayer—personally or corporately. What is your hunch?**

Didache 8:2-3—Neither pray ye as the hypocrites, but as the Lord commanded in His Gospel, thus pray ye:

Our Father, which art in heaven, hallowed be Thy name; Thy kingdom come; Thy will be done, as in heaven, so also on earth; give us this day our daily bread; and forgive us our debt, as we forgive our debtors; and lead us not into temptation, but deliver us from the evil one; for Thine is the power and the glory for ever and ever.

[3] Three times in the day pray ye so.

4. **What other emphases in prayer do you observe in *The Didache*?**
    Didache 1:3 — Now of these words the doctrine is this. Bless them that curse you, and pray for your enemies and fast for them that persecute you; for what thank is it, if ye love them that love you? Do not even the Gentiles the same? But do ye love them that hate you, and ye shall not have an enemy.

    Didache 2:7 — Thou shalt not hate any man but some thou shalt reprove, and for others thou shalt pray, and others thou shalt love more than thy life.

    Didache 4:14 — In church thou shalt confess thy transgressions, and shalt not betake thyself to prayer with an evil conscience. This is the way of life.

    Didache 15:4 — But your prayers and your almsgiving and all your deeds so do ye as ye find it in the Gospel of our Lord.

268

The Didache on FAST DAYS

1. **Who are "the hypocrites" *The Didache* cites here?**

2. **What days were the early Christians urged to fast?**

3. **What seems to be the reason for using these days?**
    Didache 8:1 — And let not your fastings be with the hypocrites, for they fast on the second and the fifth day of the week; but do ye keep your fast on the fourth and on the preparation (the sixth) day.

C. PLINY'S LETTER AND EARLY WORSHIP

Pliny the Younger was governor of Pontus-Bithynia from 111-113. He exchanged letters with the emperor Trajan on a variety of matters. Two letters are especially relevant to the practice of Christian worship at the turn of the first century, for they record an "outsider's view" of Christian worship and lifestyle practice. Pliny, Letters 10.96-97

PLINY TO THE EMPEROR TRAJAN

It is my practice, my lord, to refer to you all matters concerning which I am in doubt. For who can better give guidance to my hesitation or inform my ignorance? I have never participated in trials of Christians. I therefore do not know what offenses it is the practice to punish or investigate, and to what extent. And I have been not a little hesitant as to whether there should be any distinction on account of age or no difference between the very young and the more mature; whether pardon is to be granted for repentance, or, if a man has once been a Christian, it does him no good to have ceased to be one; whether the name itself, even without offenses, or only the offenses associated with the name are to be punished.

1. How would you outline Pliny's practice to date in dealing with the Christians?

Meanwhile, in the case of those who were denounced to me as Christians, I have observed the following procedure: I interrogated these as to whether they were Christians; those who confessed I interrogated a second and a third time, threatening them with punishment; those who persisted I ordered executed. For I had no doubt that, whatever the nature of their creed, stubbornness and inflexible obstinacy surely deserve to be punished. There were others possessed of the same folly; but because they were Roman citizens, I signed an order for them to be transferred to Rome.

269

2. What were the simple escape routes for people accused of being Christians at this time?

Soon accusations spread, as usually happens, because of the proceedings going on, and several incidents occurred. An anonymous document was published containing the names of many persons. Those who denied that they were or had been Christians, when they invoked the gods in words dictated by me, offered prayer with incense and wine to your image, which I had ordered to be brought for this purpose together with statues of the gods, and moreover cursed Christ—none of which those who are really Christians, it is said, can be forced to do—these I thought should be discharged. Others named by the informer declared that they were Christians, but then denied it, asserting that they had been but had ceased to be, some three years before, others many years, some as much as twenty-five years. They all worshipped your image and the statues of the gods, and cursed Christ.

3. **When did these Christians meet?**

4. **List the "order of service" for these meetings.**

5. **Describe the second meeting of the Christians and what happened to it.**

6. **How did Pliny try to discover further facts about the Christians?**

7. **What might have been these "excessive superstitions"?**
They asserted, however, that the sum and substance of their fault or error had been that they were accustomed to meet on a fixed day before dawn and sing responsively a hymn to Christ as to a god, and to bind themselves by oath, not to some crime, but not to commit fraud, theft, or adultery, not falsify their trust, nor to refuse to return a trust when called upon to do so. When this was over, it was their custom to depart and to assemble again to partake of food—but ordinary and innocent food. Even this, they affirmed, they had ceased to do after my edict by which, in accordance with your instructions, I had forbidden political associations. Accordingly, I judged it all the more necessary to find out what the truth was by torturing two female slaves who were called deaconesses. But I discovered nothing else but depraved, excessive superstition.

270

8. **What indication do we have of the size and makeup of the Christian church at this time?**

9. **Describe the effect of the Christians on the pagan temples.**

10. **What do you suspect is Pliny's plan to "reform" these Christians?**
I therefore postponed the investigation and hastened to consult you. For

the matter seemed to me to warrant consulting you, especially because of the number involved. For many persons of every age, every rank, and also of both sexes are and will be endangered. For the contagion of this superstition has spread not only to the cities but also to the villages and farms. But it seems possible to check and cure it. It is certainly quite clear that the temples, which had been almost deserted, have begun to be frequented, that the established religious rites, long neglected, are being resumed, and that from everywhere sacrificial animals are coming, for which until now very few purchasers could be found. Hence it is easy to imagine what a multitude of people can be reformed if an opportunity for repentance is afforded.

REPLY FROM TRAJAN TO PLINY

11. Describe Trajan's recommended approach for dealing with the Christians.

You observed proper procedure, my dear Pliny, in sifting the cases of those who had been denounced to you as Christians. For it is not possible to lay down any general rule to serve as a kind of fixed standard. They are not to be sought out; if they are denounced and proved guilty, they are to be punished, with this reservation, that whoever denies that he is a Christian and really proves it—that is, by worshiping our gods—even though he was under suspicion in the past, shall obtain pardon through repentance. But anonymously posted accusations ought to have no place in any prosecution. For this is both a dangerous kind of precedent and out of keeping with the spirit of our age.

12. Summarize everything we learn about worship in a list format from Pliny's letter and Trajan's response.

271

23
Worship Time Line
Important Dates for Reference

Most people who have been forced to take a history course groan when they recall the dates they had to memorize. True, memorizing a collection of historical dates is of relatively minor educational value. But knowing the general flow of history can be helpful in "telling the story." And, of course, that is what history does.

Occasionally the reader may wonder *what* fits *where* in history. If so, this time line should help, as well as the additional resources included as a ready reference—much like the glossary of terms which follows it. Few people read a glossary or an index. Few people will read this time line (although if you are actually reading this introduction you might be an exception!). It is here primarily for reference—to get the feel of what was happening in each century. At least you'll want to read the last few lines—we are always most interested in the "history" we have personally lived through!

(c.) denotes circa "about" or approximate date of event; all dates are A.D.

1ST CENTURY 30–100
Resurrection of Jesus Christ (c. 30)
Beheading of James, son of Zebedee (c. 44)
Christians greet one another with a kiss (60+)
Martyrdom of James of Jerusalem (c. 62)
A fire destroys half of Rome (c. 64)
Peter and Paul are martyred (c. 67)
Nero commits suicide (June 9, 68)
Fall of Jerusalem to Rome (70)
Romans move into Scotland (78)
The Didache is written (c. 100)
First Clement is written by Clement of Rome (c. 95)

2ND CENTURY 100–200

Polycarp writes to the Philippians (c. 110)

Christians urged to pray Lord's Prayer three times a day (c. 100)

Pliny the Younger, governor of Bithynia (111-113)

Communion starts separating from agape meal (early 100s)

Marcion is excommunicated (July 144)

The Shepherd written by Hermas (c. 150)

Papias writes *Sayings of the Lord* (c. 150)

Second Epistle of Clement written (c. 150)

Christian weddings are a family affair (100s)

Clement of Alexandria is born in Athens (c. 150)

Controversy over when to celebrate Easter (c. 150)

Tertullian is born in Carthage (c. 155)

Polycarp of Smyrna is martyred (c. 155)

The Great Plague in the Roman Empire (c. 160-180)

Justin is martyred (c. 165)

Origen is born in Alexandria (c. 185)

Tertullian is converted to Christianity (c. 193)

Irenaeus writes *Proof of the Apostolic Preaching* (c. 195)

3RD CENTURY 200–300

Irenaeus dies (c. 202)

Cyprian of Carthage is born (c. 205)

Tertullian argues against kneeling on Sunday (205)

Tertullian writes "Against Marcion" (c. 207-212)

Some practice infant baptism (early 200s)

Martyrdom of St. Alban (c. 207)

Clement of Alexandria dies in Cappadocia (c. 214)

Hippolytus writes *The Apostolic Tradition* (c. 217)

Christians urged to pray seven times a day (c. 217)

Origen writes *On First Principles* (c. 220-230)

Cyprian is consecrated bishop of Carthage (c. 248)

Anthony the hermit born [Father of monasticism?] (c. 251)

Synod of Carthage (lapsed and heretic baptism) (252)

Origen dies in Tyre (253)

Earliest known Christian church building destroyed by fire (256)

Cyprian of Carthage martyred (258)

Eusebius of Caesarea is born (263)

Athanasius is born (c. 298)

4TH CENTURY 300-400

Eusebius of Caesarea, *History of the Church* (300-325)

Christians meet daily, morning and night for prayers (c. 300)

Final Roman persecution (Diocletian) (303-311)

Constantine is made emperor of the Roman Empire (306)

Edict of Milan, establishing tolerance of Christianity (313)

Christmas emerges in Rome (c. 336+)

Eusebius of Caesarea becomes bishop of Caesarea (313)

Christians are given Basilicas for worship (early 300s)

Arius writes Letter to Eusebius of Nicomedia (c. 320)

Pachomius organizes the first monastery (c. 320)

Constantine builds Constantinople (324-330)

People commanded to cease work on Sunday (321)

First Ecumenical Council (Arianism, Nicene Creed) (325)

First mention of "Lent" (325)

Agape meal has disappeared (early 300s)

Constantine moves capital to Constantinople (331)

Gregory of Nyssa is born (c. 331)

Constantine baptized at death by Eusebius of Nicomedia (337)

Ambrose is born in Treves (339)

Roman Empire divided after the death of Constantine (340)

Eusebius of Nicomedia dies (c. 341)

Jerome is born (c. 347)

Christmas practiced regularly in the West (c. 350)

Augustine is born at Tagaste (November 13, 354)

John Chrysostom is born (c. 345)

Pelagius is born in Britain (354)

Anthony the hermit dies (356)

Huns conquer Goths in Russia (370)

Augustine goes to Carthage to study (371)

Athanasius dies (373)

Egeria visits Jerusalem; keeps journal (late 300s)

Emperor Theodosius establishes Catholicism as the religion of the empire (c. 377)

Second Ecumenical Council (Constantinople) (c. 381)

Birth of St. Patrick (c. 385)

Augustine baptized by Ambrose; death of Monica (387)
Augustine writes *The True Religion* (c. 390)
Gregory of Nyssa writes *The Life of Moses* (c. 390)
Augustine is ordained to the priesthood (391)
Ambrose introduces antiphonal singing (late 300s)
Gregory of Nyssa dies (396)
Augustine is consecrated bishop of Hippo (396)
John Chrysostom is consecrated bishop of Constantinople (398)

5TH CENTURY 400-500

Augustine writes *Confessions* (397-401)
Gladiator contests abolished (404)
John Chrysostom deposed (403)
John Chrysostom dies (September 14, 407)
Augustine writes *The City of God* (411)
Pelagius excommunicated for "pelagianism" (418)
John Cassian writes *The Incarnation of Christ* (429)
Augustine dies (430)
Patrick begins his missionary work in Ireland (432)
John Cassian dies in France (c. 435)
Saxon rebellion in England (442)
The Vandals invade Rome (455)
Death of St. Patrick in Ireland (c. 461)
St. Benedict born (480)

6TH CENTURY 500-600

Birth of St. Columba, Ireland (c. 521)

Benedict develops eight daily services (early 500s)
John II is bishop of Rome (533-535)
Gregory I (the Great) is born in Rome (c. 540)
Benedict dies (c. 543)
Germanic invasions of Britain (c. 550)
Organ first appears and is rejected by church (500s)
Founding of monastery at Derry, Ireland (551)
The Fifth Ecumenical Council (553)
Founding of the monastery at Kells, Ireland (554)
Founding of the monastery at Durrow, Ireland (556)
Founding of additional monasteries in Ireland (559)

Founding of the monastery at Iona, Scotland (563)

John the Faster elected Patriarch of Constantinople (582)

Gregory I (the Great) becomes bishop of Rome (590-604)

Pope Gregory gathers "Gregorian Chants" (late 600s)

Death of John the Faster, Asia Minor (595)

Death of St. Columba, Scotland (597)

7TH CENTURY 600-700

The first St. Paul's Church, London (603)

Essex in England returns to pagan worship (626)

Conversion of King Edwin of Northumbria, England (627)

Birth of St. Cuthbert, England (634)

Benedict's relics transferred to St. Benedict's Church (640)

Birth of Bede in England (c. 672)

Rebuilding of St. Paul's Cathedral, London (c. 675)

Battle of the Trent (678)

The Sixth Ecumenical Council (680-681)

Boniface born (680)

8TH CENTURY 700-800

The iconoclastic controversy (726-787)

Charles Martel defeats Arabs at Tours (732)

John of Damascus dies (749)

Boniface dies (754)

The organ emerges in church (700-900s)

9TH CENTURY 800-900

Charlemagne heads German "Holy Roman Empire" (800)

Earliest detailed wedding ceremony [Pope Nicholas I] (866)

10TH CENTURY 900-1000

What is often called the "Dark Ages" (875-950)

The organ introduced in Benedictine monasteries (900s)

11TH CENTURY 1000-1100

Anselm is born, father of scholasticism (1033)

East and West churches split (1054)

277

Scholasticism develops (1050-1350)
Peter Abelard is born (1079)
Muslims resist Christian pilgrimages (1079)
Monastery reformer Bernard of Clairvaux is born (1093)
The First Crusade (1096-1099)

12TH CENTURY 1100-1200

Polyphonic (parts) music emerges (1100s)
Peter Lombard, scholar-author is born (1100)
Anselm dies (1109)
The organ now widely accepted in the church (1100s)
Peter Waldo (pre-Luther Protestant) born in France (1140)
Peter Abelard dies (1143)
The Romanesque style displaces Byzantine (1100-1150)
The Second Crusade (1147-1148)
The greeting kiss becomes kissing the paten (1100s)
Bernard of Clairvaux dies (1153)
Francis of Assisi is born (c. 1182)
Muslims retake Jerusalem (1187)
Third Crusade to retake Jerusalem (1189-1192)

13TH CENTURY 1200-1300

The Fourth Crusade (1200-1204)
Children's Crusade (1212)
Fourth Lateran Council [Transubstantiation] (1215)
Preaching order (Dominicans) established (1216)
The Fifth Crusade [St. Francis] (1219-1221)
St. Francis's Stigmata (1224)
Thomas Aquinas born (c. 1224)
Francis writes "All Creatures of Our God and King" (1225)
Francis dies (1226)
Sixth Crusade [Frederick II] (1229)
Seventh (last) Crusade [St. Louis IX] (1248)

14TH CENTURY 1300-1400

The Black Death kills 1/3 of Europe (1300-1400)
"Babylonian Captivity of the Church" (1309-1377)
John Wycliffe is born (1330)

Hundred Years' War begins (1337-1453)

Woman's vow to "obey husband" added (late 1300s)

John Huss is born (1371)

The Great Schism—two competing popes (1378-1417)

Thomas à Kempis born, author of *Imitation of Christ* (1380)

Wycliffe dies (1384)

15TH CENTURY 1400–1500

Council of Constance burns John Huss (July 6, 1415)

Council of Constance deposes both popes for a new one (1417)

Catholic Church burns Wycliffe's bones (1428)

Savonarola, the great orator is born (1452)

Fall of Constantinople (1453)

Gutenberg prints 42-line Bible (1453)

Hundred Years' War ends (1453)

Thomas à Kempis dies (1471)

Martin Luther is born (1483)

Columbus sails to America (1492)

Savonarola dies (1498)

16TH CENTURY 1500–1600

Luther is ordained a priest at Erfurt (1507)

Henry VIII becomes King of England (1509)

John Calvin is born (1509)

Zwingli rejects all music in worship (early 1500s)

John Knox is born, Scotland's Reformed leader (1514)

Luther nails 95 Theses to church door in Wittenburg (1517)

279

Luther is excommunicated (1521)

Luther begins penning hymns (1523)

William Tyndale Publishers translation of New Testament (1529)

Ulrich Zwingli dies (1531)

John Calvin is converted (c. 1533)

Luther completes translation of Bible into German (1534)

Henry VIII declares himself head of Church of England (1534)

Calvin rejects music in worship, then relents (1500s)

Anabaptists take over Muenster (1535)

Menno Simons becomes an Anabaptist (1536)

William Tyndale burned at the stake (1536)

First edition of Calvin's *Institutes* (1536)
Jesuit order is founded [Catholic Reformation] (1540)
John of the Cross is born (1542)
Released: Cranmer's *Book of Common Prayer* (1549)
John Knox converted (c. 1543)
The Catholic Council of Trent begins (1545)
Martin Luther dies (1546)
Mary Tudor (Bloody Mary) reigns, reformers flee (1553)
Elizabeth crowned, the reformers return (1558)
New Book of Common Prayer required in England (1559)
Jacobus Arminius is born (1560)
Church of Scotland rejects celebrating Christmas (1560)
Menno Simons dies (1561)
John Calvin dies (1564)
Puritans reject vestments in Church of England (1567-1568)
Puritans discard ring in wedding ceremony (late 1500s)
John Knox dies (1572)
Whole wedding ceremony moved inside church (late 1500s)
John of the Cross dies (1591)

17TH CENTURY 1600–1700

Arminius: predestination based on foreknowledge (1603)
James I [of Bible fame] becomes King (1603)
Jacobus Arminius dies (1609)
Brother Lawrence [*Practicing the Presence*] is born (1610)
Arminians list five points of disagreement (1610)
King James Version of the Bible printed (1611)
Synod of Dort answers Arminians with five points (1618-1619)
Plymouth, Massachusetts colony founded by Puritans (1620)
John Bunyan, Puritan, born (1628)
Puritans come to Salem (1629) and Boston (1630)
Puritans found Harvard (1636)
George Fox founds Friends/Quakers (1647)
Anglican church cracks down; Puritan pastors leave (1662)
Philip Jacob Spener helps launch Pietist Movement (1675)
Protestantism becomes illegal in France (1675)
J.S. Bach is born (1685)
Brother Lawrence dies (1691)

Pietism shifts lyrics toward experience (late 1600s)

18TH CENTURY 1700-1800

John Wesley is born (1703)
Jonathan Edwards is born (1703)
George Whitefield is born (1714)
Moravian revival [Count Zinzendorf] (1727)
Moravian missionaries sent out (1727+)
Beginning of the First Great Awakening in N.J. (1720-30)
First Great Awakening [Jonathan Edwards] (1734-1737)
George Whitefield preaches to 75% of U.S. (1739-1741)
Isaac Watts writes non-quoting Scripture hymns (1700s)
John Wesley's Aldersgate experience (May 24, 1738)
John Wesley begins the Methodists in London (1739)
The Wesleys totally transform church music (late 1700s)
Brethren and Wesley reintroduce the agape meal (mid 1700s)
Presbyterians found Princeton (1746)
Jonathan Edwards dies (1758)
William Carey, missionary, is born (1761)
Baptists found Brown University (1764)
Dutch Reformed found Rutgers (1766)
George Whitefield dies (1770)
John Wesley discards wedding ring in service (late 1700s)
Wesley eliminates "giving away of the bride" (late 1700s)
Olney Hymn book ["Amazing Grace"] (1779)
Methodists start separating from Church of England (1784)
John Wesley dies (1791)
Baptist Missionary Society founded (1792)
Revivalist Charles Finney born (1792)
London Missionary Society founded (1795)

281

19TH CENTURY 1800-1900

Red River revival in Kentucky (June 1800)
The Cane Ridge Camp Meeting in Kentucky (1801)
Princeton Seminary founded (1812)
David Livingston, Africa missionary, is born (1813)
African Methodist Episcopal Church founded (1816)
Charles Finney and the Second Great Awakening (1824)

Charles Finney first used "altar call" (1825)

Fanny Crosby is born (1825)

Finney publishes *Lectures on Revival* (1835)

Oxford Movement prods Anglicans to roots (1833-1841)

Catholics confirm Immaculate Conception of Mary (1854)

Darwin publishes *The Origin of Species* (1859)

Dwight L. Moody begins revival work (1860)

Spurgeon preaches to 5000+ per week (1861)

Vatican I; Papal Infallibility stated (1870)

David Livingston dies (1873)

Charles Finney dies (1875)

Thomas Harrison gives stand-up invitation (1875)

Student Volunteer Movement launches (1886+)

Charles Spurgeon dies (1892)

The Gideons are founded by a group of businessmen (1898)

20TH CENTURY 1900-2000

C. S. Lewis born (1900)

First modern day speaking in tongues (1901)

George MacDonald dies (1905)

Azusa St. Revival launches Pentecostal movement (1906)

Gypsy Smith gives "raised hand" altar call in Boston (1906)

Fanny Crosby dies (1915)

Billy Sunday's crusades at their peak (1917-1920)

Billy Graham is born (1918)

Bill Bright is born (1921)

Paul Rader uses radio for evangelism in Chicago (1922)

Aimee Semple McPherson opens L. A. Tabernacle (1923)

Scopes's "Monkey Trial" [Fundamentalism] (1925)

Billy Graham converted (1934)

James Rayburn organizes Young Life (1941)

Dawson Trotman founds the Navigators (1943)

Torrey Johnson organizes Youth For Christ (1945)

Dietrich Bonhoeffer executed by the Nazis (1945)

Fuller Theological Seminary founded (1947)

C. S. Lewis begins *Chronicles of Narnia* (1950)

Bob Pierce organizes World Vision (1950)

Full Gospel Businessmen's Fellowship International (1951)

Bill Bright organizes Campus Crusade for Christ (1951)

Richard Niebuhr writes *Christ and Culture* (1951)

Francis Schaeffer founds L'Abri Fellowship (1955)

Henry Dusen calls Charismatics "Third Force" (1958)

Pentecostal worship spreads to mainline churches (1960)

Vatican II prompts changes in Catholic worship (1962-1965)

C. S. Lewis dies (1963)

"Jesus people" popularize Scripture choruses (1960s)

Peter Wagner popularizes term "Third Wave" (1983)

Bill McCartney founds Promise Keepers (1990s)

For Further Time Line Reference

For further study of worship and church history time lines, consider a good church history text first. After that, try the following resources and web sites:

Clay McKinney's Church History Time Line

http://www.churchtimeline.com/

This was originally created as a project for a church history class at Covenant Presbyterian Seminary, the seminary for the Presbyterian Church in America (PCA). Clay McKinney was in that class and has posted a helpful resource. McKinney is a web designer himself. You can have your history two ways: through a searchable database or listed by periods.

The Ecole Project

http://cedar.evansville.edu/~ecoleweb/chronol.html

283

This initiative is led by Anthony F. Beavers, Associate Professor of Philosophy and Religion and Director of the Internet Applications Laboratory for the University of Evansville, Indiana. This resource includes a searchable database as above. However, the Ecole initiative is not limited to data collection but also includes ancient documents, essays, and an impressive collection of links to classical religious art. Perhaps the most interesting aspect of this web resource is that users can select history regionally if they want (one can click on "Spain," for instance, and collect all the important dates in church history related to Spain). And to boot, once you have before you the list of dates, many of the names are "clickable"—that is, you can click on "Marcion" and get a short biography of Marcion. The list of all historical figures in alphabetical order can also be found at: http://cedar.evansville.edu/~ecoleweb/glossary.html

Wall Chart of World History

There are dozens of other web sites with various time lines posted for your reference—like most sites they come and go faster than church hoppers. Besides these web sites you may also want to consult the Wall Chart of World History by Edward Hull. This old British chart has been picked up recently and published by Barnes and Noble. The chart attempts to present all of history—from Adam and Eve through John F. Kennedy on a single, foldout chart in accurate perspective. Many of the early dates are silly guesses, but the dates since the first century are pretty good. The fourteen-foot-long chart does give a sense of space when looking at history. (*The Wall Chart of World History*, ISBN: 0-88029-239-3)

24
Glossary of Worship Terms

a capella

Singing without accompaniment.

agape meal

Early church common meal ending with the Eucharist.

absolution

A remission of sins pronounced by a priest.

Advent

A season of anticipation the four Sundays before Christmas.

Agnus Dei

A liturgical prayer addressed to Christ as the Lamb of God.

altar call

An invitation to come forward and pray to receive or renew one's commitment to Christ.

alleluia

A song of thanksgiving or praise—from Hebrew "Praise the Lord."

285

anointing

To apply oil as a sacred rite—especially for consecration or healing.

anthem

A song of praise sung in parts—often performed by a choir.

antiphonal

Describes singing responsively back and forth, usually on alternating verses of a hymn.

Apostles' Creed

Affirmation of faith intended to summarize the core teachings of the Apostles.

apostolic

Having the authority of the fathers of the church.

ascension

The final action of Christ's earthly life, His return to heaven.

Ash Wednesday

The first day of Lent.

Ave Maria

"Hail Mary" based on Luke 1:28, 42, a common text in music written for the church and a common prayer in Roman Catholic worship.

banns

Public announcement in church of a proposed marriage, usually three successive Sundays in a row to invite any objection to the marriage.

baptism

The application of water to a person as a sacrament or religious ceremony, usually to demonstrate induction into the church.

baptismal

A service that includes the act of baptism.

baptistery

A pool or basin or part of a church (or separate building) used for baptism.

benediction

A blessing pronounced on God's behalf—usually at the close of a service.

call to worship

An invitation to set aside other concerns to focus on God—usually at the beginning of a service.

cantor

A trained reader of Scriptures in the Jewish synagogue and later in the Christian church; an ordained position in the Eastern Church.

canticle

A scriptural hymn or chant sung in church—from books of the Bible other than Psalms.

catechism

Systematic lessons in Christian doctrine used to train individuals for baptism, later leading to confirmation.

catechumen

A new convert to Christianity, in training.

catholic

Means the "universal" church—emphasizes all Christians as one body.

celebrant

One who celebrates or officiates at the Eucharist.

chalice

The goblet used as the Eucharist cup.

chancel

The front of a church; includes the altar and seats for the clergy and choir.

Charismatic

A religious group that stresses direct divine inspiration throughout their worship services.

chrism

The sanctified oil used in special anointing services.

Christendom

The part of the world in which Christianity prevails and there is a culture that is pervasively Christian in its elements.

chorus

The part of a hymn sung repeatedly; more recently, a short simple melody repeatedly projected for the congregation.

closed Communion

Communion/Lord's Supper rite closed to nonmembers of that particular denomination or sect.

collect

Prayer of illumination—that God would open our ears to the Scripture about to be read.

compline

The final evening service of the schedule of daily services, as one might have in a Catholic monastery.

commital

The gravesite service committing the body to the ground as the final rite in a funeral.

288

Communion

Eucharist, the Lord's Supper.

confirmation

Ceremony administered to baptized persons that admits them into full communion with a church.

congregationalism

The system of church government in which "the people" rule instead of a religious hierarchy.

consecration

Making something sacred, such as the Communion elements or a leader in the church.

Convergence movement

A movement associated with "generation X" that combines three streams: evangelical, charismatic, and high church.

covenant

A way of viewing our relationship with God as a community bound to God by mutual promises.

cruciform

A design for a church or cathedral in which the floor plan is in the shape of a cross: the long beam of the cross is the *nave*, the arms are the left and right *transepts*, and the head of the cross is the *chancel*.

Daily Office

A schedule of services performed each day, as in a monastery.

darshan

The synagogue preacher (literally "searcher") who explained what had just been read from the Torah.

diaspora

The Jews who were scattered; also Christians who spread out from Jerusalem after Stephen's death.

Didache, The

An early Church manual (A.D. 100?) containing the order of services and instructions for baptism, Communion, and new convert lifestyle.

doxology

A song of praise (the *Gloria Patri, Gloria in Excelsis Dei,* and *Praise God from Whom All Blessings Flow*); sometimes concludes the service.

Easter

The Christian festival celebrating the Resurrection of Christ.

eastern

Usually refers to the "Eastern" part of Christianity which later became the Orthodox Church, as compared to the "Western" or Roman part of the church, which became the Roman Catholic Church.

ecumenical movement

Movement with the goal of the visible unity of the international church and integration of its mission.

elements

The bread and the wine for taking Eucharist or Communion.

elevation

Lifting the elements for the Eucharist.

Epiphany

January 6th feast celebrating the "revealing" of Jesus—His birth, the visit of the Magi, and His miracle at Cana; later merged into Christmas season, except in the East.

epistle

A letter to a church from one of the Apostles or Paul, usually read second in the customary three-part reading of the Old Testament, Epistles, and Gospels.

eschatological

Referring to the last days or end times.

Eucharist

Communion, the Lord's Supper.

evangelical

Worship that is focused on the Gospel or being "born again."

evensong

The evening service in the daily office, also called Vespers.

extreme unction

Roman Catholic last rites; anointing for death.

fraction

The rite of breaking bread in the Eucharist.

free church movement

Movement centered on the spirituality of worship: frees up worship from signs, symbols, and bodily postures, simplifying it.

genuflect

Bowing toward the altar upon arrival or departure at worhsip as an act of respect

gospel

The first four books of the New Testament: Matthew, Mark, Luke, and John; the third reading of the three-part Scripture reading of the Old Testament, Epistles, and Gospels.

Gloria Patri

"Glory be to the Father, and to the Son, and to the Holy Ghost, world without end, Amen"; the text for many musical arrangements written for the church.

Good Friday

Christian holiday celebrating the day on which Jesus Christ was crucified.

holy week

"Great week" or Easter week, Palm Sunday to Easter Sunday.

homily

A short sermon, usually contains only one point.

hymn

A song of praise to God, not taken directly from Scripture.

iconoclasm

Attitude of those who seek the destruction of images used for worship.

icons

Paintings or artistic objects of devotion, especially used for worship in the Eastern Church.

illumination

Prayer that God will open the Scriptures to the hearers; the "collect."

intinction

The dipping of the bread into the cup for the Eucharist.

introit

A song used during the entrance of the minister or priest.

invocation

The opening prayer invoking God's presence in worship.

kerygma

Preaching; Greek word that means "proclamation, announcement."

Kyrie Eleison

Greek for "Lord have mercy," used in most Christian liturgies.

lectern

A reading podium where scriptural passages are read during worship.

lectionary

A year's schedule of Scripture passages to be read during worship.

Lent

The forty weekdays from Ash Wednesday until Easter; observed by Christians as a season of fasting and penitence in preparation for Easter.

litany

A liturgical prayer recited by a leader with alternating fixed responses by the congregation.

liturgy

A formula for public worship; the usual order of worship.

liturgical

Related to liturgy, usually referring to high church worship.

Lord's Supper

Communion, Eucharist.

Magnificat

The first word in Latin of Mary's psalm of praise (Luke 1:46-55) and thus the title of the psalm—"My soul does magnify the Lord . . . "; a common text in church music.

mass

The set form of worship in Catholic churches, including Scripture and Eucharist.

Maundy Thursday

The Thursday of Holy Week; commemorates Jesus' Last Supper.

293

means of grace

A God-ordained channel through which God's grace is made known.

missal

A handbook used by worshipers for saying mass.

mysteriological

A style of unexplained, almost eerie worship that was especially prevalent in the Middle Ages and has returned recently.

narthex

The entrance hall leading to the nave of a church.

nave

The main or central part of a church building where the people sit (or stand) between the aisles, rear wall, and choir area.

Nunc Dimittis

Latin "now dismiss," Simeon's song when he greeted the baby Jesus (Luke 2:29-32) with "let thy servant depart in peace . . .";
a text in church music.

offertory

A selection of music played or sung during the collection of the offering.

ordinance

A worship practice or rite done as part of worship; considered "less than a sacrament."

orthodox

Usually refers to the Eastern Orthodox Church of Christianity; also refers to straight or conventional doctrine.

294

pall

The cloth used to cover a coffin at a funeral; also the cloth used to cover the chalice in a Roman Catholic mass.

Palm Sunday

The Sunday before Easter; commemorates Jesus' entry into Jerusalem.

passing the peace

The "greeting" with which members of the congregation,

including the clergy, greet one another; one says, "Peace be with you," and the other replies, "And also with you."

passion narrative

The chapters of the synoptic Gospels that tell the events of Jesus' betrayal, arrest, and death on the cross.

paten

A metal or ceramic plate on which the bread for the Eucharist is placed after the server or member of the congregation presents it; in the Middle Ages, a paten was presented to the congregation to kiss, replacing the earlier holy kiss greeting.

Pater Noster

Latin for "Our Father"; begins the Lord's Prayer.

pedagogical worship

Teaching worship; stresses preaching as the dominant part of worship—especially aimed at the mind.

Pentecost

The seventh Sunday after Easter, it celebrates the descent of the Holy Spirit upon the Apostles.

postlude

The closing piece of music in a church service.

prelude

The opening piece of music before the beginning of a service.

295

psalm

A song from the Old Testament book of Psalms.

psalter

A collection of Psalms for liturgical or devotional use.

pulpit

An elevated platform or table/desk used for preaching

Requiem

A mass for the dead; also the title of music written specifically for those services.

relics

Sacred things preserved and sometimes venerated for their memory or magical effect, such as body parts of a great saint.

responsive reading

A reading, usually of Scripture, that is read back and forth by leader and audience.

ritual

A set procedure for church ceremonies such as funerals, weddings, Communion, or baptism; often published in a book of rituals for the pastor.

rood screen

The separation screen or fence between the chancel and the nave distinguishing the proper places for the clergy and the laity.

sacrament

A rite ordained by Christ, held as a "means of grace."

Sanctus

Ancient Christian hymn of adoration, sung immediately before the prayer of consecration.

seeker service

A service designed to create a nonthreatening environment for the nonbeliever; usually leads to the removal of signs, symbols, and anything that might confuse.

Semper Reformada

Latin for "Always Reforming"; i.e., the church is in a continual state of reforming and change; sometimes credited to a reformed mind-set but not always true today.

Shema

A Jewish confession of faith that affirms monotheism.
(Deuteronomy 6:4)

sign-acts

Christian gestures with deeper meanings that are used as confessions of faith; signs of being consecrated to Christ; e.g., the
sign of the cross.

synagogue

The local Jewish congregation's place of worship and study.

Talmud

Jewish literature and teaching for living as a Jew; it contains
both text and commentary and stems from Jewish oral law.

Tenebrae

Celebrating a service in the dark, usually in the latter part of
Easter week to commemorate Jesus' suffering.

transept

The two "arms" of the church when the design is in the shape
of a cross; part of a "cruciform" design.

transubstantiation

Roman Catholic doctrine that the elements in the Eucharist
literally become the blood and body of Christ, though not in
appearance.

unction

A term for anointing, originally in the ritual of baptism, but also
for confirmation and holy orders/ordination.

vespers

Evening service in the daily office, also called evensong.

vestments

Liturgical outer dress in "high church" worship.

vigil

An all-night "waiting" or "looking for" service held before certain feasts, festivals, or special events; e.g., baptism.

watchnight

An all-night gathering for prayer and praise started by Methodists who were looking for Saturday night alternatives to drinking; later popularized in the U. S. as a substitute New Year's Eve celebration.

Whitsunday

The English term for Pentecost derived from the white robes worn by those newly baptized on that day.

word and table

Early church services consisting of two parts: Scripture and the Lord's Table.